Iftekhar Iqbal
THE BENGAL DELTA
Ecology, State and Social Change, 1843–1943

Brian Ireland
THE US MILITARY IN HAWAI'I
Colonialism, Memory and Resistance

Robin Jeffrey
POLITICS, WOMEN AND WELL-BEING
How Kerala became a 'Model'

Gerold Krozewski
MONEY AND THE END OF EMPIRE
British International Economic Policy and the Colonies, 1947–58

Javed Majeed
Autobiography, Travel and Post-National Identity

Francine McKenzie
Redefining the Bonds of Commonwealth 1939–1948
The Politics of Preference

Gabriel Paquette
ENLIGHTENMENT, GOVERNANCE AND REFORM IN SPAIN AND ITS EMPIRE 1759–1808

Sandhya L. Polu
PERCEPTION OF RISK
Policy-Making On Infectious Disease in India 1892–1940

Jennifer Regan-Lefebvre
IRISH AND INDIAN
The Cosmopolitan Politics of Alfred Webb

Sophus Reinert, Pernille Røge
THE POLITICAL ECONOMY OF EMPIRE IN THE EARLY MODERN WORLD

Ricardo Roque
Headhunting and Colonialism
Anthropology and the Circulation of Human Skulls in the Portuguese Empire, 1870–1930

Jonathan Saha
LAW, DISORDER AND THE COLONIAL STATE
Corruption in Burma c.1900

Michael Silvestri
IRELAND AND INDIA
Nationalism, Empire and Memory

John Singleton and Paul Robertson
ECONOMIC RELATIONS BETWEEN BRITAIN AND AUSTRALASIA 1945–1970

Miguel Suárez Bosa
ATLANTIC PORTS AND THE FIRST GLOBALISATION C. 1850–1930

Julia Tischler
LIGHT AND POWER FOR A MULTIRACIAL NATION
The Kariba Dam Scheme in the Central African Federation

Aparna Vaidik
IMPERIAL ANDAMANS
Colonial Encounter and Island History

Jon E. Wilson
THE DOMINATION OF STRANGERS
Modern Governance in Eastern India, 1780–1835

Cambridge Imperial and Post-Colonial Studies Series
Series Standing Order ISBN 978–0–333–91908–8 (Hardback)
978–0–333–91909–5 (Paperback)
(*outside North America only*)

You can receive future titles in this series as they are published by placing a standing order. Please contact your bookseller or, in case of difficulty, write to us at the address below with your name and address, the title of the series and the ISBN quoted above.

Customer Services Department, Macmillan Distribution Ltd, Houndmills, Basingstoke, Hampshire RG21 6XS, England

---

Atlantic Ports and the First Globalisation, c. 1850–1930

Edited by

Miguel Suárez Bosa
Departamento de Ciencias Históricas, Universidad de Las Palmas de Gran Canaria, Spain

First published 2014 by
PALGRAVE MACMILLAN

Palgrave Macmillan in the UK is an imprint of Macmillan Publishers Limited,
registered in England, company number 785998, of Houndmills, Basingstoke,
Hampshire RG21 6XS.

Palgrave Macmillan in the US is a division of St Martin's Press LLC,
175 Fifth Avenue, New York, NY 10010.

Palgrave Macmillan is the global academic imprint of the above companies
and has companies and representatives throughout the world.

Palgrave® and Macmillan® are registered trademarks in the United States,
the United Kingdom, Europe and other countries.

ISBN 978–1–137–32797–0

This book is printed on paper suitable for recycling and made from fully
managed and sustained forest sources. Logging, pulping and manufacturing
processes are expected to conform to the environmental regulations of the
country of origin.

A catalogue record for this book is available from the British Library.

A catalog record for this book is available from the Library of Congress.

Typeset by MPS Limited, Chennai, India.

Contents

List of Tables, Figures and Maps

Tables

Figures

Maps

Preface and Acknowledgements

The contributions in this book have been written with the aim of helping us to understand better the meaning of the First Globalisation (c. 1850–1930), with its associated industrial development and new migrant and commodity flows, from the perspective of the Global South. Ports have long attracted the enthusiastic attention of historians, as they were the means through which cultural and economic exchange took place, connecting different continents and cultures. What distinguishes this work is its focus on the ports of Brazil, the Caribbean, West Africa, the Canary Islands and Cape Verde islands. Most of these ports belonged to territories either governed or dominated by France, Britain, Spain or Portugal, and they participated in the global economy and society on very different terms from those cities in northern Europe where major merchant and banking interests were headquartered. Likewise, ports in independent American countries offered an original response to the challenges with which they had to deal.

The chapters observe how the working and management of the ports became 'modernised', how trade grew and diversified, commodity specialisation arose and new energy sources were introduced – first coal and then oil. Port hierarchies are investigated, together with the linkages to their respective hinterlands. Entrepreneurial, labour and institutional organisations are described in detail.

Atlantic Ports and the First Globalisation, c. 1850–1930 is the result of a long-term collaborative and comparative project involving a group of port historians based at a number of Atlantic universities, the majority of whom participated in the research and development project 'Models of Port Management and the Port Community in the Atlantic World, 19–20th Centuries', funded by the Spanish Ministry of Science and Technology, under reference number HAR2010-17408.

Over the past few years, this group has organised panels at a number of history conferences, including Ghent in July 2012, at the 6th International Congress of Maritime History, in the 'Port and Cities in the Atlantic World' session. Likewise, it met in the '4th Symposium, Ports and Port-cities of the Atlantic in Historic Perspective' during the 3rd Latin-American Congress of Economic History (CLADHE, Bariloche, Argentina, October 2012).

We would like to thank all the authors who, working on both shores of the Atlantic, have devoted their knowledge and efforts to this task. This book would not have been possible without the diligent work of Daniel Castillo Hidalgo and Francisco Suárez Viera. Likewise, we would like to thank the translators, especially Heather Adams, who translated chapters 1, 4, 5 and 7 and proofread the whole book. Finally, we are indebted to the History Department of the University of Las Palmas de Gran Canaria for its collaboration.

Miguel Suárez Bosa
May 2013

Notes on Contributors

Catalina Banko is Lecturer in History at the Central University of Venezuela. She is interested in the development of sugar production and distribution, port economics and the economics of public administration in Latin America. She has also studied the impact of external trade on the urban economies of Venezuela.

Luis Gabriel Cabrera Armas is Lecturer in Economic History at the University of La Laguna. His research interests concentrate on port traffic in the Middle Atlantic and the configuration of island economics. He has analysed the coal markets in the Canary Islands and the other Macaronesian archipelagos. In addition he is interested in the history of entrepreneurship in Spain.

Daniel Castillo Hidalgo is a postdoctoral scholar at the University of Las Palmas de Gran Canaria whose research focuses on the economic history of West Africa, mainly on the continental ports and their port communities. In addition, he is interested in the impact of port activity on urban economies and how this has influenced the economic development process.

Luiz Cláudio Ribeiro is a lecturer at the University Federal do Espirito Santo. His research focuses on Brazil's foreign trade and related institutional evolution, custom duties in Espirito Santo and the port of Santos. His works include an integral view of the Atlantic market, where seaports have played a key role.

Cezar Honorato is a lecturer at the University Federal Fluminense and a specialist on the economic history of Brazil. He has developed research projects examining the introduction of Brazil into the global market and the way in which seaports and their traffic have impacted the economy.

Leila Maziane is a lecturer at Hassan II Mohammedia/Casablanca University. She has been awarded the prestigious Corderie Royal/ Hermione. Her research interests include the history and the maritime heritage of Morocco, with publications such as *Salé et ses corsaires 1666–1727 un port de course marocain au XVIIe siècle* (2007), voted the best

French book about the sea in 2008. She is currently Secretary General of the Moroccan History Maritime Commission (CMHM).

Ayodeji Olukoju is a professor at the University of Lagos. His research interests focus on the economic history of Nigeria. He has made contributions to the way in which the European colonial empires impacted on African social and economic structures and has worked on the economic and technological evolution of the port of Lagos.

Ana Filipa Prata is a researcher at the Institute of Contemporary History, New University of Lisbon. Her research focuses on Portuguese port development and policies (nineteenth and twentieth centuries). She is extending her interest into the Portuguese overseas empire. She is also interested in the history of European port engineering and development.

Miguel Suárez Bosa is Lecturer in Economic History at the University of Las Palmas de Gran Canaria. His first research was focused on port community studies, especially labour issues. He subsequently extended this to cover entrepreneurial and institutional history in ports and their impact on the urban economies on the Canary Islands and West Africa.

Francisco Suárez Viera is a postgraduate student at the University of Las Palmas de Gran Canaria. His main research interests are linked to Atlantic history and focus on migration chains and labour markets. His areas of specialisation include the Canary Islands, West Africa and the Caribbean, especially Cuba.

1
Atlantic Ports:
An Interpretative Model

Miguel Suárez Bosa

1   Port Reforms and Globalisation

Ports play an essential role in maritime transport, which, in turn, is a key element for the economy (Ville, 1990). This can be seen in a significant number of ports located on the African and American coasts and on Atlantic islands. The expansion of a port requires sufficient resources to mobilise assets and production factors, such as raw materials, goods or people. These ports were built in different countries to meet the needs of their developing economies and to enhance their profits.

As in the cases studied, the network of maritime routes connecting Europe, Africa and America was used by many vessels belonging to the major maritime transport companies. On the one hand, we can find African continental coastal ports, such as Casablanca in Morocco, Dakar in Senegal and Lagos in Nigeria, as well as those on the Macaronesian African islands (the Canary Islands and Cape Verde); and, on the other hand, South American ports (Santos and San Salvador in Brazil, La Guaira in Venezuela) and the Caribbean port of Havana. This book will try to clarify the features of these ports, most of which are located on the periphery of the capitalist world-economy of the time.

Many Atlantic ports have already been analysed by different schools of thought and numerous studies have been conducted on various topics, yet few studies have examined the areas indicated and the specific features of these particular ports in depth. In carrying out of this analysis we have mainly, but not exclusively, taken into account the following parameters: port infrastructure and its evolution, each port's specific functions and features, institutions, administration and port activity. Port management acts as the thread that links the analysis of the different ports.

The aim of this book is to enhance our knowledge of African and Latin American ports, particularly during the period between the mid-nineteenth century and the first third of the twentieth century, the so-called First Globalisation. Generally speaking, this process featured the free circulation of goods, services and production factors (labour and capital), although both ideas and culture should also be borne in mind as indicators of globalisation. Although this process covered the whole of the planet, the phenomenon presented some distinctive characteristics in the geographic area studied here, that is, the Mid-South Atlantic. For this reason, we use the term 'Global South' in a more conceptual than strictly geographical sense, as the liberalising measures taken in the nineteenth century gave rise to unequal trade relations, dependence, acculturation and political dominance, all of which are aspects that can be associated with this process of globalisation and imperialist expansion.

In this framework, transport infrastructure played a key role providing crucial assets for expansion and the opening up of new markets. The 'tools of the Empire' (Headrick, 1989) can clearly be identified with three aspects: railways, steam vessels and the telegraph. Steam ships, which used ports, were essential in the imperial expansionist policies in Western Africa and Latina America, as they spearheaded the penetration of the capitalist system into the inland areas of the continent (Hopkins, 1988). At the same time, the main railways were built in the areas surrounding the ports, thereby enabling raw materials to be exported: the phosphates from Khouribga and cereal crops from Chaouia were shipped through Casablanca; Dakar was the embarkation point for peanut production – especially from the 1930s onwards – and constituted the last stop on the current Mali line; the coffee grown in Sao Paulo was shipped through Santos; Venezuela's cacao and coffee through La Guaira; Nigeria's precious wood and palm oil, through Lagos; and, finally, Havana was the major export port for Cuban sugar.

So, clearly, some of the ports studied played a leading role in the export of their countries' products. Likewise, the bananas and tomatoes produced in the Canary Islands were shipped to England and other European countries, as return freight, on the boats that brought coal from the English mines to supply vessels covering the ocean routes. Meanwhile, the telegraph made communication between the different ports much easier, thereby bringing transaction costs down.

Thus, the ports channelled hinterland export products and helped to make farming activities more dynamic, acting as a tool in the extraction of raw material in exchange for an increased dependence on imported foodstuffs, for example. In some cases, the ports specialised in the import of metropolitan manufactured goods such as cotton textiles, tools, alcohol, flour, construction material, machinery and others. Other specialised fields included the massive export of wood, gum Arabic, rubber, textile fibres, peanuts and other colonial commodities whose market value was very low in comparison with the volume exported and, above all, with the value of goods imported through the same port.

The new market drove forward the two major port reforms that have taken place from the mid-nineteenth century to date. This process began when the old ports had to be transformed and some others built to meet the new demands. This was the origin of the first reform that endeavoured to adapt ports to the new needs created as a consequence of the changes generated by the use of steamboats, larger vessels and higher vessel speeds. The second reform started in the 1960s–70s with the birth of containers and other novelties such as the ro-ro system or forklift trucks, which demanded new infrastructure. However, some other factors such as the triumph of neoliberalism in the 1980s and the ensuing privatisation policies should also be taken into consideration, although in this text we will focus only on the first batch of reforms.

A multidisciplinary approach could be used to study these ports. Evolutionary economics provide us with concepts such as the technological path and path dependence that help us to understand development and technological change (Rosenberg, 1992) as an internal variation of the economy with its own distinguishable dynamics, rather than something the value of which is determined solely by the resources and relative prices generated in the markets. Institutional and economic theory complements anthropology and sociology in the analysis of people working in ports.

Institutional theory enables us to clarify the limits between the private and public management of port infrastructure because this economic activity, linked to a social and cultural context, takes place in a changeable but specific institutional and legal framework (North, 1990; Temin, 1997; David, 1985). This framework may also refer to established laws and agreements regarding individual and group performances. This perspective refers to the quantitative efficiency of institutions and their management styles, but it is also interesting to consider the theoretical contributions that highlight the way these institutions are shaped. For example, we should take path dependence into account, which is determined by the course of history rather than by rational and universal economic laws. This is the case with the maritime connection that links Atlantic island ports, Canary Islands and Cape Verde with America and Africa, just as the commercial routes had done during previous centuries.

Ports can act as transport exchange hubs, creating networks or chains in many cases. Modern European historiography has focused on the analysis of port systems and intercontinental networks. For this reason, concepts such as network, hierarchy and complementarities are essential if we are to understand the complex relations established between ports (Polònia, 2010). The concept of 'hierarchy' is relative as there are no unequivocal and universal hierarchies. In this case, we should define the variables that mark a port's relative position in relation to others. The major task is to define what we are going to compare and how we are going to do so. We could consider the amount of trade and maritime transport but a specific port may have worked simultaneously on local and interregional levels, not serving only its country but also others. Within the network of ports there were also sometimes winning and losing ports (Martner Peyrelongue, 1999). Thus, for example, Las Palmas port became the leading island port of Macaronesia, Dakar replaced the other Senegalese ports, some of which were in fact more consolidated than Dakar, such as Saint Louis, while Casablanca quickly outran other Moroccan ports.

These networks were served by major shipping companies that controlled port activity, such as Blandy Brothers & Co.,Chargeurs Reunis, Elder Dempster, Woermann Linie and the Compagnie Générale Trasantlantique, among others, who 'often played a decisive role in colonial expansion policy' (Miège, 1975, p. 5). They often reached collusive agreements in fixing freight prices, giving rise to monopolies arising from the agreements signed at maritime conferences. Thus, the West African Shipping Conference (1859) was made up of the English Elder Dempster company and the German Woermann Linie, who operated along the western coasts of the African continent. This system of agreements became the norm in transoceanic maritime transport, as we can see from the numerous conferences held, which included the China Conference (1879), those of South Africa (1886), North Braliz (1895) and River Plate and South Brazilia (1896) (Davies, 2000; Kirkaldy, 1919), among others.

However, this macro-level analysis may not take the internal study and the specificities of each port sufficiently into account. This work is framed within what is known as 'Atlantic History' (Armitage, 2002),[1] which ties in with the world system (Braudel, 1994; Wallerstein, 2006). Therefore, local or regional micro-level studies could be considered to be useful for determining the existence or not of port models. Furthermore, we should bear in mind the complementary elements that play a vital role in ensuring that the major ports maintain their position. In the period studied we can identify a broader network in the Atlantic, which links Europe with Africa and America through maritime connections (Kirkaldy, 1919; Zimmermann, 1983) as well as some other networks linking specific areas, such as that of the Northwest of Africa, which connects Casablanca-Dakar and Lagos ports and, at the same time, such ports with those of the Canary Islands and Cape Verde. On the other hand, Brazilian ports constitute another network while Havana, which is historically linked to Canary Islands' ports, is now more focused on its connection with the Caribbean islands and the Gulf of Mexico.

2   Technological Change and Port Reform

The technological and socioeconomic changes that have taken place since the Industrial Revolution and the expansion of capitalism have entailed many profound transformations in navigation. The use of steam and of steel hulls, together with many other innovations, made the construction of larger vessels possible. These vessels needed adequate port infrastructure to berth, refuel, take on water or carry out urgent repair work as well as access agency services, insurance, shipping agency and other services. The growth in navigation had the following effects: (1) a considerable increase in the number of passengers and cargo volume (for this reason, larger port warehouses were required, leading to the specialisation of ports areas); (2) this revolution in maritime and ground transport required an improvement in port access and sufficient space to facilitate the reception and mobility of large vessels, conditioning the location of ground terminals, canals and rail networks; and (3) the creation of a continuous international transport network to ensure the permanent flow of goods and people, which led to the disadvantages in breaking bulk being reduced to a minimum. In the Mid-South Atlantic, this process took the shape of the construction or renovation of ports, aimed at ensuring they would act as strategic points of support for European fleets, as well as channelling the massive import and export of goods.

The technological changes that emerged from the Industrial Revolution enabled transport costs to be reduced, although to a some-what lesser extent in maritime transport than in other areas: at the end of the nineteenth century, maritime transport costs had fallen to about a sixth of those recorded at the beginning of the century, while land-based transport costs fell by 90 per cent between 1800 and 1910 (Crafts and Venables, 2005, pp. 323–9). Likewise, as authors such as North (1958) and Harley (1988) point out, an annual fall of approximately 1.5 per cent in maritime transport costs was recorded up until

1913, giving rise to an overall drop of 45 percentage points (Finley and O'Rourke, 2005, pp. 35–7). However, it took time for these changes to become consolidated given that, in 1860, sailing ships still prevailed over steamships, but the last third of the century was decisive, and in 1870, steam ship tonnage was more than double that of sailing ships (Fletcher, 1958).

Thus, as of the late nineteenth century, ports ceased to be conditioned by nature. But the size of the vessels and the speed at which they travelled, together with the need for regular services, made it necessary to carry out significant remodelling work at the ports. This was further necessitated by the complexity of the continental coastline, particularly in Africa, and Casablanca and La Guaira are good examples of how new building techniques helped to address these challenges. The ports played a new economic role, and became immersed in a continuous process of modernisation that required considerable financial backing, constituting a further challenge for the public authorities. Moreover, a modern port required both the space and the capacity to install the necessary infrastructure for shipping services, such as coal warehouses, ship repair yards or navy bases to enable military presence to be increased or to act as a base for penetration inland. In almost all cases, massive investment was put in place; indeed, it became one of the characteristics of port reform. Technical progress was to make it possible to access these bays, which were duly remodelled, where necessary, with the necessary docking equipment to facilitate transhipment as well as connections with other means of transport, above all trains. Thus, good economic relations with the hinterland were established.

If we examine the technological requirements and challenges, many countries put port modernisation plans in place (Guimerá and Romero, 1996). In the United Kingdom, ports had to adapt to the speed and size of steam vessels and ensure their capacity to export coal and other commodities (Jackson, 1983). In France, reforms were based on the Freycinet plan, designed by the Minister for Public Works in 1878, which included the possibility of assigning a direct budget and concentrating investment in a limited number of ports (Marnot, 1999), from which Casablanca subsequently benefitted. In Spain (Chapter 2), significant investment was made as of the middle of the century, particularly after the passing of the Port Law in 1880 (Alemany Llovera, 1991); in almost all cases, the works were carried out directly by the state or by the so-called Boards of Port Works, whose resources originated in the levying of taxes or subsidies and loans authorised by the Government.[2] In Brazil, during the Brazilian Empire, ports began to receive a different treatment to that received since 1869 (Chapter 7). First, the port exploitation services were open to concession through public tender, in which interested individuals could participate, leaving the government to approve the projects and other labour-related issues as well as prices of services. Foreign capital could be accepted provided that there were officials in Brazil.

Generally speaking, new infrastructure was funded by government and building work was normally carried out by large companies headquartered in the imperialist countries. Sometimes, such work was contracted out to private companies for the concession of the exploitation of port services. In these latter cases, the concessionaries aimed to maximise their profits, but were not always efficient in carrying out their work, in which case the concessions were rescinded, with the inevitable disputes that this process led to, as was the case in La Guaira or Santos.

On the other hand, a port is not an isolated infrastructure but rather it also tries to compete with other ports to attract vessels to its facilities. Port development is clearly influenced by the surrounding environment and activity levels, which in turn are conditioned by changes in the port's volume, nature and the origin of its traffic. At the same time, and despite the fact that many ports carry out the same kinds of activities, the development of a particular port also depends on the degree of autonomy of its managers and on the financial regulations imposed on them. Since the first half of the twentieth century, the main aim of a port has been to establish links with its sphere of influence. This is why a regional analysis and a systemic structural approach that takes into consideration the relations and flow of goods and services with the hinterland and the foreland or (*Vorland*) is so important. The same can be said of the financial networks and the loading and unloading networks for goods that come and go from the port.

Ports should not be considered as a microeconomic unit or business centre but as part of an economic region with its own potential, resources, enterprises and economic and social agents, all competing for the economic benefits generated. There are some other useful contributions to an economic analysis, such as the new field of economic history. This is important as the phenomena studied in the global economy refer to a territory and the economic relations established between countries, geographical regions and central or peripheral places, following the proposals of economic geography (Crafts and Venables, 2005).

The ports analysed decisively constituted the shaping of many of the cities in which they are located; indeed, some of the cities' origins actually lie in the fact that the port existed, as is the case of Mindelo on the island of San Vicente, or Dakar. Most of the other cities dealt with here owe their growth and modernisation to their close relationship with modern ports. The association between cities and ports is a recurring subject in the history of European civilisation. The anyport model (Bird, 1963) describes the evolution of port structures in time and space and the close relationship between the port and the city, leading to the concept of the city-port (Broeze, 1997; Hoyle and Pinder, 1992; Kovietz, 1978). In terms of space and time, port cities and their surrounding areas constitute 'a fundamental element in the spatial structure, organization and re-organization of economies and societies, and in relationships between those societies and their environments' (Hoyle, 1997, p. 264).

Ports were also the point of entry and exit of migrants or passengers in transit to new destinations. Port cities constituted areas of settlement for ethnic minorities originating either in the metropolitan countries or the colonial territories, which in turn made these cities more dynamic. In this sense, we need look no further than the Jews and Palestinians in Casablanca and Dakar or the Hindustani minorities in the cities of the Canary Islands. We should bear in mind that they were the source of slave labour in those countries in which slavery had not been abolished, such as the coffee and sugar plantations in Brazil and Cuba respectively. Once slavery had been declared illegal by the French and the British, no slaves could be embarked in the major ports in French and British colonies, giving rise to the post-slavery period in Lagos, for example (Chapter 6). However, slaves were still shipped clandestinely from small ports to Portuguese or Spanish colonies.

3 Port Management Models

Port organisation includes many aspects that need to be mentioned, as ports are gigantic enterprises with a life of their own along with their own problems. A port is essentially a human creation and hence its location is determined more by economic needs than by natural conditions. Based on a holistic conception, ports are valuable not just because of their buildings or equipment but also because of the people who work in them: ship agents, insurance companies, police, mooring men, freight forwarders, maritime brokers, the essential qualified workforce and its respective management team. Taken as a whole they make up what we call the port community.

However, we should underscore the importance of port management models as they constitute the connecting thread linking our chapters.

Around the world, port exploitation problems tend to be dealt with by a range of simpler to more complex solutions; hence the importance of a comparison between the different methods used. To a greater or lesser extent, all ports have a port body responsible for management, but the different models vary depending on a number of elements: the services offered, be they private, public or both; the scope (local, regional or global); the ownership of infrastructure, including port areas and superstructure, especially those dedicated to the handling and storage of goods; effectiveness and harbour management and so forth (Jarvis, 1999; Musso, Parola and Ferrari, 2012; González Laxe, 2002).

In the last third of the nineteenth century, a legislative framework was created to shape port management models and define the performance of port agents. As a consequence of this process, the performance model changed from one of liberal capitalism to a more corporatist approach. Since then, many different management and ownership models have been developed, the variations between them depending on their institutional context.

The specialised literature tends to use a classification created by the American Association of Port Authorities that distinguishes between the few private ports and those in public hands. At the same time, public ports are subdivided into three types: in (1) service ports, port authorities offer all necessary services for the port to function properly, the port owns the infrastructure and superstructure and port services are controlled by public authorities; in (2) tool ports, the same applies, but services are offered by a private entity; finally, in (3) landlord ports, port authorities provide only basic infrastructure.

But this classification is excessively rigid and does not faithfully reflect the complexity of the real situation. The classification may be determined by a number of factors including history, economic development or the government in power's political ideology, so the concept of embeddedness (Granovetter) involves the idea of a necessary social contextualisation of economic processes, and entails multiple scales as well as local dimensions (Debrie, Lavaud-Letilleul and Parola, 2013, p. 58) is of particular relevance here. The texts included in this book suggest that traditional social conditioning comes into play in the choice of a particular management model for each port. It is no coincidence that the management model in Casablanca or Dakar is similar to that of French metropolitan ports, as well as those of the Canary Islands and Cape Verde ports. Meanwhile, the Lagos model of management is similar to the English one. However, there were also some shifts from tradition, as in the case of Santos and La Guaira; the reasons could be that they have been dependent on British Empire economies since the nineteenth century.

However, this classification is somewhat rigid and prevents us from deducing the characteristics of each port. Reality is more complex and a more flexible framework would be more useful. There are two discernible trends in the field of ports (Musso, Parola and Ferrari, 2012, pp. 116–17), depending on whether private or public interests predominate. On the one hand, according to a public conception, ports must be socioeconomically relevant and must serve the good of the local community; that is, they constitute a factor in economic development. This trend was important in countries such as France or Spain, as well as in their colonies, and examples can be found in Casablanca and Dakar and was also seen in Lagos.

The Government gave power to autonomous organisations or public entities such as Chambers of Commerce in France or the Port Works Board, which enjoyed considerable autonomy in the management of Spanish ports. The colonial ports management depended heavily on the mother country and on its institutions. The port was, as in the mother country, directly operated by the state, which did not just build the infrastructure and the platforms but also the superstructure, the sheds and the cranes. However, the state gave power to some private enterprises to carry out some activities. Chambers of commerce and business associations were crucial, acting as pressure groups; the presence of both businessmen and workers gave this institution a corporate nature.

On the other hand, the private sector conception dictates that ports should function in the same way as any other enterprise of any other sector. An acceptable balance must be struck to offset the risks run by investors and businesses. Rio de Janeiro and La Guaira ports follow this trend. In this case, operations are run by port authorities, with administrative autonomy and responsibility. The Brazilian *doca* port companies are a clear example here as this kind of management is frequent in countries that have formed part of the British Empire, such as Nigeria, and also in ports such as Puerto de Santos, La Guaira, which depended on European capitalism. In this case, profitable infrastructure is the most important factor, and they were managed following business criteria.

It is not easy to choose between the two trends but the conclusion reached in the 10th International Congress of Navigation, which took place in Milan in 1908, could be useful. In the third declaration on the topic of 'different port administration and exploitation models: influence on traffic development', it was said that 'Any management system that favours port prosperity and growth in its traffic should be considered good, as long as said management is honourable.'³

This book draws together a group of studies that present the processes described as we will analyse in the corresponding chapters. Links with central administration were vital for those ports dependent on the mother country (Chapters 2, 3, 4 and 5). These ports were managed by the state, which gave power to more or less decentralised local entities such as the Port Works Board in Spain or the Public Works Administration in France. The state controlled port management through local authorities that established prices, within limits, and private participation in the port through concessions and licenses. Essential activities and services in the port were public and included the following: maritime traffic, pilot service, port equipments and authorisations to load and unload cargo (De Raulin, 1941; Celce, 1952; Marnot, 1999).

The situation in the Macaronesian archipelagos regarding coaling supplies to those vessels crossing the Atlantic is a good example of how sound institutions and a clear institutional framework clearly promote economic activity. Macaronesian islands such as the Canary Islands and Cape Verde, which were politically and economically linked to a European country, aimed principally to provide coaling, water and agency services shipping (Chapters 2 and 3). In Portugal, the port administration model was established later, as the model adopted did not become clear until 1910. There was no one single institution to provide srtucture to the ports and many of the powers were divided among different ministries. Ports were owned by the state, which granted concessions to companies in exchange for certain services, while customs, also owned by the state, was responsible for charging import and export duties. Meanwhile, Mindelo, a port in Cape Verde, in turn a Portuguese colony, also provided service to shipping. It was a state-owned port run by private companies, some of which, such as the English companies, were very large.

Due to its strategic location, Mindelo's Porto Grande was a fundamental port of call in the historic cycle of coal. However, the Portuguese colonial authority's inability to invest in other advantageous sources, and to properly manage and administer its colonial ports, determined the end of the expansionist cycle of Port Grande as a coaling station, and gave rise to an increased openness to the participation of the private sector.

What is considered the first phase of the contemporary development of port services took place from the 1850s onwards. Initially, Portuguese colonial ports in Cape Verde benefited from the income that came from supplying 86.6 percent of coal between 1856 and 1880, compared with

13.4 percent in the Canary Islands (Suarez Bosa and Cabrera Armas, 2012). The need to obtain a profit from merchandise and passenger transport, along with reducing fuel costs, led the shipping companies to purchase only the coal needed to reach Cape Verde, where the price was lower than in South American ports.

In addition to this, the Canary Islands' free-port status gave the region a considerable advantage compared to competing Atlantic way-stations. Operating costs in the Canary Islands were comparatively lower, both in comparison with Cape Verde and Madeira. In 1894, for example, ships arriving in the Canary Islands to restock coal avoided taxes if they entered port for 'coal, water or victualling', paid just 3s.4d. to enter and leave port, 28s.2d. for pilotage and a 4s.2d. consular fee. In 1896, ships were paying just 25s. per tonne of coal supplied.

The complete consolidation of Canary Island ports as a logistical platform took place from 1880 onwards. Alongside institutional aspects, other factors should be added: technological advances made steam engines more efficient, giving ships a wider navigational range, and placed the Canary Islands in a favourable position; the intensification of public investment in navigational infrastructure (in contrast to that carried out by the Portuguese in Cape Verde); individual business strategies boosted commerce as a wider and more competitive range of services was offered for which the price and stopover time became determining factors; the shipping lines' preference for the Canary Islands, especially by the British Elder Dempster and the German Woermann Linie as a way-station in the Europe–Africa–Europe routes; and finally, the possibilities that the business could offer, above all, after a fiduciary system was introduced in 1883.

Similarly, the outcome was different in the Canary Islands, despite the oligopoly in port activity. Competition from San Vicente and Madeira meant that business strategies were accompanied by other key elements in attracting traffic in this zone: coal, water and food supplies were offered at an inferior price along with technical support and improving a general set of services; the layover time in Canary Island ports was considerably reduced in the last third of the nineteenth century; and, equally importantly, the Canaries offered lodging for crew and passengers wanting shore leave. The entry of new companies of British origin in supplying coal and freshwater supplies played a key role in these developments, a tendency which shifted to German firms in the twentieth century.

At the same time, coaling companies had a number of ways of attracting customers, such as price reductions or preferential treatment of ship captains. In any case, such competitiveness as existed was relative since most of the time the Atlantic ports were governed by cartels that emerged from the agreement known as Atlantic Island Depot Arrangement (AIDA) which survived into the 1930s.

However, the multiple entities of the government departments and the Elder Dempster Shipping Line company in charge of management at Lagos, the main port of British West Africa, constituted a problem and gave rise to inefficiency. Chapter 6 details how, in a region with a few natural harbours, Lagos, a lagoon port cut off from the open sea by a sand bar, the 'Bugbear of the Bight', became West Africa's leading seaport by 1914. Situated within the broad context of transport infrastructure development under British imperialism, it details the policy and strategic calculations behind port development, which was synchronised with railway development to facilitate the export of raw materials to Europe and the import of European manufactures to the colonies. Port engineering, revenue from colonial resources, imperial and colonial official policy, and the mercantile pressure-group politics of European chambers of commerce and shipping lines, all combined to shape the development of Lagos, especially between 1892 and 1914, the height of port development.

Havana's port (Chapter 7) is an atypical case as, on the one hand, it first adopted the typical Spanish management system, albeit modified because of its condition as a colony; while, on the other hand, after independence, the port was conditioned by its dependence on the United States of America. Some colonial institutions, such as the Board of Trade and, subsequently, the Chamber of Commerce (Lonja de Comercio) played a vital role in the management of this port. The Port of Havana faced important challenges during this period. At first, the port was heavily involved in African slave traffic, with the bulk of export trade directed to Europe. After 1850, Havana stopped trafficking slaves and received a large amount of European immigrants who were directed into the booming sugar and tobacco industries. Cuba, first a Spanish colony, experienced a further colonial experience during the American occupation of the island. This helped to redirect the economy and trade of the island: the USA controlled the bulk of Cuban exports and imports, and US companies also invested heavily in sugar production. In short, they displaced all other competitors, placing Havana port within the sphere of US expansion. However, the Port of Havana had undergone a robust institutional development during the late nineteenth century, under the Spanish tradition, which survived US occupation. This development was strongly linked to a growing trade oligarchy in Havana.

Meanwhile, in developing countries (Chapters 8 and 9), management tended to be private. In Latin American republics and in ports such as those in Brazil and Venezuela, port management was also private and companies were granted concessions if they built the infrastructure. In some cases, the management of these companies, which were often foreign, generated problems, or government nationalist policies made public management inevitable.

La Guaira Port (Chapter 8) required a major overhaul in order to cope with the growing volume of exports, especially cacao, and to supply its capital, Caracas, with products. For this reason, the state awarded the port's construction and conservation to an English company, Punchart, McJaggart and Lowther and Co. The concession, approved by Congress in 1885, leased the running of this port exclusively to an enterprise called the La Guaira Harbour Corporation (Compañía del Tajamar) for 99 years. Subsequently, the Port Corporation had some exclusive privileges, such as not having to pay some custom duties. In any case, this corporate management system caused conflicts with the state and with local businessmen and port workers' interests. It was eventually nationalised in 1936.

In Brazil (Chapter 9), enhanced port infrastructure was required and so the government decided to look to private investors because of the high expense involved and the Paraguayan war debt (1864–70). The law govering the Brazilian port system was passed in 1869 (Siqueira Silveira, 1984) and it established a concession system for port construction and commercial exploitation. This model was also adopted by the Port of Santos.

In summary, the trends adopted differ but we cannot affirm that any one is superior or more efficient than any other. However, we can see that numerous conflicts arose in those ports where legislation was not clear about exactly what each private agent must do. This occurred because private enterprises clearly gave priority to their profits without respecting the conditions of the concession. On the other hand, in those ports where the rules were clear, activities were performed efficiently.

By the end of the 1930s, models attributing more power to public administration seemed to be gaining ground. We could say that this was the general tendency after the Second World War and it continued until the 1980s, when waves of neoliberalism imposed privatisation reforms.

Table 1.1 Summary of port typologies

Port name	Country	Port's main function	Port authority	Building of infrastructure	Equipment and superstructure	Provision of services to vessels and goods
Las Palmas/Sta Cruz de Tenerife	Spain	port of call/services to navigation	owner of infrastructure and superstructure; private services	public	public	private
Porto Grande-Mindelo	Cape Verde	port of call/services to navigation	owner of and responsible for the port and its services	public	private	private
Casablanca	Morocco	trade/export of raw materials	owner of infrastructure; private services and superstructure	public	public	private
Dakar	Senegal	trade gateway	owner of infrastructure; private services and superstructure	public	mixed	private
Lagos	Nigeria	trade gateway	owner of infrastructure; public service	public	mixed	public
Havana	Cuba	trade gateway	owner of infrastructure; private service	public	private	private
La Guaira	Venezuela	trade	owner of and responsible for the port and its services	private	private	public
Santos	Brazil	trade/export of raw materials	owner of and responsible for the port and its services	private	private	private

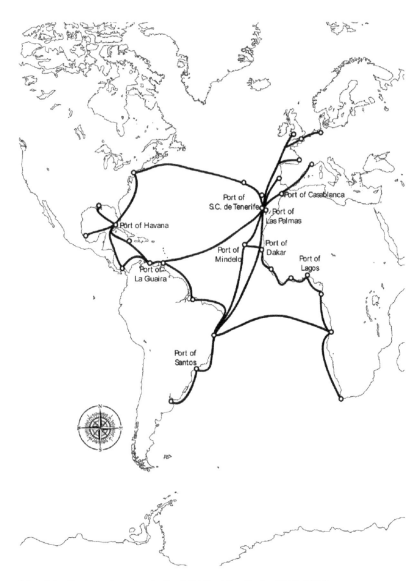

Map 1.1 Ports and routes in the Middle Atlantic (c. 1850–1930)

Notes

1. See Luis Molini and Fernando García Arenal (1908), 'Los puertos españoles (I)', in *Revista de Obras Públicas*, 1689, p. 61.
2. The bibliography on the concept of Atlantic history is fairly extensive. We consider it opportune for the purposes of our work here to apply the category of 'Cis-Atlantic', i.e. 'national or regional history in a broad sense', coined by D. Armitage (2002).
3. 'X Congreso Internacional de Navegacion', *Revista de Obras Públicas*, 1596, 26 April 1909, p. 207.

Bibliography

Alemany Llovera, J. (1991) *Los puertos españoles en el siglo XIX* (Madrid: CEHOPU).
Armitage, D. (2002) 'Three Concepts of Atlantic History', in D. Armitage and M. J. Braddick (eds), *The British Atlantic World, 1500–1800* (Basingstoke: Palgrave Macmillan), pp. 11–27, 250–4.
Bird, J. (1963) *The Major Seaports of the United Kingdom* (London: Hutchison).
Braudel, F. (1994) *La dinámica del capitalismo* (Santiago de Chile: Fondo de Cultura Económica).
Broeze, F. (ed.) (1997) *Gateways of Asia: Port Cities of Asia in the 13th–20th Centuries* (New York: Kegan Paul International).
Celce, G. (1952) 'Le port de Casablanca et l'economie marocaine', doctoral thesis. Faculté de Droit de Paris.
Crafts, N., and A. J. Venables (2005) 'Globalization in History: A Geographical Perspective', in M. D. Bordo, A. M. Taylor and J. G. Williamson (eds), *Globalization in Historical Perspective* (University of Chicago Press), pp. 323–72.
David, P. A. (1985) 'Clio and the Economics of QWERTY', *American Economic Review*, 75, 332–6.
Davies, P. N. (2000) *The Trade Makers: Elder Dempster in West Africa, 1852–1973–1989* (Newfoundland: International Maritime Economic History Association).
Debrie, J., V. Lavaud-Letilleul and F. Parola (2013) 'Shaping Port Governance: The Territorial Trajectories of Reform', *Journal of Transport Geography*, 27, 56–65.
De Raulin, G. (1941) *Les ports de Commerce: construction, organisation, exploitation* (Paris: Sociéte d'Éditions géographiques, maritimes et coloniales).
Finley, R., and K. H. O'Rourke (2005) 'Commodity Market Integration, 1500–2000', in M. D. Bordo, A. M. Taylor and J. G. Williamson (eds), *Globalization in Historical Perspective* (University of Chicago Press), pp. 13–64.
Fletcher, M. E. (1958) 'The Suez Canal and Work Shipping, 1869–1914', *Journal of Economic History*, 18, 556–73.
González Laxe, F. (2002) 'Economía marítima y tipologías portuarias', *Boletín Económico ICE*, 2717, 3rd February, 21–33.
Guimerá, A., and D. Romero (eds) (1996) *Puertos y Sistemas portuarios (Siglos XVI–XX)* (Madrid: Ministerio de Fomento).
Granovetter, M. (1985) 'Economic Action and Social Structure: The Problem of Embeddedness', *American Journal of Sociology*, 91(3), 481–510.
Harley, C. K. (1988) 'Ocean Freight Rates and Productivity, 1740–1913: The Primacy of Mechanical Invention Reaffirmed', *Journal of Economic History*, 48, 851–76.

18   *Atlantic Ports: An Interpretative Model*

Headrick, D. (1989) *Los instrumentos del Imperio* (Madrid: Alianza).
Hopkins, A. G. (1988) *An Economic History of West Africa* (London: Longman).
Hoyle, B. S. (1997) 'Cities and Ports: Concept and Issues', *Revista Vegueta*, 3, 262–78.
Hoyle, B. S., and D. A. Pinder (1992) *European Port Cities in Transition* (London: Belhaven Press).
Kovietz, J. W. (1978) *Cities and the Sea: Port Cities Planning in Early Modern Europe* (Lanham, MD: Johns Hopkins University Press).
Jackson, G. (1983) *The History and Archeology of Ports* (Surrey: Tadworth).
Jarvis, A. (1999) 'Port History: Some Thoughts on Where It Came from and Where It Might Be Going', in L. F. Fisher and Adrian Jarvis (eds), *Harbours and Havens: Essays in Port History in Honour of Gordon Jackson* (Newfoundland: International Maritime Economic History Association), pp. 13–34.
Kirkaldy, A. W. (1919) *British Shipping: Its History, Organization and Importance* (London: Kegan Paul Trench & Trubner).
Kovietz, J. W. (1978) *Cities and the Sea: Port Cities Planning in Early Modern Europa* (Baltimore, MD: Johns Hopkins University Press).
Marnot, B. (1999) 'La politique des ports maritimes en France de 1860 à 1920', *Histoire, économie et société*, 18(3), 643–58.
Martner Peyrelongue, C. (1999) 'El puerto y la vinculación entre lo local y global', *Revista Eure*, 25(75), 103–20.
Miège, J.-L. (1975) *Expansión europea y descolonización de 1870 a nuestros días* (Barcelona: Labor).
Musso, E., F. Parola and C. Ferrari (2012) 'Modelos de gestión portuaria', *La economía del Transporte Marítimo, Papeles de Economía Española*, 131, 116–27.
North, D. C. (1958) 'Ocean Freight Rates and Economic Development 1750–1913', *Journal Economic History*, 18, 538–44.
North, D. C. (1990) *Institutions, Institutional Change, and Economic Performance Prosperity* (Cambridge University Press).
O'Rourkeand, K., and H. G. Williamson (1999) *Globalisation and History: The Evolution of Nineteenth-century Atlantic Economy* (Cambridge, MA: MIT Press).
Polònia, A. (2010) 'European Seaports in the Early Modern Age: Concepts, Methodology and Models of Analysis', *Cahiers de la Méditerranée*, 80, availablet at: http://cdlm.revues.org/index5364.html (accessed 2 Dec. 2012).
Rosenberg, N. (1992) *Progreso técnico: análisis histórico* (Barcelona: Oikos-Tau).
Siqueira Silveira, H. (1984) 'A concessao de portos no Brasil', *Portos e Navios* (March), 30–3.
Suárez Bosa, M., and L. Cabrera Armas (2012) 'La competencia en los servicios portuarios entre Cabo Verde y Canarias (1850–1914)', *Anuarios de Estudios Atlánticos*, 58, 363–414.
Temin, P. (1997) 'Is It Kosher to Talk about Culture?', *Journal of Economic History*, 57(2), 267–87.
Ville, S. (1990) *Transport and the Develoment of the European economy, 1750–1918* (Basingstoke: Macmillan).
Wallerstein, I. (2006) *Análisis de sistemas-mundo. Una introducción* (Madrid: Siglo XXI Editores).
Zimmermann, E.W. (1983) *Zimmermann on Ocean Shipping* (London: Sir Isaac Pitman & Sons).

2
The Ports of the Canary Islands: The Challenges of Modernity

Luis Gabriel Cabrera Armas

1 Introduction

The evolution of the archipelagos of the Canary Islands, Madeira and Cape Verde, has been conditioned by their insularity, small size and scarcity of land resources. However, this has not been an insurmountable obstacle to economic growth. On the contrary, from the beginnings of European overseas expansion, their privileged geographic position in the African Atlantic, along with institutional factors, allowed them to become fully integrated in the Atlantic trade networks. Since the mid-nineteenth century, with the expansion of free trade and the beginnings of steam navigation, the role of the Islands as stopover platforms between Europe, America, Africa and Oceania increased, consolidating their position as communications nodes along with the triumph of steam navigation and imperialist expansion. The demand generated enabled new growth potential in these areas allowing, as can be seen in the Canary Islands, the diversification of production structures thanks to the growth and development of port services.

The present chapter is structured in four sections after this introduction. In the second section the main characteristics of the activity in the ports of La Luz-Las Palmas and Santa Cruz de Tenerife in the Canary Islands between 1850 and 1929 are analysed and compared with competitors such as Funchal (Madeira), San Vicente (Cape Verde) and Dakar (Senegal), using different indicators (traffic, fuel supplies and goods movement). The purpose is to measure certain factors affecting the role of ports as communications nodes in the mid-Atlantic. In the third section the endowment of infrastructures of the ports of Santa Cruz de Tenerife and La Luz-Las Palmas de Gran Canaria and the role of central government (public sector) and enterprises (private sector) in this process are studied. In the fourth section the most significant changes in public and private management of ports are commented on, focusing on the business response to them and the consequent influence on demand and competition between ports. Finally, the last section contains the most relevant conclusions.

2   Port Activity

Port activity has been essential for the economic development of the islands, as they lack alternative infrastructure, especially for the entry and exit of goods and, for the period in question, passengers. Moreover, the intensification of the international movement of goods, passengers and capital in the Atlantic sparked interest in certain island spots as communications nodes depending on several variables, such as geographic location, openness to trade and the availability of resources and labour (Carreira, 1982; Correia e Silva, 1998; Câmara, 2002; Suárez Bosa and Cabrera Armas, 2012). The analysis of port activity reveals three major phases, corresponding to changes in Atlantic navigation.

In the first phase, from the mid-nineteenth century to the beginning of the 1880s, we witness the gradual expansion and transformation of port services due to the development of steam navigation and the need to provide coal, water and food. This led to a change in the design and functions of the ports. Steamers required specific physical and material conditions: deeper waters, large bays and sheltered harbours or places to carry out operations and, in general, more complex and expensive infrastructure and material resources (Zimmermann, 1983). The growth of port activity in the ports of La Luz-Las Palmas on the island of Gran Canaria and Santa Cruz de Tenerife on the island of Tenerife at this stage, unlike other mid-Atlantic ports (Mindelo on the island of San Vicente in Cape Verde and Funchal in Madeira), was not specifically linked to international transit traffic, but to internal factors such as the fishing and commercial activity generated by the cultivation and commercialisation of cochineal in Europe in 1852 and the passing of a decree (which became law in 1870) which declared the main ports of the Canary Islands Free Ports (Puertos Francos), liberalising exports and almost all imports (Bourgon Tinao, 1982; Cabrera Armas, 1997). By contrast, in the port of Mindelo and to a lesser extent that of Funchal, the majority of port activity was linked to the supply of coal to steamers in transit, as can be observed in the 97-per cent correlation between the two variables between 1855 and 1885 (Suárez Bosa and Cabrera Armas, 2012). In that period (1855–85), Mindelo supplied around 65 per cent of coal in the mid-Atlantic and Funchal 23 per cent, while Canary ports provided only 12 per cent of the total (see Tables 2.2 and 2.3).

The prominence of Mindelo, which grew from a marginal and sparsely populated area to a dynamic centre of population and economic growth in Cape Verde, can be attributed to its favourable position, the conditions of its bay and its enterprise policy (Fundo de Desenvolmiento Nacional, 1984). This helped to overcome obstacles such as (1) a higher tax on coal than in the Canaries, (2) the weakness of its domestic market, (3) the scarcity and therefore high price of water, and (4) the monopoly of the main services to ships. In fact, technical limitations, together with the different wind patterns encountered in the two hemispheres after crossing the equator, resulted in increased consumption of coal and water, forcing steamers to stopover in Mindelo, where cheaper coal than in the USA also led to steamers carrying just enough to reach Cape Verde. Besides, the characteristics of the Bay of Mindelo allowed supply operations without large fixed capital requirements (piers and embankments). Finally, the business commitment to modern naval assets, together with the availability of cheap labour, enabled the port to be very competitive despite being controlled by British companies. In fact, between 1858 and 1874, coal supply was controlled by Millers & Nephew, between 1875 and 1880 by the aforementioned and Cory Brothers & Co. Ltd These two companies would subsequently merge to found Millers, Cory & Co. in 1881 (since 1889 Millers & Cory Cape Vert Islands Ltd) (Fundo de Desenvolmiento Nacional, 1984; Suárez Bosa and Cabrera Armas, 2012).

In the second phase, from the early 1880s until the First World War, the process of globalisation consolidated, driven by a sharp drop in freight rates and the expansion of communications. In general, as reflected in the traffic figures and coal supplies, the triumph of steam navigation in commercial shipping benefited these island ports in the African Atlantic area (see Tables 2.2 and 2.3). Although Mindelo maintained its prominence in telegraphic services (Fundo de Desenvolmiento Nacional, 1984), the ports that performed the best in the rest of port services were those of the Canaries, registering an increase from 87,000 tons of coal supplied in the early 1880s (6 per cent of the total supplied in the three Archipelagos) to over 52 per cent in the 1890s, reaching an average of 1.7 million tonnes in the five years preceding the First World War (representing 62 per cent of the total supplied including Dakar) (Table 2.3). There are three main reasons for the duration of this primacy (excepting the period of the First World War) until the 1930s.

First, the increased competitiveness of port services offered in the Canaries was decisive in attracting regular traffic, aided by the increase and modernisation of private services, the increase in public investment (harbours, lighthouses and beacons) and the reduction in health and administrative barriers, which allowed costs and time of the ship in port to be cut. Parallel to this, the cereal crisis and decrease in cochineal demand increased manpower supply and reduced labour costs, together with lower fuel taxation than in the Portuguese archipelagos, as consignees' margins were reduced due to the increased size of the shipping companies and resolutions adopted at the freight conference by shipping (Kirkaldy, 1914; Dyos and Aldcroft, 1969; Morton, 1977). Finally, we should not forget the positive effect for the whole of the island's economy caused by the establishment in 1883 of a trust system in Spain (Martín Aceña, 1990), unlike in Portugal (which had a system of fixed exchange rates), to lower the cost of service vessels and encourage speculation in the exchange rates of the peseta, offsetting the reduction in margins in coaling and watering.

Second, the geographic position now benefited the Canaries, especially Las Palmas, as a result of imperialist expansion in Africa. British, French, German or Belgian carriers opted preferably for the Canary Islands, due to lower service costs and fuel saving thanks to the proximity to the continent and to the reduction of the price paid at origin as bargaining power increased (Cabrera Armas and Díaz de la Paz, 2008). In addition, cost reduction and technical advances in navigation (Harley, 1971) decreased the relative advantage of Funchal and Mindelo on other routes, thus part of such trade was diverted to Canary ports (Sousa Machado, 1891; Martín Hernández, 1991, Câmara, 2002) (Table 2.2).

Third, the growth and diversification of the economy in Las Palmas and Santa Cruz helped to maintain this leadership. The coal business, water supply and food led to an increase in the number of hotels, bed and breakfasts and restaurants and ended up promoting other service activities such as insurance and banking or, in the industrial sector, docks, shipyards and construction workshops for ship repair and, as technology progressed, cold storage for preservation of meat, fish and vegetables. Variations in the price of transportation and European demand increased the Islands' supply, which was mainly agricultural (bananas, tomatoes and potatoes) and handmade items (cigars and embroidery), and access to the imports demanded by the Islands flourished (Suárez Bosa and Cabrera Armas, 2012). This stimulated and diversified traffic, commercial development and port services (Davies, 1995). This trade favoured the arrival of steamers looking for freight (especially those returning to Europe), and shipping companies that linked various ports of the Atlantic and Mediterranean, such as Compagnie de Navigation Armenienne et Marocaine or Forwood Brothers & Co., with an extensive presence in the islands, joined among others by Yeoward Brothers Line, Otto Thoressen Line, Fred Olsen & Co., Elder & Fyffes in the twentieth century. Moreover, coastal shipping experienced strong growth due, firstly, to the establishment of several maritime postal services subsidised by the government, and, on the other hand, to the expansion of domestic demand for transport, especially after 1907 when the ban on foreign flag vessels providing inter-insular navigation came into force.

Commercial activity reached its highest volume between 1910 and 1914 when, excluding the import of coal and supplies to ships, the two ports handled a total of 502 thousand tonnes per year, 64.1 per cent of which corresponded to the port of Las Palmas (Table 2.1). The leadership of Las Palmas can be attributed to increased urban concentration, a higher income level and its role as a redistribution centre for domestic and African markets, reflected in the volumes imported by both ports, where the 237 thousand tons per year on average registered for Las Palmas doubled the figure corresponding to Santa Cruz (115,639 tons per year). The volume exported also increased, reaching an average of 84,600 tons per year in Las Palmas and 64,300 tons per year in Santa Cruz. In this case, the leadership of Las Palmas can be explained by the strength of its fishing and agricultural sectors and the centralisation of traffic in that port, while Santa Cruz competed, in addition to Las Palmas, with Puerto de La Cruz in the same island (Table 2.1).

The First World War had a ruinous effect on economies such as the Canary Islands or Madeira, part of the agricultural production,

Table 2.1 Movement of goods at Canary Islands (1910–29) (five-year averages in tons)*

Period	Exports			Imports		
	Las Palmas	Santa Cruz	Total	Las Palmas	Santa Cruz	Total
1910–14	84,581	64,299	148,879	237,046	115,639	352,685
1915–19	47,475	49,592	97,066	61,656	78,139	139,795
1920–24	109,071	126,044	235,120	159,679	152,175	311,854
1925–29	239,441	167,695	407,136	216,640	202,691	419,331

*Excluding fuel import
Source: Juntas de Obras de Puertos de La Luz-Las Palmas and Santa Cruz de Tenerife, *Memoria*, years indicated; Cámara de Comercio, 1930. Self-made elaboration.

manufacturing and services of which was linked to maritime traffic and external demand (bananas, tomatoes, wine, tobacco products and embroidery). Trade, shipping and, in general, all port services, contracted sharply in Funchal, Las Palmas, Santa Cruz and, to a lesser extent, Mindelo. By contrast, increased activity in the new Dakar port complex was due to diversion to this port of the Allied merchant and war fleets (see Tables 2.2 and 2.3).

After the First World War, the Canary Islands' economy entered a period of growth that was slow until 1922, as a result of the general decline in traffic amid falling freight and shipment shortages, but then quickened until the beginning of the Second Republic (1931–36), thanks to the recovery of the island's agricultural export sector and port services, although companies and workers faced new challenges resulting from changes in transportation and domestic and international maritime trade. First, trade movement increased as a result of the recovery in external and domestic demand. Second, there was a decrease in transit traffic, an increase in captive traffic and a partial transformation of fishing. Third, in terms of supplies, we can observe the partial recovery of coal, after a sharp drop during the war period, and the emergence of a new product for navigation: petroleum.

Commercial activity in the ports experienced a sharp increase that explains the interest in changing the length and width of the docks and warehouses. In the Canaries, exports, mainly of perishable agricultural products (bananas, tomatoes and potatoes) grew to an average of 407,100 tons per year in 1925–29, 59 per cent of which corresponded to the port of Las Palmas (Table 2.1). Imports, by contrast, performed differently. In the 1920s, the entry of products in both ports tended to balance out due to the lesser role of the port of Las Palmas in redistributing goods. This trend is reflected, with respect to the five years preceding the war, in an average decline between 1920 and 1924 of 77,300 tons in the goods unloaded in Las Palmas (−32 per cent), and an increase of 26,500 tons in Santa Cruz (+32 per cent). In the second five-year period, the increase in internal demand due to the growth of the tertiary sector and the urbanisation process (in the early1920s, the cities of Las Palmas and Santa Cruz were home to a quarter of the region's population), there was a general recovery in imports, with an average volume in both ports of 419,300 tons per year (Table 2.1). This increased volume of trade constituted another advantage of the Canaries, as a pull factor for traffic, against rivals like Funchal port and Mindelo, although not with respect to Dakar and Casablanca, places where colonial trade increased after the war.

The increase in trade contrasts with the variation in the number of vessels using the ports. In the 1920s all ports posted increases compared to the War years, but not in relation to the pre-war period (with the exception of Dakar, which increased in vessel numbers and, to a lesser extent, in tonnage) (see Table 2.2). The decline in traffic in the three Atlantic Archipelagos was influenced by several factors: (1) the reduced requirement for intermediate ports due to higher vessel tonnage and improvements in propulsion with the shift from coal to liquid fuels; (2) the shift of the economic axis from London to New York and variations in Atlantic trade; (3) the decline in the price of coal and fuel in the ports of South America; and (4) the fall in port visits by British and German vessels, with decreases for the 1910–14 and 1925–29 periods of 47.9 per cent and 41.6 per cent respectively for Las Palmas, while Santa Cruz saw a decline of 46.7 per cent for UK vessels, and 25.3 per cent for German boats. Other markets such as the French (−15.9 per cent) and Italian (−8.4 per cent) were also affected. These decreases were counterbalanced by entries of vessels from other nations; Spanish vessels in particular were favoured by the application of differential flag rights and increased subsidies for domestic shipping, which intensified commercial bonds between mainland Spain and the Canaries as an alternative to growth in European protectionism. The share of domestic traffic in total inflows in 1925–29 reached 49.5 per cent in Las Palmas and 65.7 per cent in Santa Cruz. However, in terms of tonnage, vessels flying the Spanish flag only accounted in the same period for 10.2 per cent (Las Palmas) and 20.8 per cent (Santa Cruz) of the total, due to the increased presence of vessels with a lower average tonnage. By contrast, in the second half of the twentieth century, the tonnage of foreign vessels increased by an average of 4500 tons, representing an increase of 25.9 per cent in Santa Cruz and 10.7 per cent in Las Palmas compared with the five year pre-war period (Cabrera Armas and Díaz de la Paz, 2011) (see Table 2.2).

The importance of steam navigation for the growth and transformation of the ports, especially in terms of the ensuing major indirect effects, should not hide the fact that an important part of port activity was also linked to sailboats registered in the Islands. In the 1925–29 period, the number and tonnage of boats entering the ports stood at 1781 units per year in Las Palmas, while Santa Cruz recorded 942 sailboats per annum. We cannot differentiate between merchant and fishing vessels but, according to the Chamber of Commerce, Industry and Navigation of Las Palmas, in 1923 the boats engaged in fishing accounted for 55.4 per cent of income, a figure that dropped to 51.8 per cent in 1929.

This decrease was primarily due to the modernisation of the sector with the introduction of steamers and motorisation of ships. Thus, in 1923, 1027 left Las Palmas with the Canary and African fishing grounds, with a register of 32,324 tonnes. An increase in number but especially in tonnage was the result of the incorporation of steamers, rising from only 7 units in 1923, to 377 in 1929 (31.5 per cent of the total), with 39,679 registered tonnes (57.2 per cent of the total) (Cámara de Comercio, 1924 and 1930).

As mentioned above, in the interwar period, the port regained a lease of life thanks to the recovery of fuel supplies, water and to a lesser extent of ship repairs. However, the characteristics of the supplies differed from those of earlier stages. Between 1914 and 1935 the energy sources in shipping diversified and the number of ships consuming petrol derivatives rose from 11.2 per cent to 49.8 per cent of the total world fleet. The ports analysed also incorporated this restructuring process, with Santa Cruz in the 1930s the last to incorporate the service of petroleum supply and Las Palmas the first, with Sociedad Petrolifera Española, a subsidiary of Royal Dutch-Shell (Mindelo and Las Palmas in 1920, Dakar in 1925 and Santa Cruz in 1930).

Oil companies opted for the port of Las Palmas, as in the case of coal, due to the advantages of its geographical location, to several projects aimed at improving port facilities and especially to lower fuel costs. Fuels for export and local consumption were exempt from taxes through the system of free ports. However, the rates stipulated by the newly created Board of Works per unloaded ton and wharfage (charge on loading and unloading in terms of navigation: cabotage, big cabotage and height), as well as the transportation tax levied as of 1920, had to be paid.

In this area of the Atlantic, records indicate that in the 1920–24 period, 94.9 per cent of the heavy oil (*mazut*) was provided by Las Palmas. This value decreased in the period 1927–29 to 61.3 per cent of the total, due to increased consumption in Mindelo (23.1 per cent) and Dakar (20.3 per cent) (Table 2.3). This new product was essential to retrieve foreign transit traffic, as Spanish steamers continued to consume coal (Valdaliso Gago, 1997). It is not known which vessels took coal and which fuel but the high correlation between the entry of vessels and fuel supply (94 per cent in Las Palmas and 83 per cent in Santa Cruz), can confirm the modernisation in port services, especially in Las Palmas. In 1929, fuel consumption, in terms of coal equivalent (tce) accounted for 50.8 per cent of total supplies in Las Palmas, 30.5 per cent in Mindelo and 26.0 per cent in Dakar (Table 2.3).

The emergence of the port's oil services contrasts with the downward trend in coal and shipbuilding (Table 2.3). In the 1920s, in comparison with the 1910–14 period, an average of 135,200 fewer tons per year of coal (−46.3 per cent) were imported, while the decline in Las Palmas stood at 388,400 tons per year (−51.3 per cent). However, the Canary ports managed to maintain their primacy in coal supplies, as other ports also declined (Mindelo by 11.0 per cent and Funchal dramatically by −64.4 per cent), except for Dakar, which registered a consumption similar to the pre-war period (203,000 tons per year on average in the decade). This prominence of the Canaries was related to the competitiveness and diversity of services offered, especially in Las Palmas, where new coal companies were installed, and the adoption of a concerted corporate policy together with imposed cartelised benchmark supply prices for all ports, absorbing competing companies in certain cases. In terms of construction and ship repairs, the lower demand for coal and, to a lesser extent, water, caused a decline in the construction of coal barges and boat cisterns. The construction of both merchant and fishing boats also fell back, as many assemblers acquired foreign vessels powered by coal or oil with an iron or steel hull. However, the recovery of international traffic and the motorisation of the island fleet ensured the creation and expansion of repair workshops.

3   Infrastructure and Port Management in the Canary Islands

3.1   Port Characteristics

Until the mid-nineteenth century the island ports were simple piers where only small boats could operate, weather permitting; as a result, most of the operations related to trade and fisheries were conducted in the bay and coastal beaches. The beginnings of capitalist expansion changed the design of the port facilities. The increasing globalisation of production, trade and migration flows, technological advances in navigation, vessel size and specialisation required new infrastructure and naval resources in ports. The natural harbour gave way to an artificial version where stowage and loading and unloading operations could be carried out more quickly and therefore at a lesser cost. Island ports have to include traditional activities such as trade and fishing, as well as playing the role of ports of call, in which steamers obtain basic supplies such as coal and water and a place for the crew and passengers to rest. In the development process, public and private involvement was fundamental.

3.2   Development of Port Infrastructure

3.2.1   *Public Initiatives*

In Spain, the success of liberalism in the mid-nineteenth century led to a new conception of the role of government in economic growth (Comín Comín, 1996), in which government should be involved in the generation of economic infrastructure that would strengthen the country's wealth and productivity (Frax Rosales, 1996). These ideas were expressed in 1848 in the Canary Islands in the order of the Ministry of Commerce, Education and Public Works to develop a General Plan of Communications and Public Works for the archipelago at the hands of engineers of roads, canals and ports.[1] The Plan, adopted in 1849, established the ports of Las Palmas de Gran Canaria and Santa Cruz de Tenerife among the priority projects, providing them with state and local funds. Subsequently, the 1851 Decree (Royal Decree of 17 December) clarified the areas in which the administration was to act, classifying the ports into two categories: of general interest (state funding only) and of local interest (state and local government funding); once the above-mentioned decree had been further developed, these, in turn, were subdivided into ports of first- and second-order interest (Alemany Llovera, 1991).

In the ports of Santa Cruz and Las Palmas public intervention took the form of the approval of new projects carried out directly by the administration or, more often, by contractors (after being duly put out to tender). These first interventions did not lead to the results expected. Long administrative project procedures and the lack of financial resources limited government achievements. The projects for the extension of the old docks of Santa Cruz and Las Palmas, or the construction of a new pier at La Luz in the Isleta Bay (6 miles from the main town of Las Palmas) were not completed. In some cases, they were paralysed after a modification in the project, in other cases, as a result of being rejected by contractors, all combined with a lack of funds, as a result of the state budget cuts policy since 1864 (Cuéllar Villar, 2002).

The construction of a pier was started in Santa Cruz in 1849 and declared of general interest in 1852. Initially, it had an annual subsidy of 50,000 pesetas but it was suspended in 1866 when only 343 metres were built (200 of which were usable, with an average width of 12 metres; Junta de Obras del Puerto de Santa Cruz de Tenerife, 1930). In 1852 the extension of the old harbour of San Telmo in Las Palmas started after several delays with an annual assignation of 25,000 pesetas and it too was paralysed in 1872 upon termination of the contract, barely reaching 56.0 per cent of the projected work (150 metres of quay and part of the front nose). Finally, the proposed protection dock and pier in La Luz started in 1863 in the same municipality, to be suspended in 1869 when only 22.0 per cent of the budget had been invested (León y Castillo, 1909; Martín Galán, 1983) (Figure 2.1).

The second phase of the evolution of the Canary Island ports started in the 1880s, lasting until 1914, after years of paralysis during which the government only invested in conservation works. During this period, both public and private sectors funded the means required by navigation, enabling them to become some of the main Atlantic ports in only ten years.

With the ratification of the Ports Act of 7 May 1880 and especially as the state took responsibility for funding the ports declared of public interest, public intervention began (Alzola Minondo, 1994). This was a turning point for the port works and therefore (by extension) for their surrounding areas, which started to play a more important political, social and economic role.

Thus, a plan for the expansion of Santa Cruz, declared a port of general interest of second order in 1880, was approved in 1881. This plan included the construction of the so-called North Pier and the extension of the old pier and breakwater in order to increase the surface and docking operations in the bay and to correct defects of the frustrated 1864 project: including the path of the seawall, the lack of berthing areas

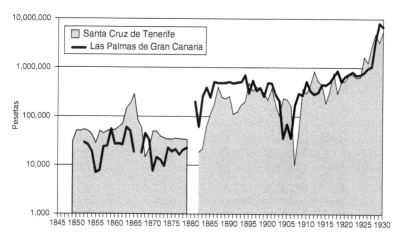

Figure 2.1 Public investment in Santa Cruz de Tenerife and La Luz-Las Palmas (1845–1930)
Sources: Cabrera Armas (n/d), ms.

and the reduced size of the dock (Junta de Obras del Puerto de Santa Cruz de Tenerife, 1930, 19). The work was put out to tender in 1884 for 4.3 million pesetas, and planning was completed by 1896, and the construction work took a considerable length of time. The North Pier was completed in 1909 and the South Pier in 1916, at an increased cost of 2.7 million pesetas, giving Santa Cruz two available quays: the North, with an approximate length of 200 metres, and the extension of the dam-quay south to 735 metres, thereby increasing the total area for all kinds of winds to 51.6 hectares and for storms (strong winds from the East) to 63.2 hectares. However, according to the port authority, the port had still two serious problems: 'A reduced surface area (7,052 m2) for loading and unloading, with the consequent delay in these operations, and, what was worse, a very small dock, which made it difficult to build future wharfs, docks, shipyards and other complementary elements' (Junta de Obras de los Puertos de La Luz y Las Palmas, 1929).

   In Las Palmas, state projects focused on the extension of the pier of La Luz that had been paralysed since 1869, with the old port of San Telmo[2] deemed not worthy of attention. Construction was initially commissioned out to a Board of Las Palmas Port, allocating means and a single grant of 200,000 pesetas drawn on the state budget (Royal Order of 10 May 1881). This Board performed the works through the public administration until April 1882, at which point the state took over responsibility for them, together with their conservation, when La Luz was declared a refuge harbour, and therefore, of general interest (Spanish Act of 27 April 1882). Subsequently, the granting of the work to British company Swanston and Co. was approved. In 1903, after 19 years of implementation, the work was finally completed at a total final cost of 8.4 million pesetas (León y Castillo, 1909; Martín Galán, 1983).

   The third phase in the island's port modernisation took place after the First World War (Cuéllar Villar, 2002).[3] The public administration found that existing infrastructure facilitated the coal supply services, water supply and passenger transit. But on the other hand it did not satisfy most of the requirements posed by petroleum, larger ships and the movement of goods on a larger scale. In the early 1920s in both Las Palmas and Santa Cruz new projects and services were undertaken, with the subsidies granted by the state and the new rates and means required by the respective port authority playing a major role. Due to the large amount of funding required for the works, higher incomes were needed. In 1925, under the decree of 24 July, the state approved the proposal of a special grant of 10 million pesetas for each port authority, distributed over 12 years (750,000 pesetas per year from 1926, and 1,085,000 pesetas for the last 3-year period), with the condition that the Island Councils of Tenerife and Gran Canaria contribute the same amount and that the Port Authorities would cover any expenses that exceeded the subsidies. However, the Councils, despite creating bonds to this end, did not initially comply with the agreement and therefore neither did the state. The rejection of the Councils was due, in addition to a lack of resources, to the inclusion of the ports of Las Palmas and Santa Cruz in an extraordinary budget in 1926, which assigned to the Spanish port system 600 million pesetas (Melguizo Sánchez, 1979; Gómez Mendoza, 1997). The state aid, along with higher incomes from the Port Authorities and the recovery in the level of vessel traffic, allowed the budget to multiply by 3 to over 8.3 million per year on average in the 1925–29 period. The projects for the expansion of both ports were put out to tender in 1927 (Figure 2.1).

Among the works in Santa Cruz we could highlight the south pier extension and completion of the first harbour basin following the 1918 project, approved in 1923. The first work, which included the obliga-tion to complete the dam that the Port Authority had been in charge of since 1917, 1924 was taken over by Siemens-Schuckert Electric, SA for 5.6 million pesetas and not completed until 1930. The second, more ambitious work, was awarded to the Sociedad Metropolitana de Construcción, SA and envisaged a construction time of 15 years, but after several renovations and extensions was finally concluded in 1944 with a final cost of 38.2 million pesetas. The works included the exten-sion of the South dike-pier (to 1319 m length), the widening and exten-sion of the North Pier (270 m long by 60 wide), extending the surface area of the dock substantially, and dredging it (Junta de Obras del Puerto de Santa Cruz de Tenerife, 1930). In Las Palmas, the main project, also awarded to the Sociedad Metropolitana, which after its merger with the Matschapp Nederlanskhe voor Havenwerkn, would result in the Comunidad de Obras para el Puerto de Las Palmas (Coppa), included the construction of a new 2581-meter dike, the expansion of the dock shelter to 243 hectares, 5455 metres of linear berthing and 240 m^2 of terrace for deposits (Junta de Obras de los Puertos de La Luz y Las Palmas, 1929; Martín Galán, 2001). The execution, which lasted until 1936, had a final cost, after successive enlargements and modifications, of 45.3 million pesetas (Figure 2.1).

3.2.2 *Private Initiatives*

The growth of port activity depended not only on public intervention. Private capital played an important role in port development as it was not limited to the consignment and agency tasks but, in the age of steam navigation, also invested in land deposits and floating material in order to meet both foreign demand and that generated by the island's economy. These essential services in the transport chain required a space on the docks and, given their limited capacity, it was necessary to include a maritime–terrestrial strip where, following the British model, activities could be concentrated in one place to build coal and freight service esplanades and a sheltered bay space in which to locate floating material (tugboats, cargo barges, tankers and boats), as merchant ships could not operate in the 'private' docks and should, therefore, perform operations in public docks or, more often, in the bay. To access these spaces it was first necessary to develop a project and obtain the corresponding administrative concession, which was always temporary, from the state. Second, the capital, both fixed and variable, had to be deployed for the heavy investments required by such facilities. In this sense, although what could be considered the first stage in the development of the ports of Las Palmas and Santa Cruz took place in the 1850s, it was not until the 1880s that they started to consolidate as intercontinental logistic platforms (see Tables 2.2 and 2.3).

Among these elements it is important to point out that the services had to be competitive, not only to obtain and sell coal, water, food and technical support at a lower price than competing ports, but also to improve the overall efficiency, from the speed at which coal, water and goods were supplied to the services and leisure (banks, hotels, inns, restaurants, boarding houses) for crews and passengers who required them (Cabrera Armas, 2007). At this point, the amount of investments made by the consignee companies in ports is not known, but an approximation of the amounts dedicated to the construction of the projects, together with the floating material, allows us to calculate the average annual investment from 1880–1929 at over 500,000 pesetas. To reach such a high-value participation of local consignees was essential, such as Hamilton and Co. (Guimerá Ravina, 1989), Ghirlanda Hermanos and Juan Cumella Monner in Santa Cruz or Miller and Co. and Salvador Cuyás y Prat in Las Palmas (Miller, 1994), together with the entry of new players from the UK and Germany that had mining interests in the supplies of coal, water, food and so forth as in the cases of the British Elder Dempster and Co. and the German Woermann Linie and Deutsche Kohlen Depot. We also can differentiate new players in the field with ship-owner interests. These included companies like Blandy Brothers and Co., Cory Brothers & Co., Wilson, Sons & Co., Hull Blyth & Co., Elder Dempster, Woermann Linie, Deutsche Kohlen and, after the Great War, the Canary Islands Depots Coal & Oil Co. Ltd, the Oceanic Coal Co. Ltd, Royal Dutch-Shell, British Petroleum and, of course, companies and entrepreneurs who, although not involved in the supply of fuel, played their role as consignees with an active presence in the port movement: Hardisson Hermanos, H. Wolfson, J. Ahlers, Yeoward Brothers, Otto Thorensen, Elder and Fyffe, M. Curbelo and so forth (Suárez Bosa, 2004; Martín Hernández, 2004; Cabrera Armas and Díaz de la Paz, 2008; Suárez Bosa and Cabrera Armas, 2012).

Finally, among private initiatives we could highlight those related to the supply of liquid fuels whose service was offered by companies, subsidiaries of multinational or national companies, who paid the Port Authorities a canon in order to be able to offer said services. These suppliers included the Sociedad Petrolifera Española, a subsidiary of Anglo-Dutch Shell, which in 1920 obtained a concession to install pipes and tanks for fuel oil and diesel oil in the port of Las Palmas, while they supplied a vessel from the pontoon to perform the basic services to navigation (Burriel de Orueta, 1974). To a lesser extent, companies such as British Petroleum (represented by Cory), Vacuum Oil Company, Compañia de Petróleos Porto-Pi (50 per cent-owned by the banker Juan March and the French financial group Baver Marchal et Cie. from Paris), with a pontoon vessel in the Bay of Gando in Gran Canaria, also participated in port growth. In Santa Cruz, the fuel supply to navigation was delayed until 1930, despite the concessions granted by the state from the early 1920s, with the installation by Sociedad Petrolifera Española of a pontoon vessel in the pier of Santa Cruz, while the Compañía Española de Petróleos, S.A. (CEPSA) inaugurated the first oil refinery in Africa.

4 Institutions and Port Management

Until the early nineteenth century, the port management in the ports of Santa Cruz de Tenerife and Las Palmas de Gran Canaria corresponded to different local organisations. The State's role was to supervise work and contribute subsidies to complement the taxes levied locally to finance the work. After the rise of the Liberals to power in 1845 the powers of the state in land–maritime areas were defined more clearly. By declaring this national property for public use, the state held the property and influence of the docks and marine–terrestrial space, while private agents, which could also have docks, warehouses or esplanades in those areas, held their property on the basis of a temporary administrative concession. Therefore, the port type responded to the so-called landlord model in which the port authority – in this case the state – is the owner of the infrastructure of public use, approving public and private projects affecting the terrestrial maritime zone, permitting these spaces to be occupied and the management (docking, mooring etc.) of merchant ships in port. Private agents, meanwhile, were responsible for providing support services to ships, crew and passengers.

4.1   Governance

Public administration of the ports in the Canaries was structured from the mid-nineteenth century under four ministries:

1. The Ministry of the Navy, whose General Command had, in the past, served as the harbour master, with control over tuition and fees regime and inner harbour traffic.
2. The Ministry of Development, through the Provincial Public Works, was in charge of developing and managing construction projects, repairs, maintenance and the cleaning of the ports, and they were entrusted with everything to do with the policing and organisation of activities in the docks, as of the 1851 Royal Decree of 17 December 17.
3. The Ministry of Government, through the Civil Government, responsible as of 1855 (Health Act on 28 November) for monitoring the health status of ships (crew, passengers and cargo) and for issuing the corresponding documentation.
4. The Ministry of Finance, whose customs administrators and, in the case of the Islands from October 1852 onwards, free ports collected the charges established relating to customs and product taxes, mooring, and loading and unloading created in 1851 to replace the existing excise taxes to fund the works in ports, but its application was delayed until 1868 in the Islands for travellers and unloading and until 1874 for loading.

The main changes in governance occurred in the twentieth century when, according to the rules adopted in 1903 (General Regulation of 17 July), two Port Authorities were created, one for each port. The first Port Authority of La Luz and Las Palmas was ordered in 1905 (Royal Order of 16 June). Subsequently, although Las Palmas was not a provincial capital, and given the importance of the port, it was equated in composition to that of the provincial capitals (Royal Order of 15 January 1906), becoming one at the end of 1906. The following year, the constitution of the Port Authority of Santa Cruz de Tenerife was ordered, although it was not definitively established until mid-1908.

The organisation of the Port Authorities was structured around two decision-making bodies: the Board and the Executive Committee. The Board's Plenary Committee was made up of 20 members, including representatives of the central government in the Islands, specifically the Civil Governor or the Deputy Government, Navy Commander, Finance Officer, State Attorney, Regional Development Commissioner, Director of Maritime Health and the Engineer-Director of the Port Authority, members of local authorities representing the City and Town Councils, and a representation of institutions such as the Chamber of Commerce, Industry and Navigation (recognised in 1911, with the publication of the Basic Law of 29 June, as public corporations under the Ministry of Development, they should be heard in all matters affecting them), a representative of the Chamber of Agriculture and the Maritime League. Moreover, the Executive Committee, in which the number of members was reduced to 10, made up the Civil Governor (chairman *ex officio*), the port director-engineer, Commander of Navy, Maritime Health Director, Manager of ports, the President of the Island Council and five members of the Chamber of Commerce, Industry and Navigation, which normally acted as effective Presidency, the Vice President, the two participating representatives and the Secretariat. Finally, the port authority structure was divided into two sections. The Project Manager, headed by the figure of an Engineer-Director appointed by the state, was responsible for developing and managing construction projects, maintenance and operation, and the Secretariat for the management of the entity.

The creation of the Port Authorities in Spain pursued economic port self-sufficiency and improved coordination of work in them. State concern for the financial autonomy of the Port Authorities was subsequently reflected in a specific law in 1911 (Law of 7 July). The new entities assumed some of the powers held by the Ministry of Development, in particular the management of public infrastructure (quays, lighthouses, sheds), as well as matters related to the police and docks service, with the government reserving the ownership of fixed capital, the approval of projects and plans of the Port Authorities and occupancy permits for the maritime zone until the late twentieth century. To revitalise the works and services at ports, along with state government subsidies, they authorised the levy of excise taxes on passengers and goods (to finance the works), fees for navigation services and the issuance of debt securities, with or without government guarantee, also to cover the cost of intended works.

In the 1920s, concern as to the competitiveness of the ports increased, after the Chief Engineer/Board Directors indicated the rudimentary nature of the means employed and the inadequacy of the infrastructures given the changes in maritime transport (Harley, 1971; Mokyr, 1993). The model was similar to the tool model, in which the Port Authorities were not limited to the construction, conservation and exploitation of the port but also aimed to provide reasonably priced equipment and services, acting as 'regulator for the, not always strictly fair, prices, often charged by the private facilities often wear' (Junta de Obras del Puerto de Santa Cruz de Tenerife, 1930, 121). It was, ultimately, a way of putting an end to the private sector monopoly to which the Port Authorities attributed the ports' loss of prominence.

However, except for the establishment of public water supply service at the docks, many of the initiatives promoted by the Port Authorities never actually materialised. In some cases this was due to the lack of funds, in others, the changes of criteria in the direction of the Port Authorities and, in the majority, the opposition of private utilities, sometimes with the connivance of local and national authorities. This was what happened, for example, with the attempts to provide public cranes in Las Palmas as a result of the 'tough opposition' of companies (that owned cranes, both in floating barges as in coal piers) and delayed approval of projects: 'For reasons of superiority, perhaps as a result of having stopped over at an official centre in the Islands before arriving in Madrid ' (Junta de Obras de los Puertos de La Luz y Las Palmas, 1929, 18–19). The same thing happened in Santa Cruz with the project presented in 1927 to acquire a public ships tank service to reduce prices demanded by the trust in the bay, which 'to date (1930), has been sleeping [...] the sleep of the just' (Junta de Obras del Puerto de Santa Cruz de Tenerife, 1930, 110).

Nevertheless, the Port Authority of Santa Cruz managed to launch initiatives such as the building of a small yard and workshop (1919), public-service cranes and, given the lack of private sector interest, in 1930 it funded and awarded the construction of facilities for the supply of oil derivatives on the docks to the Sociedad Petrolifera Española.

4.2   Private Management

As for private management in ports, a heterogeneous group of entrepreneurs (agents, merchants, shipowners etc.) co-existed with workers (sailors, chargers etc.). These professions were regulated to different extents. Entrepreneurs, from 1821 onwards, had to be registered in the industrial and commercial registers to engage in intermediation activities in the ports. Besides, the exploitation of a concession on the docks or in the maritime zone required the development of a project and administrative authorisation. In terms of port tasks, the most important was loading and unloading, as well as those carried out on board ships, and they could only be carried out by those enrolled in the Guild of Merchants until this privilege was abolished in 1849, at which point only those specifically registered persons could take them on (Royal Orders of 21 January and 9 November 1849 and Royal Decree of 15 March 1850).

The first changes in this organisation affected the labour force in those ports engaging in foreign trade. In 1859, the Royal Order of 5 February established that if no marina-registered persons were available, 'land-based' persons – that is, those not enrolled – could be recruited for the tasks of loading and unloading. In 1864, the Royal Decree of 15 June declared loading and unloading operations to be free, suppressing the rates in force. Finally, in 1873, the compulsory registration of all those who worked in any kind of marine-related activity, the so-called Maritime Registry (Matrícula de Mar), was abolished and replaced by mandatory registration for all sailors and fishermen, entitling all inhabitants of Spain to freely practise maritime industries as long as they observed the regulations outlined by public agencies.

Since then, the relationship between employers and workers would depend on individual negotiation and on collective negotiation (with or without arbitration from the Administration) as class consciousness developed, which would result in the signing of the first formal agreements between employers and workers in the working rates for stowage, unloading and reloading. Indeed, the largest concentration of workers in the islands in the Canary ports took shape in the late nineteenth century. As traffic increased, moving supplies and trade, many workers found jobs in port work, mostly in the work of loading and unloading, but the range of professions was complex. Given the discontinuity of shipping, dock work tended not to be a regular occupation, especially in the case of loading and unloading. Therefore, the number of workers varied over time, as can be observed in the transfer of labour from one specialty to another. These variations were due also to the introduction of technological innovations and their influence on the organisation of work. These aspects would lead to a port work culture, where the term 'temporary' is a constant feature. 'Masculinisation' is also an important concept; this port culture was transmitted to some city neighbourhoods like La Isleta or Los Riscos in Las Palmas of Gran Canaria (Martín Galán, 2001) or San Andrés, Valleseco, Toscal and El Cabo in Santa Cruz (Cioranescu, 1979), where most of these workers lived, often in conditions of deplorable hygiene.

Dock workers have a recognised tradition of association, and the first working organisations in the Canaries appeared around port work, where they have the highest rate of enrolment and mobilisation capacity, probably because this field includes significant nuclei of salaried workers and class consciousness. There are reports of associations in the Port of Las Palmas in the last decades of the nineteenth century, driven by the large number of workers that had no formal organisation, successors of the ancient port chargers. However, both in Santa Cruz de Tenerife and Las Palmas, the first trades unions were constituted at the beginning of the twentieth century, after strikes staged to demand wage increases and an eight-hour working day. They were, in general, worker associations linked to certain port activities: shipwrights, carpenters, mechanics, sailors and, the largest, coal loaders (black load) and general merchandise (white load). Back in the 1920s, a framework to regulate the organisation of work was put forward by the unions, with their proposal to supply a work force from closed lists, and by the administration, supported by the enterprises, with their proposal of a specific labour relationships framework, in an expression of the Joint Committees of Maritime Transport formed during the dictatorship of Primo de Rivera that gave rise, after conflicts from the mid-1920s, to two separate agreements on loading and unloading rates between employers and workers (Suárez Bosa, 2003; Martín Hernández, 2003).

Another remarkable aspect of private management in ports is related to how entrepreneurs were represented and to their responses to changes in the characteristics of organisation and traffic. Business interests from the late nineteenth century were channelled through the Chambers of Commerce, Industry and Navigation and the representation, by virtue of their membership of the same, in different institutions such as the Port Authority. But employer organisations were also constituted in the Canary Island ports, in line with the trend in most European societies since the end of the nineteenth century, to set up interest organisations. Perhaps the most significant example in this regard, within the corporatism of the dictatorship of Primo de Rivera, was the formation in 1925 of two consignees' employer organisations to defend corporate interests against labour demands, tariff increases imposed by the Port Authority and Island Councils and so forth.

Organisational changes were also critical in companies and markets. Business strategies, regardless of the port analysed, were generally characterised by business diversification (supplies, insurance, agency, commercial and financial intermediation etc.) from the core activity of vessel consignment. Without the representation of the shipping company, owner or renter of the vessels, the services required by the ship while in port could not be outsourced to third parties. However, the scale and strategy of shipping lines, traffic characteristics and competition between ports and agents conditioned the organisation of companies providing port services. The shipping companies formed societies to ensure high investment and reduce uncertainty in the business; the accumulated turnover generated economies of scale and these societies were grouped together in maritime freight conferences (New Zealand Agreement, South African Conference, African Shipping Conference, West African and the North Brazilian, Brazil and River Plate Conference, River Plate Conference etc.) to ensure price stability and, therefore, the return on investment (Kirkaldy, 1914; Marx 1953; Dyos and Aldcroft, 1969). These agreements had an impact on freight service providers, especially for fuel, forcing them to adjust to prices accepted by the association. In addition, to avoid uncertainty in the business, it was necessary to ensure their shipment by signing a contract, usually on an annual basis, with the shipping company which established the service prices.

But organisation and business management was modified in line with regular navigation impositions and increased demand for services. The family-based consignee company lost ground to big service providers. But this did not lead to its demise, as family-based companies retained an active presence in the Canaries in supply companies like Miller and Co. in Las Palmas or Hamilton and Co. in Santa Cruz, thanks to their economic and business strategies. Both companies established their own branches in London, or alliances with family companies, responsible for negotiating the purchase of mineral, shipping contracts and so forth. Moreover, as in the case of Hamilton, agreements were established with other competitors for services where higher capital requirements were needed (coal, water, transport etc.). As a result, each company maintained its corporate body and, of course, its consignment contracts, expanded their own business size, economised on management costs and established an administrative unit in order to reduce costs and risk, increase competitiveness as well as control the market (Cabrera Armas and Díaz de la Paz, 2008).

From the 1880s onwards, as traffic growth and business expectations sharpened, this family structure was modified due to the entry of large companies mostly linked to mining interests and, to a lesser extent, shipping interests. Clearly, the emergence of a new supplier in the market disrupted the status quo. This can be seen in the case of Santa Cruz with the entry into the coal business of the British Cory Brothers and Co., with a minority share (37.5) in which Hamilton and Co. continued to control the majority of the business and its management until the termination of the agreement between the two companies in the 1910s; although they maintained the agreements on the purchase and transportation of coal to Santa Cruz (Cabrera Armas and Díaz de la Paz, 2008). In most ports, however, the company opted to open a branch to grab a share of the business. This is what happened, for example, in the port of La Luz with the installation of Miller and Co., Blandy Brothers and Co., Elder Dempster and Co. and Swanston and Co. in the 1880s, or in Santa Cruz, Elder Dempster in the 1890s. This situation would change from the late 1890s with the emergence of coal houses, as in the case of Cory and to a much lesser extent, Blandy (whose headquarters was in Funchal), in other ports of the world. The tactics of these companies altered the port market in both ports. Thus, while increased competition resulted in an incentive for upgrading facilities and equipment, old firms ceded parts of the port business to new companies. The end result of this process was the signing of collusive agreements, giving rise to cartelised supply in activities that required increased investments in fixed and variable capital. However, while in the water supply, passenger transportation or maritime rescue, the process was characterised by the integration into a trust of the companies in the respective port in which each company contributed their material resources and provided service at a given price. Under collegiate leadership, the coal service was transformed as a result of the agreements reached by the coaling companies. In Las Palmas, the first such transformation, and therefore the first agreement between consignee coal houses, took shape in the late nineteenth century between Wilson, Sons and Co., a mining company that owned numerous coal deposits, and companies established since the 1880s in the port of La Luz: Miller, Blandy, the Grand Canary Coaling Co. (Elder coal subsidiary), and Swanston & Co. Wilson's managers, shortly after opening their facilities,

> approached the owners of other deposits requesting a percentage from their shipping companies, threatening them with crude competition otherwise. The companies handed over 20 per cent of their contracts and since then have continued in the same vein, taking over the contracts of others when the opportunity arose.[4]

The second round of market-sharing agreement also took place in Las Palmas in the early twentieth century, after the failure of the efforts made by the supplier companies and the British government to prevent the opening of a deposit owned by German shipping company Woermann Linie:

> [They] began by offering severe competition to the British firms established there, reducing the prices of coal to a profitable figure, but eventually the British firms, in order to avoid severe losses, had to arrange to give the Germans a certain entire percentage of the trade at the said port, considerably decreasing the business held for years by Britons. (Martín Hernández, 2004, 64)

In Santa Cruz, however, three major coal companies (Hamilton, Cory and the Teneriffe Coaling Co.) managed to ensure that, apart from the S.A. Depositos de Carbones de Tenerife, whose majority shareholder was the German Deutsches Kohlen Depot Gesellschaft, no other company was to offer coal or related services (in water vessels, sea rescue etc.). Nevertheless, although they did not participate directly in the coal business, some companies obtained economic compensation from the established companies. This was the case with Wilson Sons & Co., Hull Blyth & Co. or, after the First World War, Compañía General Canaria de Combustibles, SA (majority-owned by Britain's Canary Islands Depots Coal & Oil Co. Ltd). This company, which after integration in 1921 in the coal association of Las Palmas, in 1925 handed over their conces-sionary rights in Santa Cruz to the companies operating in that port in exchange for 7500 pounds in cash, together with

> 12 per cent of total annual coal sales (in Santa Cruz), in addition to an extra 3/6d for each ton per year below the tonnage represented by that 12 per cent, and by contrast, we will pay 3/6d per ton for each ton that surpasses said percentage.[5]

Agreements between enterprises were not limited to the one-off sur-render of the coal business in ports. In 1903, in a context of growing regional traffic and increased competition, the coal houses promoted the establishment in London of the Atlantic Island Depot Arrangement (AIDA) cartel that was maintained until the end of the period under analysis, except during the so-called coal 'war' in Las Palmas in 1912 and during the First World War (Quintana Navarro, 1985). The agree-ment, renewable annually, set a reference price for the sale of coal in the Atlantic ports (Las Palmas, Santa Cruz, Mindelo, Funchal and, later, Dakar), and assigned a percentage of the business to coal-based car-riers representing each consignee in a port, so that on any coal that

exceeded this percentage remaining financial compensation had to be paid (always in sterling), and conversely, they would perceive payment, if sales did not reach the agreed quota.

However, market deals did not always guarantee price stability if new competitors appeared or operating costs did not fall. This was the case in 1928 when companies of the cartel of Las Palmas decided to avert falling prices by purchasing the Shipowners Society with coal deposits in Dakar and Oran (Algeria) by 100,000 pounds that was not part of the cartel in that Senegalese port. As for operating costs, reduced activity in the coal deposits, shipyards and workshops led companies to implement a dual policy. On the one hand, they reduced labour costs through wage cuts and layoffs, especially for black load, which resulted in increased labour unrest (Suárez Bosa, 2003; Martín Hernández, 2003). On the other hand, they tried to reduce costs by arranging certain activities, such as the agreement signed in 1925 to partner in the coal and goods unloading between Blandy Brothers Las Palmas and Compañía General Canaria de Combustibles, or the one adopted in 1929 to extend the agreement to the entire process (from buying to selling coal), including most coal operating in Las Palmas. In fact, in 1930 the Condor Limited holding was founded in London with a capital of 10.8 million pesetas, put up by the consignees with deposits in Las Palmas: Miller (18.6 per cent), Blandy (12.1), Grand Canary Coaling (20.8), Compañía Carbonera de Las Palmas, S.L. (controlled by Hull Blyth & Co., 9.3), Compañía Nacional de Carbones Minerales, S.A. (a subsidiary of Wilson, Sons & Co., 16.0), Compañía General de Combustibles Canarias, S.A. (Quéret property since 1929) and Llewellyn & Merrett, Ltd (23.2), with Cory Brothers & Co. staying out of the holding (and subsequently joining in 1946), along with Oceanic Fuel Company, Ltd (whose majority share-holder was the Oceanic Coal Co. Ltd) and the German Depósitos de Carbones de Tenerife, which in 1925 had acquired a majority stake in the Woermann Linie in Las Palmas. Changes in the coal market in Las Palmas contrasted with the stagnation in Santa Cruz as the market was controlled by the same companies until the end of the period, except for Cory Brothers, which ceased to supply fuel at the end of 1920s in the wake of the port expansion works.

5   Conclusion

Historically, the purpose of the ports was to provide services and infra-structure that would enable navigation, while also requiring manage-ment to be as efficient and competitive as possible to reduce budget expenditure and investment. In the ports of La Luz-Las Palmas and Santa Cruz de Tenerife, both the public and private sectors contributed to increased management efficiency, especially from the 1880s onwards, thanks to increased investment in the provision of fixed and variable capital. Taking advantage of the favourable geographic situation in the context of the colonial race, the Canary Island ports enjoyed a leading

Table 2.2 Entry of vessels and tonnage in Mid-Atlantic ports (1880–1929) (five-year average)

	Number of vessels							
	Canary Islands				Cape Verde Mindelo	Madeira Funchal		Senegal Dakar
	Santa Cruz		Las Palmas					
Period	Steam	Total	Steam	Total	Tránsito	Tránsito	Total	Total
1880–84	391	1436	224	1259	1255	727		
1885–89	660	1555	732	1642	1397	747		
1890–94	964	1828	1624	2468	1140	703		
1895–99	1346	2272	2025	2945	1409	794		
1900–04	1852	2972	2344	3634	1435		1345	
1905–09	2476	3604	2858	4816	1510		1377	715
1910–14	3236	4068	4548	6257	1435		1251	1176
1915–19	1301	2042	1518	2956	923		341	1583
1920–24	2112	3156	2891	4575	964		683	1732
1925–29	3010	3952	4105	5885	1308		927	2461

	Tonnage in thosands							
	Canary Islands				Cap Verde Mindelo	Madeira Funchal		Senegal Dakar
	Santa Cruz		Las Palmas					
Period	GRT	Net	GRT	Net	Net	GRT	GRT	Net
1880–84		520	476			872		
1885–89		859	n/a	1906	1649	923		
1890–94	1824	n/a	n/a	3407	n/a	1065		
1895–99	2955	1887	n/a	4607	4697			
1900–04	5290	3061	8214	4856	7602			
1905–09	6718	4031	9009	5500	n/a		5991	1128
1910–14	8295	4949	16277	9674	n/a		7209	2120
1915–19	1932	1457	5401	3020	n/a		1266	3758
1920–24	5967	3657	10866	6663	n/a		4159	2621
1925–29	7754	4687	14818	8760	5820		n/a	3683

Source: Almeida (1938); Bebiano (1933); Cabrera Armas y Suárez Bosa (2012); Câmara (2002); Martín Hernández (2004); Murcia Navarro (1975); Pawlowski (1918). Self-made elaboration.

position among the mid-Atlantic ports as a tri-continental communications node. In the transition from the nineteenth to the twentieth century, the need to improve the financial management of the ports, the strengthening of the domestic market and increased competition due to the establishment of large companies with mining interests and, to a lesser extent, shipping interests, would result in new changes to port management. In the public sector the most remarkable events were the creation of Ports Authorities and the endowment of a new infrastructure related to changes in domestic and foreign demand in the first third of the twentieth century. In the private sector, the formation of cartels and trusts in port services that required greater investment, together with the dynamism of the domestic market and lower transaction costs, made it possible to maintain the competitiveness of the Canary ports in the Atlantic context.

Table 2.3　Coal and fuel supplies in Mid-Atlantic ports (1855–1929) (five-year average in thousands of tonnes)

	Canary Islands			Cape Verde Mindelo		Madeira Funchal*	Senegal Dakar	
	Santa Cruz	Las Palmas						
	Coal	Coal	Fuel	Coal	Fuel	Coal	Coal	Fuel
1855–59		5.1		23.3		9.1		
1860–64		11.5		42.5		12.8		
1865–69		9.9		50.9		15.5		
1870–74		6.9		58.9		28.6		
1875–79		5.4		71.0		30.3		
1880–84	20.5	6.0		160.5		49.4		
1885–89	60.7	83.6		216.2		65.0		
1890–94	98.8	210.9		180.6		63.9		
1895–99	152.4	260.1		282.2		87.9		
1900–04	236.7	306.4		317.0		181.0		
1905–09	217.6	342.8		289.8		148.9		
1910–14	292.0	757.1		268.4		119.5	206.6	
1915–19	78.1	158.1		218.1		35.5	340.9	
1920–24	145.6	356.8	89.6	221.5	12.0	44.0	190.8	
1925–29	168.0	380.7	181.4	267.6	80.4	41.1	215.2	39.1

* Funchal fuel supply data is not available.
Sources: Almeida, 1938; Bebiano, 1933; Suárez Bosa and Cabrera Armas, 2012; Lopes de Figueiredo, 1913; Nadal Farreras, 1978; Pawlowski, 1918. Self-made elaboration.

Notes

1. Civil engineers first took control of the direction of public works in the Canary Islands in 1848 in the port of Santa Cruz de Tenerife, and subsequently also in Las Palmas de Gran Canaria as of 1851.
2. In 1880, despite the importance of San Telmo docks in the coastwise trade and fisheries, the conservation works were transferred to the Board of Docks under the control of Las Palmas City Town Hall, which barely made investments in its conservation, and even less in its expansion. In 1888, it was declared port of general interest of second order, transferring the conservation works again to the state.
3. In 1885 the first reform was approved with the replanting due to increased work in the North Pier. In 1893 the budget was increased to 367,392 pesetas. The first part of the South-dike was modified, turning it into a dock-dike, joining the second and the third part to form a stretch of 464 m. In 1898, a new additional budget of 245,693 pesetas was approved to reform the basements of the second piece and the concrete used in the entire construction. In 1902, after the failure of the second piece of the south dike, further expenditure of 390,492 pesetas was authorised for the repair works, while its length was reduced from 464 to 250 m. In 1907, an additional sum of 640,929 pesetas was authorised to convert the 250 m of the dike in dike-dock, with a width of 21 m over the first 70 m and 7.4 m for the remainder. Finally, in 1911, the budget was increased to 1,138,050 pesetas to prolong the south-dike to the original length of 464 m and increase the width of the entire piece to 21 m.
4. Archivo Histórico Provincial, Santa Cruz de Tenerife, Fondo Hamilton, correspondence, 1902.
5. Compañía General Canaria de Combustibles, proceedings, 3 February 1925.

Bibliography

Alemany Llovera, J. (1991) *Los puertos españoles en el siglo XIX* (Madrid: CEHOPU).
Almeida, J. (1938) *O Porto Grande de S. Vicente de Cabo Verde* (Lisboa: Ed. Imperio).
Alzola Minondo, P. (1994) *Las obras públicas en España* (Madrid: Colegio de Ingenieros de Caminos, Canales y Puertos).
Bebiano, J. B. (1932) 'Alguns aspectos económicos do Arquipélago de Cabo Verde', *Boletim Geral das Colónias*, 82, 3–20.
Bebiano, J. B. (1933) *La colonie du Cap Vert et la crises*, Institut Colonial International (Bruselas: Établissement Généraux d'Imprimerie).
Bourgon Tinao, L. P. (1982) *Los Puertos Francos y el Régimen Especial de Canarias* (Madrid: Instituto de Estudios de Administración Local).
Burriel de Orueta, E. L. (1974) *El puerto de la Luz en Las Palmas de Gran Canaria* (Las Palmas de Gran Canaria: Centro de Investigación Económica y Social de la Caja de Ahorros de Gran Canaria).
Cabrera Armas, L. G. (1997) 'La Reforma de Villaverde y el Régimen de Puertos Francos de Canarias', *Situación. Serie de estudios regionales. Canarias*, 17–28.
Cabrera Armas, L. G. (2007) 'El impacto del desarrollo portuario en el mundo urbano: Canarias, 1870–1914', *XXVI Meeting of the Portuguese Economic and Social History Association*, Punta Delgada (Azores).

Cabrera Armas, L. G., and A. Díaz de la Paz (2008) 'El tráfico marítimo en la era del Imperio: cartel, monopolio y oligopolio: el caso de Santa Cruz de Tenerife, c. 1870–1914', *IX Congreso de la Asociación Española de Historia Económica (AEHE)* (Murcia-Cartagena).

Cabrera Armas, L. G., and A. Díaz de la Paz (2011) 'El apogeo del nuevo modelo de crecimiento económico', in A. Millares et al. (eds), *Historia Contemporánea de Canarias* (Las Palmas de Gran Canaria: Obra Social de La Caja de Canarias), pp. 197–235.

Câmara, B. (2002) *A Economia da Madeira (1859–1914)* (Lisboa: Imprensa de Ciências Sociais).

Cámara de Comercio, Industria y Navegación de Las Palmas (1924) *La navegación y el comercio de Las Palmas en el año 1923–1924* (Las Palmas: Tip. High-Life).

Cámara de Comercio, Industria y Navegación de Las Palmas (1930) *Memoria comercial correspondiente a 1929* (Las Palmas: Tip. El Diario).

Cámara de Comercio, Industria y Navegación de Las Palmas (1931) *Memoria comercial correspondiente a 1930* (Las Palmas: Tip. El Diario).

Carreira, A. (1982) *Estudos de Economia Caboverdiana* (Lisboa: Imprensa Nacional-Casa Da Moeda).

Cioranescu, A. (1979) *Historia de Santa Cruz de Tenerife*, Vol. IV (Santa Cruz de Tenerife: Lit. A. Romero, S.A.).

Comín Comín, F. (1996) *Historia de la Hacienda Pública en. España* (Madrid: Crítica).

Correia, C. (1996) 'A cidade do Mindelo nos séculos XIX–XX', *Africana*, 4, 99–112.

Correia e Silva, A. L. (1998) *Nos Tempos do Porto Grande do Mindelo* (Praia-Mindelo: Centro Cultural Português).

Cuéllar Villar, D. (2002) 'Política de obras públicas y políticas liberales: El Ministerio de Fomento (1851–1874)', *Transportes, Servicios y telecomunicaciones*, 2, 43–69.

Davies, P. N. (1984) 'The British Contribution to the Economic Development of the Canary Islands with Special Reference to the Nineteenth Century', *V Coloquio Historia Canario Americano*, 3, 353–80.

Davies, P. N. (1995) 'Relaciones comerciales entre Gran Bretaña y las Islas Canarias desde 1850 a nuestros días', in idem et al., *Canarias e Inglaterra a través de la Historia* (Las Palmas de Gran Canaria: Cabildo Insular de Gran Canaria), pp. 217–69.

Dyos, H. J., and D. H. Aldcroft (1969) *British Transport: An Economic Survey from the Seventeenth Century to the Twentieth* (Leicester University Press).

Frax Rosales, E. (1996) 'Las leyes de bases de obras públicas en el siglo XIX', *Revista de Estudios Políticos*, 93, 513–28.

Fundo de Desenvolmiento Nacional (1984) *Linhas gerais da história de desenvolmiento urbano da cidade do Mindelo* (Praia: Ministério da Habitaçâo e Obras Públicas).

Gómez Mendoza, A. (1997) 'Las obras públicas, 1850–1935', in F. Comín Comín and A. Gómez Mendoza (eds), *Los fundamentos de la España liberal (1834–1900). La sociedad, la economía y las formas de vida*, Historia de España de Menéndez Pidal, 33, 467–515.

Guaíta, A. (1984) *El Ministerio de Fomento, 1832–1931* (Madrid: Instituto de Estudios de Administración Local).

Guimerá Ravina, A. (1989) *La Casa Hamilton. Una empresa británica en Canarias, 1837–1987* (Santa Cruz de Tenerife: Litografía Romero).

Harley, C. K. (1971) 'The Shift from Sailing Ships to Steamships, 1850–1890: A Study of Technical Change and Its Diffusion', in D. N. McCloskey (ed.), *Essays on a Mature Economy: Britain after 1840* (Princeton University Press), pp. 215–34.

Junta de Obras de los Puertos de La Luz y Las Palmas (1929) *Memoria correspondiente al año 1928* (Madrid: Vicente Roca).

Junta de Obras del Puerto de Santa Cruz de Tenerife (1930) *Memoria relativa al progreso y desarrollo del puerto* (Santa Cruz de Tenerife: Lib. y Tip. Católica).

Kirkaldy, A. W. (1914) *British Shipping: Its History, Organization and Importance* (London: Kegan Paul Trench, Trubner).

León y Castillo, J. de (1909) *Orígenes del Puerto de refugio de La Luz en Las Palmas de Gran Canaria*, Archivo Histórico Provincial de Las Palmas, Fondo Juan de León y Castillo, 14.

Lopes de Figueiredo, A. (1913) *O Carvâi na economia de Cabo Verde* (Lisboa: Tip. Industrial Portuguesa).

Martín Aceña, P. (1990) 'The Spanish Money Supply, 1874–1935', *Journal of European Economic History*, 19(1), 7–33.

Martín Galán, F. (1983) '1852–1883: antecedentes del Puerto de Refugio de La Luz', *Aguayro*, 146, 4–9.

Martín Galán, F. (2001) *La formación de Las Palmas: ciudad y puerto* (Las Palmas de Gran Canaria: Fundación Puerto de Las Palmas).

Martín Hernández, U. (1991) 'Los archipiélagos atlánticos de Canarias, Madeira, Cabo Verde y Azores (1880–1919). Una aproximación al estudio de las relaciones a través de los informes consulares Británicos', *Actas VIII Coloquio de Historia Canario-Americana, Las Palmas de Gran Canaria*, 2, 97–132.

Martín Hernández, U. (2003) *Cien años de lucha portuaria: aproximación histórica al sindicalismo en el Puerto de Santa Cruz de Tenerife* (Santa Cruz de Tenerife: Portuarios de Tenerife).

Martín Hernández, U. (2004) *Puertos Canarios y Navegación Internacional* (Santa Cruz de Tenerife: Idea).

Marx, D. (1953) *International Shipping Cartels: A Study of Industrial Self-regulation by Shipping Conferences* (Princeton University Press).

Melguizo Sánchez, A. (1979) 'El presupuesto de Calvo Sotelo', *Cuadernos económicos de ICE*, 10, 401–42.

Mokyr, J. (1993) *La palanca de la riqueza. Creatividad tecnológica y progreso económico* (Madrid: Alianza Universidad).

Morton, F. Scott (1977) 'Entry and Predation: British Shipping Cartels, 1879–1929', *Journal of Economics & Management Strategy*, 6(4), 679–724.

Nadal Farreras, J. (1978) *Comercio exterior con Gran Bretaña, (1777–1914)* (Madrid: Ariel Historia).

Pawlowski, A. (1918) 'El puerto de Dakar en la colonia francesa del Senegal', *Revista de Obras Públicas*, 1(2252), 586–88.

Quintana Navarro, F. (1985) *Barcos, negocios y burgueses en el Puerto de La Luz, 1883–1913* (Las Palmas de Gran Canaria, Centro de Investigación Económica y Social de la Caja Insular de Ahorros de Canarias).

Sousa Machado, J. de (1891) *Estudo sobre o Commercio do Carvão no Porto Grande da Ilha de S. Vicente (Archipelago de Cabo Verde) e no Porto da Luz em Gran Canaria (Archipelago das Canarias)* (Lisboa, Imprensa Nacional).

Suárez Bosa, M. (2003) *Llave de la fortuna: instituciones y organización del trabajo en el puerto de Las Palmas, 1883–1990* (Las Palmas de Gran Canaria: Fundación Caja Rural de Canarias).

Suárez Bosa, M. (2004) 'The Role of the Canary Islands in the Atlantic Coal Route from the End of the Nineteenth Century to the Beginning of the Twentieth Century: Corporate Strategies', *International Journal of Maritime History*, 16(1), 95–124.

Suárez Bosa, M., and L. G. Cabrera Armas (2012) 'La competencia en los servicios portuarios entre Cabo Verde y Canarias (1850–1914)', *Anuario de Estudios Atlánticos*, 58, 363–414.

Valdaliso Gago, J. M. (1997) *La navegación regular de cabotaje en España en los siglos XIX y XX. Guerra de fletes, conferencias y consorcios navieros* (Bilbao: Departamento de Transportes y Obras Públicas del Gobierno Vasco).

Zimmermann, E. W. (1983) *Zimmermann on Ocean Shipping* (New York: Sir Isaac Pitman & Sons, 1921).

3
Porto Grande of S. Vicente: The Coal Business on an Atlantic Island

Ana Prata

1 Introduction

The situation in the Atlantic that emerged in the first half of the nineteenth century was a result of a profound revolution in maritime transportation technology and communications. Everything was in flux. The need for increased ship tonnage, brought about by the growth in traffic volume, was met by the contributions of technology that emerged as a result of the Industrial Revolution, unleashing a chain reaction of adjustments and adaptations that culminated in the substitution of sailboats with steam vessels, and the use of coal as an energy source. This heavy and voluminous fuel introduced a new travel rationale to oceanic navigation: the need for refuelling stops. This rationale overcame the need to transport large stocks of coal on board, which would entail sacrificing space designed for commercial cargo and the transportation of passengers and thereby lead to a decrease in the profitability of maritime routes (Suárez Bosa and Cabrera Armas, 2010, 5).

Navigation companies themselves, faced with the new expensive costs of steam navigation, adopted new models of performance, organisation and financing, transforming themselves into corporations that started to invest in the entire economic chain connected with maritime transportation (from naval construction to oceanic coal supply) in a vertically focused strategy (Suárez Bosa, 2004).

It is within this context that we see the number of Atlantic coal stations emerge and multiply on the long transoceanic routes. Seeing that the Atlantic was the central axis of this new global economy, the Iberian archipelagos became the object of special interest on the part of newly industrialised Great Britain. These small islands were seen by British powers as key points in the commercial and technical viability of steam navigation (Cabrera Armas, 2010). British requests to Portugal and Spain, aimed at acquiring facilities for the construction of coal stations in the Azores, Madeira, Canaries and Cape Verde, were a constant during this period (Correia e Silva, 2000, 100).

It was to be the archipelago of Cape Verde, however, specifically Porto Grande, with the natural characteristics of the port – deep, protected waters, with excellent access points and its strategic geographic location, located at a key junction for the supply of maritime businesses travelling between Europe and South America, and even for those who operated the route of the Cape – that would attain the greatest prominence during the first decades of this coal cycle.

The aim of the following pages is, therefore, to explain the integration of Porto Grande into these new Atlantic commercial systems, at a time when it was a fundamental port of call in the European expansionist policies – in the transition from the nineteenth to the twentieth century – and to understand the influence of the historic cycle of the coal industry in the development and structuring of the port itself. To carry out this analysis, our primary sources have been the statistical information available for the archipelago of Cape Verde, the *Official Bulletins* of the General Government of Cape Verde, published since 1842, and a varied set of official documentation, which includes correspondence between the entities of mainland Portugal and the colony, and various records referring to the economic performance of the Cape Verde province, available at the Ultramarine Historic Archives in Lisbon.

2 Porto Grande of S. Vicente as an Atlantic Coaling Station

Located in the archipelago of Cape Verde, on the island of S. Vicente, Porto Grande was, until the first decades of the nineteenth century, a port of somewhat lesser importance, where a few ships occasionally docked. Over a short period, however, the new configuration created in the Atlantic, the increasingly complex global economic relations and the new need for refuelling stops required by steam navigation would completely alter the importance and position of this island port, setting off a truly unique economic evolution.

Nautically speaking, from a steamship point of view, Porto Grande on S. Vicente, with its strategic location mid-way between Europe and South America and its natural characteristics that guaranteed easy access to the ever-larger vessels that now dominated the Atlantic and global traffic, effectively emerged as the most strategic port of call in the Atlantic (Table 3.1). Thus it was crucial to equip the port with the capacity to supply coal to the steam vessels in transit, a business that from its inception was linked to British initiatives. At the time of the establishment of the first coal deposits in Porto Grande, however, there were other ports in the archipelago that were in much greater use by international navigation but that, for technical reasons – low tides, exposure to winds – found themselves immediately excluded from this new reorganisation of the Atlantic.[1]

One of the decisive steps towards the creation of the first English coal companies was the signing of the Treaty of Commerce and Navigation between Portugal and England on 3 July 1842. According to this treaty, the subjects of each of the signing parties would enjoy, in the domain of the other, the status of favoured nation. Despite the formal reciprocity of the privileges conceded to both sides, in practice the real beneficiaries of the prerogatives listed in the treaty were the British, since they were the ones who held defined commercial and strategic interests in the Portuguese ports (Castro, 1890).

S. Vicente was, at the time, the least populated of the archipelago islands, the poorest in terms of fiscal income and the one least served by civil administration, military and ecclesiastical institutions (Correia e Silva, 2007). Aware of the strategic interest of the archipelago of Cape Verde and the island of S. Vicente, the Portuguese authorities started to draft a new action plan.

Seeking to reverse the situation, on 11 June 1838, the same year in which the first coal deposit in Cape Verde was registered, a settlement by the name of Mindelo was created by royal decree, near Porto Grande.[2] Three months later, the first urbanisation plan of Mindelo was published, defining the set of projects needed in terms of sanitation, the construction of public buildings, and the establishment of security and taxation forces, with the object of guaranteeing the foundations for the development of the Porto Grande port structure. However, the economic and political difficulties experienced by the Portuguese monarchy would limit the availability of capital for investment in the development of the Cape Verde colony. What could be done was done, while the new requests for the licensing and installation of coal depositories rapidly multiplied.

The structure of the first companies linked to the coal industry in S. Vicente was connected, as we have already mentioned, to the initiative of a few English families – the Rendalls and the Millers – that had settled several years previously in the archipelago of Cape Verde. Their pioneer spirit was due to their knowledge of the islands, where they had developed export businesses for raw materials, to the reputation they had earned with the local authorities over the years and the information that they received regarding the progress achieved in steam navigation.[3] However, their experience, in the beginning of the 1850s, quickly attracted more established companies, persuaded by the geostrategic value of the port.

By 1850, the Royal Mail Steam Packet, one of the most important packet businesses in the world, received authorisation from the Portuguese authorities to install a coal deposit. Seeking to make the recently established London–Rio de Janeiro route feasible, the Royal Mail decided to extend its investments to the coal supply sector of the intermediary ports. This constituted a manifestation of the vertical focus to which we have already alluded.

In 1851, Thomas and George Miller, residents of S. Nicolau, received permission to create a new deposit in Porto Grande, named Thomas & Miller. Patent Fuel followed their lead, also in 1851. In 1853, it was the turn of the prosperous Visger & Miller. Five years later, in 1858, a new deposit was established by MacLeod and Martin. Over a short period, Porto Grande's role as a coaling station was already irreversibly established.

The interest shown by the English industries and merchants regarding Porto Grande created some optimism among Portuguese authorities, who actually considered changing the capital of the archipelago from Praia, on the island of Santiago, to Mindelo, but no such change was ever made. However, on 7 December 1851, the customs office of S. Vicente was elevated to first-order customs,[4] and on 1 September 1854, the tax of 100 réis per imported ton of coal was ordered, an amount which was to be 'exclusively used towards construction on said island of S. Vicente'.[5]

Years later, in 1858,[6] Mindelo was raised to the status of village,[7] and a set of measures aimed at the development of its urban structures was prepared. The purpose was to adapt Mindelo to the reality that was being sketched out for it (Valdez, 1864, 108). The construction of several buildings was planned – customs office,[8] military barracks,[9] official residency of the governor of the island,[10] court, jail,[11] municipal hall[12] – that would be exclusively dedicated to public services, a better marking out of the port area, the installation of public lighting[13] and the creation of a water supply network.[14]

Mindelo was essentially undergoing an exceptional time of development, being transformed in a short amount of time from a marginalised, sparsely populated space to an economic and social pole, around

Table 3.1 Shipping lines with monthly calls in Mindelo (1877–80)

Company	Nationality	Route
Empresa Lusitana	Portuguese	Lisbon–Madeira–S.Vicente–S. Tiago–Bolama–S.Tomé–Angola
Royal Mail Steam Packet Co.	English	Southampton–Lisbon–Brazil–River Plate
Pacific Steam Navigation Co.	English	Liverpool–Lisbon–Brazil–River Plate–Valparaíso
Orient Steam Navigation Co.	English	London–Cape of Good Hope–Australia
Lamport & Holt	English	Liverpool–London–Brazil–River Plate
Société Générale de Transports Maritimes	French	Marsaille–Brazil–River Plate
Chargeurs Réunis	French	Havre–Brazil–River Plate
Apesteguy Frères	French	Bordeaux–Brazil–River Plate
Dufur Ebruzza	Italian	Genoa–Brazil–River Plate
Società Lavarello	Italian	Genoa–Brazil–River Plate
Rocco Piaggio & Filho	Italian	Genoa–Brazil–River Plate
Nicolo Schiafino	Italian	Genoa–Brazil–River Plate
Nord Deustscher	German	Bremen–Brazil–River Plate
Hamburg Sudamerikanische Chaft Kosmos	German	Hamburg–Lisbon–Brazil–River Plate
Dampfschiffahrt	German	Hamburgh–River Plate–Valparaíso

Source: Costa, 1880, 187.

which the life of almost all the archipelago was starting to turn (Correia e Silva, 2007).

At the same time as the requests to license coal deposits, we have also found several other requests for the construction and development of other types of structures in this period. The growing English presence in S. Vicente was felt not only on the level of the coal industry, but also on a cultural level. In 1853, Thomas and George Miller and George Rendall were to request from the Portuguese government the concession of some land for the construction of an English golf club and a football pitch.[15]

3 The Economic Rise of Porto Grande (1850–90)

The flash development of Porto Grande is part of and intrinsically associated with the cycle of alterations designed by the new system of Atlantic ports of call. This meant that the higher or lower volumes of traffic and coal commerce would have a direct influence on the island's economic performance.

The study of Atlantic ports of call reveals a division into two main periods: the first (1850–80), when the first coal companies were established, set in motion by the competitiveness and the profitability and novelty of the industry; and the second (1880–1914), when there was a progressively visible trend to form cartels and merge the various businesses in order to neutralise competition and guarantee fixed profits, a situation which would eventually lead to the rise of prices per ton of coal.

In the specific case of Porto Grande, these two periods would also mark the two major moments of commercial and economic development of the port, in which we can trace a journey from euphoria and economic ascension (1850–90) – with Porto Grande as the most important coaling station of the Mid-Atlantic – to stagnation and crisis (1890–1914), when the competition from other coal ports and the inability to overcome some endogenous structural problems led Porto Grande to surrender its place as the premier port of call of the Atlantic (Correia e Silva, 2007).

Between 1850 and 1860, five coal companies were established in Mindelo: Royal Mail Steam Packet (1850), Thomas & Miller (1851), Patent Fuel (1851), Visger & Miller (1853) and MacLeod and Martin (1858), all belonging to English ex-patriots.

However, in a few years the deposits belonging to John Rendall, Thomas & Miller and MacLeod and Martin were incorporated into economically stronger businesses. Additionally, in 1860 one of the companies clearly dominated the coal market in Porto Grande: Millers & Nephew, created that very year by merging the Patent Fuel and Visger & Miller companies. Royal Mail Steam Packet, on the other hand, would continue exclusively to refuel its own fleet (FDN, 1984).

There was therefore, from a very early time, a commercial monopoly of coal in Porto Grande, and this situation had direct consequences on the rise of coal prices; this lasted for approximately 15 years, until the time when Cory Brothers & Co. was established in Mindelo (1875).

The appearance of this new coal company caused an immediate lowering of the coal price per ton from 47 shillings to 32.[16] As a direct consequence, an increase in the number of steam vessels seeking coal refuelling was registered. According to the monthly statistics of the Port Captaincy published in the Official Bulletins of Cape Verde, in 1875, 309 long-distance merchant ships entered Porto Grande, a number which, in 1879, had already increased to 669 ships.[17]

Table 3.2 Traffic of vessels calling at Porto Grande (1851–94)

Year	Number of vessels calling
1851	153
1861	267
1871	556
1881	1158
1889	1927
1894	891

Source: Figueiredo, 1913, 8; FDN, 1984, 53–4

The prosperous coal industry activity naturally generated other branches of business, such as the supply of provisions and commodities to ships and the import of several foreign products to satisfy the new needs of the residents and visitors to the island. At the end of 1879, a total of 157 business establishments[18] were listed, the majority of which also belonged to English merchants.

The strategic position of the island of S. Vicente also made it one of the most important poles of the global telegraph system. On 10 March 1874, the first underwater telegraph cable was installed by the Brazilian Submarine Telegraph, connecting S. Vicente to Madeira. In June, the connection to Brazil was finished.[19] In 1884, India Rubber Gutta Percha and Telegraph Works connected Praia to Mindelo. On 12 December of the following year, the telegraph communication with Bolama, Bissau and other ports in Africa[20] was opened. Over the following years, the telegraph network continued to expand (FDN, 1984, 56).

The increase in navigation to Porto Grande and the commercial development of the village of Mindelo contributed significantly to the public and municipal economic development of the island of S. Vicente. From the economic year of 1869–70 to that of 1878–79, public revenue increased from 19,781$575 réis to 39,360$666, an increase of almost 100 per cent, the main source of said return being the tax of 100 réis per ton of coal imported into the deposits.[21] From 1880 to 1882, the revenue for the treasury once again registered an increase of almost 200 per cent, increasing from 72,879$846 réis to 121,020$032 réis (Table 3.3). This new rise was justified in part by the rise in coal tax to 300 réis per imported ton of 1880 raised.

Coupled with the constant increase in maritime traffic in S. Vicente, and motivated by it, we have noted a degree of reorganisation in farming production in other islands of the archipelago. The following products

Table 3.3   Revenues on the tax on coal
imported to S. Vicente (1856–90) (in réis)

Year	Revenue
1856–60	14,659$000
1861–65	22,146$800
1866–70	25,143$700
1871–75	28,427$500
1876–80	44,500$700
1881–85	250,625$166
1886–90	371,526$307

Source: Figueiredo, 1913, 13.

arrived almost daily to S. Vicente from Santo Antão and São Nicolau: maize, beans, flour, cattle, fruit, coffee, sugar and tobacco, among others, a move that was strongly supported by the central authorities.[22]

The migratory flow of the archipelago's island populations also became frequent as, encouraged by the prosperity of S. Vicente, workers would go there in search of a job, and in turn provide cheap labour for the island's merchants and industries. At the high point of this activity, between 1860 and 1870, the lack of housing in Mindelo started to become evident. Several buildings that were built then were financed or actually directly built by the English (Figueira, 1968, 160), who thus resolved the problem of finding housing for their workers.[23]

Although it was not a political capital, even on a provincial level, in 1879 Mindelo housed the largest community of foreigners in the archipelago and several countries who were interested in the oceanic routes had consular or vice-consular representation in Mindelo, to wit: Germany, Belgium, Brazil, Denmark, United States of America, England, Italy, the Netherlands, Oriental Republic of Uruguay, Russia, Sweden, Norway and Turkey (Monteiro, 1996, 113–24). The rapid economic and social growth recorded in Mindelo led the Portuguese authorities to raise the village to city status[24] in 1879, and to transfer, in 1881, the headquarters of the Port Captaincy of the Cape Verde Province from Praia to Mindelo.[25]

While the construction of public buildings peaked between 1858 and 1879, the major expansion period of port equipment and service to navigation only began after Mindelo's status had been elevated to that of a city. The customs building was enlarged (1880–82); two lighthouses (1882 and 1894) and two signalling stations were built (1886); the boundary wall was finished (1891), as was the leper colony (Lazareto) (1882–1900).[26]

It should be mentioned that in spite of the investments made, the lack of capital on the part of the Portuguese State was a constant factor, and consequently construction projects dragged out endlessly and the difficulties in fulfilling many of the intentions were the order of the day. On the other hand, the strong British presence, evident on both the commercial and the socio-cultural level, would confer on the British merchants and industries an important economic weight in the evolution of the coal business and facilitate the creation of monopolies, impeding the establishment of a competitive system. This situation, which started in 1890, as we will see below, would have grave consequences for the positioning of Porto Grande as an Atlantic coaling station.

4   The Question of Port Administration and Operations

Up until 1910, the contours of the Portuguese port administration system were not very clear, as the services related to the maritime and port jurisdiction were reorganised several times during this period (Prata, 2011, 89).

Although the Portuguese ports depended directly on the state, not only for works and improvements but also for their administration and operation, no administrative system had yet been created that linked or centralised the national ports' various needs. The diverse jurisdictions were scattered throughout various ministries and secretariats, with the result that decision-making was difficult and administration unprofitable.[27] Inexperience and uncertainty as to the way forward dogged the progress of the works required, so frequent recourse was made to the opinion and skill of foreign engineering.[28]

In port operations, the warehouse services, loading and unloading, remained under-developed, and fees were paid to the Customs house for the use of some of their equipment. In 1910, with the fall of the monarchy and the beginning of the republican regime, the Portuguese state tried out a new system for the administration and management of its ports, creating various Autonomous Port Authorities (Juntas Autónomas dos Portos).[29] These autonomous boards were local corporations, created by the government and dependent on the Ministry of Commerce. Their objectives were as follows: to execute studies and the necessary works; to administrate services, revenues and subsidies for the construction, improvement and operation of the port; and to promote the development of commercial and maritime traffic. This system was created with the intention of giving greater administrative and financial

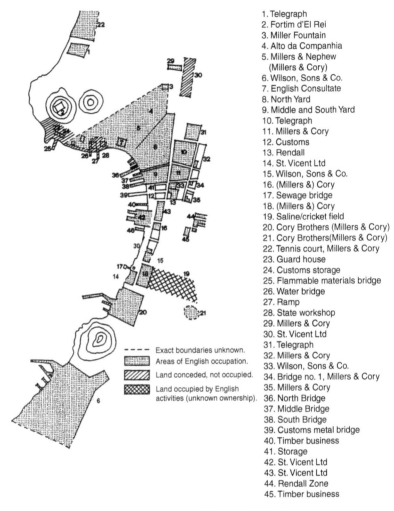

1. Telegraph
2. Fortim d'El Rei
3. Miller Fountain
4. Alto da Companhia
5. Millers & Nephew
   (Millers & Cory)
6. Wilson, Sons & Co.
7. English Consultate
8. North Yard
9. Middle and South Yard
10. Telegraph
11. Millers & Cory
12. Customs
13. Rendall
14. St. Vicent Ltd
15. Wilson, Sons & Co.
16. (Millers &) Cory
17. Sewage bridge
18. (Millers &) Cory
19. Saline/cricket field
20. Cory Brothers (Millers & Cory)
21. Cory Brothers(Millers & Cory)
22. Tennis court, Millers & Cory
23. Guard house
24. Customs storage
25. Flammable materials bridge
26. Water bridge
27. Ramp
28. State workshop
29. Millers & Cory
30. St. Vicent Ltd
31. Telegraph
32. Millers & Cory
33. Wilson, Sons & Co.
34. Bridge no. 1, Millers & Cory
35. Millers & Cory
36. North Bridge
37. Middle Bridge
38. South Bridge
39. Customs metal bridge
40. Timber business
41. Storage
42. St. Vicent Ltd
43. St. Vicent Ltd
44. Rendall Zone
45. Timber business

Legend:
- - - - Exact boundaries unknown.
▦ Areas of English occupation.
▨ Land conceded, not occupied.
▨ Land occupied by English activities (unknown ownership).

Map 3.1   Areas of British occupation at Mindelo (1879–1914)
Source: Adapted from FDN, 1984, 52.

autonomy to these corporations, the thinking being that the decentralisation of jurisdictions would allow for enhanced management and
administration of port affairs. The Juntas, however, would always continue to be heavily dependent on the central authorities for decisions
and finances. Nevertheless, we do find in the composition of these
Juntas a representation of governmental and local authorities – the
mayor of the town hall, the port captain, the director-engineer of the

port works, the customs officer – and representatives from the business and industrial sectors, chosen among the various associations and institutions with interests in the port (Prata, 2011, 123). In the end this situation made it possible for private citizens to have some say in the decisions that were made.

In the colonies, the regime for port administration and management followed the general lines of the central administration in mainland Portugal. The colonial ports were the property of the Portuguese state and it was the responsibility of the Portuguese authorities to administer the services and to carry out the needed improvements, through the Ministry of the Navy and Overseas Possessions (Ministério da Marinha e Ultramar), which was renamed the Ministry of the Colonies in 1911.

In fiscal terms, a system of customs houses was set up, responsible for collecting all the fees for the entry and departure of ships, passengers and goods. In the specific case of Cape Verde, there were two customs houses: one at Mindelo, on the Island of S. Vicente,[30] and the other at Praia, on Santiago, which were responsible for supervising all matters related to shipping, imports, exports, and transport of passengers of all the customs offices of the archipelago.[31] As early as 1 September 1854, a tax of 100 réis per ton of imported coal had been instituted, and the funds raised were to be applied to the works needed on the island of S. Vicente.[32]

The model of the Autonomous Port Authorities was never applied in the colonies. But, due to the difficulty the Portuguese authorities faced in developing all the colonial ports, there was a greater openness to the participation of private parties in the ports, not in their management, not in their administration – the Portuguese state never gave up these prerogatives – but in their operation. The Port of S. Vicente is a paradigm example of this reality. Examples of this practice include the concessions of several plots of land made to foreign businessmen and industrialists and the various licences granted for the establishment of English companies linked to the coal business (Map 3.1).

Practically the entire coastline of Porto Grande was in the hands of British private initiatives, and so it was by English initiative that various warehouses, bridges and docks were built, not for the specific purpose of developing the port infrastructures of Mindelo, but to facilitate the entrepreneurs' own businesses and activities.

The operation and equipping of the Port of S. Vicente were not properly carried out by the Portuguese authorities, either as a result of lack of capital, or simply due to lack of interest, their thinking being that the location of the port and its natural characteristics would be sufficient to guarantee the continued performance of the port. The main concern of the Portuguese was, in fact, that of controlling the tax revenues and customs.

5   The Crisis or the Lost Opportunity (1890–1914)

The demand for coal by international navigation was the fundamental condition for the functioning of the economic-social system built in Mindelo. However, at the end of 1889, the general conditions of the Atlantic market would be subverted. The source of this change lies in factors not directly connected to the dynamics of commerce; rather it was the overall situation that changed. In Rio de Janeiro, Brazil, the monarchy was deposed on 15 November 1889 by a military coup. In Argentina, the growth model based on external credit suffered a crisis in 1890, leading Chile into a turbulent civil war the following year. Consequently, as of 1890, there was a marked drop in Euro–South American traffic, as well as a drastic decrease in external demand for coal, precisely the two pillars on which the growth model of Porto Grande was based. Because of the structural connection that the coal-port sector had with the remaining sectors, the crisis generalised quickly, affecting the economy of the whole city. Together with the rapid decrease seen in fiscal revenue, there was also a reduction in the level of employment, a contraction of the internal market, and commercial bankruptcies (Correia e Silva, 2007).

To further compound this reduction in demand, a new structural element also arose in the context of the Mid-Atlantic: the development of other coal ports competing with Porto Grande – Santa Cruz, on the island of Tenerife and La Luz, on Gran Canaria. In fact, since the opening of Porto Grande to steam navigation, the Portuguese administration believed that S. Vicente's geographic position, aided by the fantastic natural conditions of the port, gave Mindelo a captive hold on the routes that connected Europe to South America. Consequently, the Portuguese developed a purely renter attitude, exploiting the profitable natural resource represented by the geographic position and thinking, naively, that the steam vessels stopped in Porto Grande because of a geographic necessity and, therefore, that they would always continue to do so.

However, if the advantages in location were decisive at the beginning of the coal cycle, over time they tended to be compensated, and even surpassed, by institutional and technological advantages. While the other ports in the Mid-Atlantic system were launching the construction of other advantageous fiscal, infrastructural, administrative, commercial strong points, the Portuguese authorities remained confident that the geographic location of Porto Grande was the only differentiation factor needed to maintain its status as the premier coaling station in the Atlantic, forgetting that, as and when its strategic location advantage ceased to be sufficiently competitive, another port would present itself as more attractive, with attractive overall conditions (infrastructures, coal prices, taxes and services) (Correia e Silva, 2007; Suárez Bosa and Cabrera Armas, 2010; Câmara, 2002). In fact, since the 1870s, when the price of coal rose in Mindelo, the navigation companies began to adopt alternative measures, seeking to transfer part of the purchases originally made there to other coal ports.

The origins of the crisis of 1890, as was to be expected, were explained differently by the Portuguese authorities and the English coal dealers. While the coal dealers advocated the theory of the external and Atlantic origin of the crisis, aggravated by the lack of fiscal and administrative flexibility by the Portuguese state and by the high tax imposed on each ton of coal, which would increase from 100 réis to 300 in 1880, the Portuguese authorities tended to attribute the responsibility for the retraction of coal navigation to the behaviour of the English companies operating in Mindelo, who, in their quest for higher profits, repeatedly increased the prices of coal.

In point of fact, steam vessels decided on their ports of call in the light of two cost components: accessibility charges, which led them to prefer ports situated on their ideal routepath, entailing fewer detours; and refuelling costs, based on the price per ton of coal and port operations (Câmara, 2002; Correia e Silva, 2007). To the extent that the first component was decisive, that is to say, the cost of the detour being more important than that of refuelling, Porto Grande enjoyed a leading position in the coal port system, but starting at the end of the 1880s, through the linking of fiscal relief mechanisms, infrastructure modernisation, business dispersion and the duplication of coal supply stations, the Canary Islands were able to significantly bring down refuelling costs to the point of nullifying their location disadvantage, thereby making it worthwhile for steam vessels to alter their routes to access that archipelago.

Apart from the fact that Porto Grande was underequipped and that there was a lack of investment by the Portuguese state in the development of modern port infrastructures, either as a result of lack of initiative or lack of capital,[33] the commercial monopoly regime that started early in Porto Grande also had grave consequences in terms of creating competitive advantages for the Cape Verde archipelago. For most of the time between 1850 and 1890, the entire coal sales market in Porto Grande was divided between only two businesses, a situation that inevitably led to the establishment of pacts and agreements between them, wiping out competition and sparking a bull market in the prices per ton of coal (Table 3.4).

As we have seen above, in 1860 it was Millers & Nephew that clearly dominated the coal market in Mindelo. With the tendency of higher coal prices, the flow of ships started to decrease and from year to year the fiscal revenue earned also fell off. Faced with this situation, the Portuguese administration sought to alter the market structure of coal sales, fomenting the licensing of new coal houses. Thus, in 1875 the Cory Brothers & Co. business entered the scene.

This arrival of the Cory Brothers on the market and the subsequent breaking up of the coal business monopoly quickly led to a marked lowering in the pricing of coal supplied to navigation, which was simultaneously accompanied by a fast relaunch of commercial traffic. In fact, the establishment of Cory Brothers in 1875 inaugurated the period of highest prosperity for Porto Grande, turning it into the most important coal port in the Mid-Atlantic. Between 1875 and 1889, the number of steamships entering Porto Grande almost tripled and tax revenues doubled.

Table 3.4   Coal companies established in Porto Grande (1850–91)

Year	Designation	Observations
1850	John Rendall	
1850	Royal Mail Steam Packet	
1851	Thomas & Miller	
1853	Visger & Miller	
1858	MacLeod and Martin	
1860	Millers and Nephew	Merging of Patent Fuel with Visger & Miller
1875	Cory Brothers & Co.	
1884	Wilson, Sons & Co.	
1885	Brewer & Co.	In 1887, yields business to Cory Brothers & Co.
1889	Miller & Cory Vert Islands Ltd	Merging of Miller & Nephew with Cory Brothers & Co.
1891	St. Vincent Cape Vert Islands Coaling Co. Ltd	The so-called Companhia Nacional de Cabo Verde
1893	Blandy Brothers & Co.	Final concession was never granted

In 1884, at the peak of prosperity, and believing in the potential of competition between coal dealers, the Portuguese administration authorised the establishment of a third firm, Wilson, Sons & Co.[34] However, despite this 'bet' on the institution of a competitive system with the existence of several companies, the coal dealers' negotiations tended to favour agreement between firms, if not mergers.

Millers & Nephew and Cory Brothers, by common agreement, decided to raise the price per ton of coal, causing part of the port flow that stopped in Mindelo to reroute to the Canary Islands as of 1884. Faced with local protests and the response from the Portuguese administration, the coal dealers justified their stance, arguing that the raise in the price of coal was a consequence of the increasing fiscal pressure on the coal industry noted since 1880.[35] According to the coal dealers, while Las Palmas and Tenerife enjoyed a strong free port regime, in S. Vicente the Portuguese administration continued to place burdens on the coal industry, the explanation of the difference in the price of coal between the two Atlantic archipelagos lying in the excess taxation by the Portuguese state.

Taking advantage of the negative impact on the local economy caused by the temporary exit of some of the more important clients of Porto Grande – Pacific Orient Line, Albinon Steam Ship Co., Chargeurs Reunis and Norddeutscher Lloyd – the two coal dealers went even further, demanding that a drawback[36] system be established in Porto Grande, similar to that which took place in the ports of Lisbon and Madeira, or even that all fiscal charges in effect be suppressed and the island of S. Vicente be declared a free port. The Portuguese state, however, did not accede to these demands (FDN, 1984, 55).

In 1885, the Portuguese authorities authorised the establishment of a floating deposit to a German company, Brewer & Co. of Bochum, Westphalia,[37] which quickly lowered the price of coal and increased the steam traffic. However, this situation lasted for only a short time. Later, in 1887, Brewer & Co. transferred all its business to Cory Brothers & Co.,[38] and two years later, to avoid competition with Wilson, Sons & Co., Cory Brothers & Co. and Millers & Nephew merged, creating a limited liability corporation called Miller & Cory Cape Vert Islands Ltd (Almeida, 1925, 158–78).

Hence, at the end of the 1880s, despite all the best efforts described, there were only two coal companies in Porto Grande, and the price of coal tended to rise once more. In 1891, we see in the Official Bulletin of Cape Verde that the steam ships would progressively avoid Porto Grande, preferring the ports in the Canaries[39] instead, where the price of coal was much lower, the port conditions far superior and the shipping charges practically non-existent.[40] In that year, a ton of coal cost 34 shillings in Porto Grande, whereas the same quantity was sold for 17 shillings at the ports in the Canaries (Almeida, 1925, 158–78).

In spite of all the sporadic recoveries, S. Vicente had definitively lost its position as the premier coal port of the Mid-Atlantic as of 1890, and all the port performance indicators showed a clear preponderance of the Canaries in the capture of the traffic of steam ships crossing the Atlantic.

Because it failed to convert an economy based on location-related revenue into a competitive one, as of 1890 Porto Grande would only function in times of heavy traffic growth, such as that witnessed during the Anglo–Boer war of the Transvaal or in the times of labour tension in the English mines. However, this growth was short-lived and did not yield profits, and S. Vicente would once again fall back as a result of its structural problems.

Faced with the accentuated retreat of navigation from 1891, and the lowering of fiscal revenue associated with coal sales, the Portuguese government, instead of opting for an economic effort to develop port technology, concentrated once again on the more immediate issue – the price of coal – and supported the establishment of yet another coal company in Porto Grande.

It is important to mention that, at the same time, some efforts were made to improve the infrastructure conditions of the port. The construction included a bridge for unloading flammable materials, a lighthouse in São Pedro, a new Customs bridge, a state office, a ramp and several storage facilities and docking points along the coastline. However, this somewhat tardy and limited-in-scope attempt did not achieve the scale

Table 3.5   Variations of the tax on coal in Cape Verde (1895–1915) (in réis)

Years	Amounts	Years	Amounts
1895–96	84,174$67	1905–06	80,629$97
1896–97	92,712$26	1906–07	117,227$35
1897–98	73,994$86	1907–08	100,227$35
1898–99	94,067$71	1908–09	64,398$28
1899–00	140,096$50	1909–10	91,837$07
1900–01	110,714$41	1910–11	69,016$26
1901–02	84,571$08	1911–12	72,479$03
1902–03	69,420$97	1912–13	75,293$65
1903–04	74,101$07	1913–14	51,840$62
1904–05	67,593$13	1914–15	65,063$09

Source: Estatística dos Rendimentos Públicos da Colónia de Cabo Verde: anos de 1895–1896 a 1914–1915, Repartição Superior de Fazenda de Cabo Verde, 1916 (Praia, Cabo Verde: Imprensa Nacional), 113.

needed to be able to place Porto Grande on a level of development equal to that already reached at other coal ports in the Atlantic. Supporting the establishment of new coal companies, seeking to promote competition and lowering the prices per ton of coal would unfortunately be the Portuguese administration's last resorts from that time onwards (FDN, 1984, 54–5).

On 23 September 1891, the new Companhia de São Vicente de Cabo Verde was formally created by royal decree.[41] The concession was granted, for a period of 99 years, in favour of António Júlio Machado, representing a group of merchants from Lisbon and Porto. This time, preference was given to the creation of a Portuguese company, which should have served as a type of regulator for the price of coal and avoided an alliance of interests with British companies.

However, in February 1894, approximately three years later, and after several protests on the part of British coal dealers, the new statutes of the Companhia were approved. The managing body would now be exclusively made up of British citizens, and the share capital, budgeted at 239,850$000 réis, divided into 410 shares, was also largely in the hands of British entities and citizens. Added to this was also the fact that, starting in 1894, the company would start using the name St Vincent Cape Vert Islands Coaling Co. Ltd in international markets. The British interference that they had tried to avoid was all too obvious.

With all the battles won by the English participants, St Vincent Ltd was, in 1895, the third coal dealer of Porto Grande, along with Miller & Cory Cape Vert Islands Ltd and Wilson, Sons & Co. The initial transactions carried out by this new company produced, as expected, a reanimating effect on the port flow, due to the accentuated fall of the price per ton of coal, which dropped from 34 shillings to 19 in 1896. The number of long-distance steam vessels entering Porto Grande rose from 891 in 1894 to 1518 in 1896 (Correira e Silva, 2000, 188).

These conditions only lasted for the short period during which the competition between the coal dealers really worked. But the new company had already established pacts with its congeners in 1897 and, once again, Porto Grande would lose its competitive edge (Table 3.5). In the meantime, the overthrow of the Portuguese monarchy on 5 October 1910, and the implantation of the republic renewed spirits. It was thought that the new political events could reverse Porto Grande's progressive loss of ground in the Atlantic coal economy. A vain hope.

In March of 1911, the newspaper *A Voz de Cabo Verde* started a campaign for the relaunching of the coal sector, calling attention to the urgent need to put an end to the competition from the Canaries, and by then also from the port in Dakar. There was some talk of the option of creating more coal deposits in Cape Verde[42] and the creation of a new deposit in Praia. However, none of that materialised.

In the following year, Blandy Brothers & Co., long since established in Madeira and in the Canaries, presented a formal request to the Government of the Republic of Portugal to build coal deposits in the archipelago of Cape Verde. Besides the obvious advantage that the creation of a new coal company would bring to bear on the fostering of competition between the businesses in Porto Grande, Blandy Brothers also had an important network of clients – Royal Mail, Pacific Line, Lamport & Holt Line, Union Castle Line, White Star Line – which would be of interest for the port. However, at the mercy of pressure brought to bear by the coal dealers Millers Cory, Wilson, Sons, and St Vincent Ltd, the concession was never actually granted.

In spite of the marked growth that was noted in terms of the number of ships entering the port and the subsequent rises in coal sales, starting in 1890 Porto Grande was no longer able to compete with the other coal ports and its structural problems tended to reproduce and grow worse.

6   Conclusion

In summary, the combined impact of all the political, economic, commercial and technological changes that occurred between the nineteenth and twentieth centuries completely changed the configuration of the Atlantic zone and would eventually convert the Mid-Atlantic archipelagos into essential ports of call on the main oceanic routes.

The advantages of location, decisive at the beginning of the coal cycle, catapulted Porto Grande into being the premier Atlantic coal port from 1850. However, as the remaining ports of the Mid-Atlantic system initiated the construction of other advantageous fiscal, infrastructural, administrative and commercial sources, the location factor ceased to be decisive. All the coal ports specialised in the same function, and so they quickly became each other's competition.

What finally dictated the end of the expansionist cycle of Porto Grande de S. Vicente as a coaling station was the inability to create other competitive advantages, be they fiscal, commercial or infrastructural, to complement the advantage of its strategic position, while also guaranteeing the sustainability of its location in the transatlantic routes. As the process evolved, this inability led Porto Grande to lose market share to the Canary Islands, and subsequently to Dakar. Porto Grande was ultimately a victim not only of the aspirations to maximise profits on the part of British coal companies, but also, more concretely, of the Portuguese colonial system, which did not have the economic resources, organisational capacity or even any political will to develop the port.

The continued strategy that lowered the price per ton of coal, which we have seen started in 1890, would be the Portuguese administration's last resort in an attempt to guarantee the positioning of Porto Grande in the Atlantic panorama. However, the window of opportunity had already been lost.

Notes

1. The ports of Sal-Rei on the island of Boa Vista, the Porto Inglês on the island of Maio and the port of Santa Maria on the island of Praia found themselves in this situation.
2. This was a floating deposit undertaken at English initiative.
3. In 1850, the British consul John Rendall received authorisation from the Portuguese government to build an on-land coal depository in Porto Grande.
4. *Official Bulletin of Cape Verde (Boletim Oficial de Cabo Verde)*, 55, 1851, Royal Ministerial Order of 7 December 1850.
5. *Official Bulletin of Cape Verde*, 27, 1858, Royal Ministerial Order 218, referring to the decree of 1 September 1854.
6. Curiously, it was only in 1858 that Praia, the capital of the archipelago, was elevated to the status of village, largely as a way of avoiding discontentment among the population.
7. The Portuguese authorities thought that 'having [...] the main settlement of the island of S. Vicente [...] experienced a contemporary growth in number of residents, and in urban construction and [seeing that] Porto Grande [...] is visited by a large number of vessels.' *Official Bulletin of Cape Verde*, 29, 1858, Regal Decree of 29 April 1858.
8. Built between 1858 and 1861. *Official Bulletin of Cape Verde*, 16, 1873, map of the public construction executed between September 1858 and June 1873.
9. Built between 1859 and 1874. Ibid.
10. Built between 1859 and 1874. Ibid.
11. Finished in 1863. Ibid.
12. Built between 1862 and 1874. Ibid.
13. Only achieved in 1874. *Official Bulletin of Cape Verde*, 39, 1874.
14. In 1864, a royal ministerial order mandated the detailed study of the problem of water supply in Mindelo. Only nine years later, in 1873, two subterranean galleries for water supply were opened and only in 1874 was a cost study done on water piping.
15. Land conceded by Portuguese authorities on 6 June 1853.
16. See *A ilha de S. Vicente de Cabo Verde. Relatório do Administrador do Concelho Joaquim Vieira Botelho da Costa, 1879*, in *Raízes*, 7(16), 1980, 156ff.
17. *Official Bulletin of Cape Verde*, 1875–70, customs monthly statistics.
18. See *A ilha de S. Vicente de Cabo Verde. Relatório do Administrador do Concelho Joaquim Vieira Botelho da Costa, 1879*, in *Raízes*, 7(16), 1980, 156ff.
19. *Official Bulletin of Cape Verde*, 25, 1874, Royal Ministerial Order 68.

20. *Official Bulletin of Cape Verde*, 41, 1884; 18, 1886.
21. *Official Bulletin of Cape Verde*, 22, 1880, Report of the County Administrator.
22. *Official Bulletin of Cape Verde*, 20, 1880, Report of the County Administrator.
23. An example of this is called the 'English Quarter', built by the MacLeod and Martin Company in 1860, later property of Millers & Nephew.
24. *Official Bulletin of Cape Verde*, 20, 1879, Royal Decree of 14 April 1879.
25. *Official Bulletin of Cape Verde*, 26, 1883, Report of the County Administrator, Decree of 25 October 1881.
26. Sanitary inspection building.
27. The services for demarcation of the ports, navigation lighting and pilots came under the jurisdiction of the Ministry of the Navy and Overseas Possessions; the collecting of taxes and fees by the customs offices came under the Ministry of the Treasury; works and improvements depended on the Ministry of Public Works, Commerce and Industry; and the maritime health services also came under the Ministry of the Navy and Overseas Possessions.
28. Various engineers provided services in Portugal, including: John Rennie, Coode, Knox, Abernethy, Freebody.
29. Between 1911 and 1928, 14 Juntas Autónomas Portuárias were created, but none of them in the Portuguese colonies.
30. Created on 7 December 1851. *Official Bulletin of Cape Verde*, 55, 1851, Royal Ministerial Order of 7 December 1851.
31. The following offices depended on the Mindelo Customs House: Ponta do Sol, on the Island of Santo Antão; Preguiça, on the Island of S. Nicolau; Santa Mara on the Island of Sal and Sal-Rei on the Island of Boa Vista. Under the Customs House of Praia were the offices of: Tarrafal, on the Island of Santiago; Porto Inglês, on the Island of Maio; S. Filipe, on the Island of Fogo; and Furna, on the Island of Brava.
32. *Official Bulletin of Cape Verde*, 27, 1858.
33. Between 1852 and 1880 the Canary Islands' ports received considerable financing by the Spanish state, budgeted at around 16.3 million pesetas. Between 1880 and 1900, the volume of investments doubled, aggravating even further the gap in relation to the other ports in the Atlantic coal system (Correira e Silva, 2007, 63).
34. *Official Bulletin of Cape Verde*, 18, 1885.
35. In that year, the tax on each ton of coal jumped from 100 réis to 300. *Official Bulletin of Cape Verde*, 47, 1880.
36. A system that consisted of the return of half of the fees paid for imported coal to the coal dealers when it was resold to ships in transit.
37. *Official Bulletin of Cape Verde*, 47, 1885.
38. *Official Bulletin of Cape Verde*, 43, 1887.
39. It should be noted that although the free port regime, established in 1852, was instrumental to the successful integration of the Canary Islands in the Atlantic steam ship routes, this instrument, as such, would have had little effect. What allowed the Canaries to perform better in capturing transatlantic steam traffic was the addition of a series of complementary stimuli, among which the investments in port infrastructures were of major importance.
40. *Official Bulletin of Cape Verde*, 13, 1891, Municipality News.
41. *Official Bulletin of Cape Verde*, 43, 1891, Royal Decree of 23 September 1891.
42. 'Depósitos de Carvão', in *A Voz de Cabo Verde*, 1, Praia, 1 March 1911, 3.

Bibliography

Almeida, J. (1925) 'O Porto Grande de S. Vicente de Cabo Verde: plano de melhoramento para valorizar este porto e atrair a Cabo Verde a navegação de longo curso', *Boletim da Agência Geral das Colónias*, 6, 158–78.
Cabrera Armas, L. G. (2010) 'El papel de las Islas Canarias en los intercambios entre Europa y América, 1845–1880', Segundo Congreso Latinoamericano de Historia Económica (Mexico).
Câmara, B. (2002) *A Economia da Madeira (1850–1914)* (Lisbon: Imprensa das Ciências Sociais).
Castro, J. F. B. de (1890) *Nova Colecção de Tratados, Convenções, Contratos e Actos Públicos celebrados entre a Coroa de Portugal e as Mais Potencias compilados por ordem do Ministério dos Negócios Estrangeiros*, I, 1840–62 (Lisbon: Imprensa Nacional).
Correia e Silva, A. L. (2000) *Nos Tempos do Porto Grande do Mindelo* (Praia, Mindelo: Centro Cultural Português).
Correia e Silva, A. L. (2007) *Os ciclos históricos de inserção de Cabo Verde na economia atlântica: o caso das cidades porto (Ribeira Grande e Mindelo)* (Lisbon: FCSH – Universidade Nova de Lisboa).
Costa, J. V. B. (1880) *Aditamento aos Relatórios da Administração do concelho de S. Vicente de 30 de Janeiro de 1877 a* 1 de Março de 1880 (Cape Verde).
Figueira, M. B. (1959) 'Subsídios para o estudo evolutivo da cidade do Mindelo de São Vicente de Cabo Verde', *Revista Agrícola*, 9, 17–20.
Figueira, M. B. (1968) Subsídios para o estudo evolutivo da cidade do Mindelo de São Vicente (Lisboa: ISCSPU).
Figueiredo, A. L. (1913) *O Carvão na Economia de Cabo Verde* (Lisbon: Tipografia Industrial Portuguesa).
Fundo de Desenvolvimento Nacional (FDN) (1984) *Linhas Gerais da História do Desenvolimento Urbano da Cidade do Mindelo* (Praia, Cape Verde: FDN).
Machado, J. S. (1891) *Estudo sobre o Comércio do Carvão no Porto Grande da ilha de S. Vicente (arquipélago de Cabo Verde) e no Porto da Luz em gran Canária (arquipélago das Canárias)* (Lisbon: Imprensa Nacional).
Monteiro, A. R. (1996) 'Movimento Consular em Cabo Verde nos finais do século XIX', *Africana, Revista do Centro dos Estudos Africanos e Orientais da Universidades Portucalense*, special issue, 4, 113–24.
Prata, A. (2011) *Políticas Portuárias na I República (1880–1929)* (Lisbon: Caleidoscópio).
Suárez Bosa, M. (2004) 'The Role of the Canary Islands in the Atlantic Coal Route from the End of the Nineteenth Century to the Beginning of the Twentieth Century: Corporate Strategies', *International Journal of Maritime History*, 16, 95–114.
Suárez Bosa, M., and L. G. Cabrera Armas (2010) 'Los Puertos Francos y las economías insulares atlánticas', VII Congreso Ibérico de Estudos Africanos (Lisbon).
Valdez, F. T. (1864) África Ocidental: notícias e considerações (Lisbon: Imprensa Nacional).

4
The Port of Casablanca in the First Stage of the Protectorate

Miguel Suárez Bosa and Leila Maziane

1 Introduction:
The Role of Ports in a Dependent Territory

The port of Casablanca quickly became the most important port in Morocco. In fact, very soon after its minimal infrastructure was completed, almost two thirds of Moroccan trade was shipped through Casablanca, so a study of the port enables us to carry out a synthesis of the territory's economy as a whole. The role it played makes it, to a degree, the image of the country at the time, and a barometer of the country's evolution. The fact is that it rapidly became a fundamental part of Morocco's expansion.

Construction had begun at the beginning of the twentieth century using advanced techniques, so it answers to a modern conception of port organisation. At the same time, it was born of the political will to serve the country's economy. For these reasons, the anyport (Bird, 1963) model is an appropriate one to use for its analysis, as this model describes the evolution of port structures in time and space. The reasons why a modest cove that was difficult to access and whipped by the big ocean waves, previously used by poor fishermen, was chosen for the construction of what was destined to become Morocco's most important port are basically linked to economic factors, although others should also be taken into consideration, such as the Protectorate authorities' wish to avoid the dispute between the two historic capitals, Fes and Marrakech.

As of the end of the nineteenth century, the Sherifian authorities had set out to create an infrastructure in line with the needs of the major naval vessels that appeared thanks to the new technology of the steam age, large ships for the transportation of raw material and goods.

Subsequently, the French administration of the Protectorate projected a national port, which entailed the centralisation of the port, as opposed to the option of a decentralised model favouring the strengthening of and investment in a network of ports located along Morocco's Atlantic coast.[1] The final decision gave rise to considerable controversy, as can be seen in the abundant bibliography, which analyses the data and concludes that Casablanca became the main port of Morocco, the winning port of the region, if we accept the existence of 'winning' and 'losing' ports, as per the regulationist approach (Veltz, 1994).

For this study of the port, we adopted a holistic view, although the overarching element is port management. We were able to source a significant amount of bibliography and documentation, which is hardly surprising, given the significance of this infrastructure. It is worth mentioning the work of Vidalenc (1928), Eyquem (1933) and Celce (1952), as general studies for the period under consideration; other books or articles looking at specific aspects of a technical nature (Laroche, 1927), on economic and social factors as featured in the bibliography; and journals such as the *Bulletin Économique et Social de Maroc*. We would also like to draw attention to the availability of abundant documentary material: reports written by the Protectorate's authorities, the British Diplomatic and Consular Reports (District of Casablanca), full sets of commercial exchanges and other elements regarding political, economic and social aspects. Moreover, we also have the documentation generated by institutions such as the Chamber of Commerce and Industry of Casablanca and the port administration itself.

This port forms part of an international network of connections that includes both the West Atlantic (Bordeaux and Nantes) and the Mediterranean (with Marseilles and Barcelona as points of contact), and further south, Las Palmas in the Canary Islands and Dakar on the African content, all joined up by various maritime routes and shipping lines. So any analysis should take into consideration not only the local context, but also the wider scope of what we could call 'Atlantic history', leading us to consider the world system, considering what occurs in peripheral or semi-peripheral countries, as Morocco was at the time.

But a port is not just a set of quays or dikes, cranes and hangars; rather it is a gigantic enterprise with a life of its own, an autonomous body with its specific problems, which include the administration itself, the concessionary companies, finance and staff. All these elements form part of a whole that we call the port community. These elements will be the subject of our analysis in this chapter.

2   The Construction of the Port of Casablanca and Its Importance in the Economy of Morocco

2.1   The Option of Port Concentration in a Hostile Fiscal Environment

The origins of the port of Casablanca lie in its geographical conditions. It is located in the central part of Morocco's Atlantic coastline,
so its hinterland was part of a dense network that stretched out in all
directions, covering 70 per cent of all transported goods and 77 per cent
of the value of imported traffic from the French zone of the Protectorate
(Protectorat, 1953, 19). Likewise, this network extended into the
foreland and linked into a network of ports that includes the nearby
Fedala-Mohammedia, specialising in fuel; to the south, it tied in with
the ports of El Jadida (Mazagán), Safi, Essaouira (Mogador), Agadir, and
to the North, with Rabat-Salé, Kénitra, Larache and Tangiers.

The appearance of the first commercial firms and the setting up of the
early shipping lines with regular services to Casablanca coincide with
the first attempts to valorise the surrounding land. Therefore, as of the
second half of the nineteenth century, the primary function of the port
was regional, and it became the point where both the rail and the road
networks converged. These networks provided access to its hinterland,
the region of Chaouia, and it also became a favourable point from
which to penetrate into the Atlas plateau as well as the ideal exit point
for agricultural and livestock products for the whole of central Morocco.
In fact, the region of Chaouia was the origin of the port of Casablanca.
The trading of grain and animals was abundant from then on, and,
together with the French intervention, led the city to grow from a small
town to a business centre (Celce, 1952, 7).

At the same time, the discovery of rich deposits of phosphates at the
beginning of the twentieth century in nearby Khouribga constitutes a key
element in the Moroccan economy, and their large-scale extraction from
the second decade of the century onwards required an exit point from
which to export them. The relative proximity of Casablanca made it the
obvious choice as the best marine access point for export. This commodity
became the main export passing through Casablanca (Table 4.1).

But the choice of Casablanca was also conditioned by political and
military motives, as the French authorities wanted to have infrastructure
as the logical exit point for the 1907 military intervention. Due to this
punitive action some workers who protested for the profanation of a
cemetery were killed and this is thought to be the prelude to French intervention. Likewise, in technical terms, this Atlantic location offered several

Table 4.1 Export of phosphates from Casablanca (1921–38) (in tonnes)

Year	All Exports	Phosphates	% of Phosphates over the total
1921	181,894	8000	4.3
1922	225,284	79,345	35.2
1923	321,052	191,596	59.6
1924	725,393	436,422	60.1
1925	1,007,632	726,537	72.1
1926	1,163,662	884,917	76.0
1927	1,601,428	1,198,077	74.8
1928	1,960,561	1,324,115	67.5
1929	1,961,032	1,577,576	80.4
1930	1,920,937	1,772,201	92.2
1931	1,279,025	965,444	75.4
1932	n/a	n/a	n/a
1933	1,374,985	1,091,052	79.3
1934	1,607,308	1,255,802	78.1
1935	1,670,038	1,192,982	71.4
1936	1,746,562	1,108,000	63.4
1937	1,724,207	1,170,457	67.8
1938	1,849,200	1,107,390	59.8

Source: Eyquem, 1933, 72; *Bulletin Économique du Maroc*, 1–24.

advantages, such as having a solid base on which to build the quays and the certainty that it would not silt up with sand (Timoule, 1988). Indeed, the port's splendour and that of the city originated from diplomatic and military circumstances. The Act of Algeciras (1906), which certified the division of Moroccan territory between the European powers, entailed the creation of a large port open to the international economy. The rate of 2.5 per cent for levies established at the Algeciras Conference was raised to 12.5 per cent *ad valorem* paid in the port, although some products such as silk, wine or cereals enjoyed more favourable exceptional rates of 7.5 per cent, as did some material destined for boat repairs, seeds or fertilisers, which only paid 2 per cent (Eyquem, 1933, 23).

The territorial division was certified with the Protectorate instigated by the Fes Treaty in 1912, whereby the central and south parts, or 'useful Morocco', came under French administration, while the north was governed by Spain. The indigenous rebellion of 1907, in which several workers who rebelled against the occupiers were killed, was quashed by the action of French troops; peace was subsequently achieved and the port windows of the Atlantic *façade* opened up. Casablanca quickly became the most important port, for economic reasons, as the

Protectorate's initial projects envisaged a major national port with a view to obtaining the maximum benefits possible.

The Protectorate's authorities and specialists opted for a major national port, an opinion that was shared by the Resident General, Marshal H. Lyautey, a centralist conception that finally won out, as it was considered that it would facilitate coordination between the different means of maritime, rail and road transport. As opposed to dispersion between several nodes of secondary importance, priority was given to the ease with which the goods originating abroad or inland could find a point of convergence from which subsequently to be sent out in different directions, serving the whole Moroccan economy. Thus, Casablanca played a predominant role, although the rest of the regional ports must also be taken into consideration.

The importance of Marshal Hubert Lyautey in the modernisation of Morocco in all aspects is well known. He was named Resident General in 1912, and one of his main concerns as of the moment he took part in the commission chaired by M. Guérard, Inspector of Bridges and Roads (Ponts et Chaussées), was the construction of a major port. From an economic point of view the commission decided in favour of Casablanca, as it responded to the two major objectives: to build a large port that was at a similar distance from the two main towns of the inland *entrepôt*, that is, Fes to the north and Marrakech to the south (Chastel, 2009, 170). In this decision, the commission was supported by Morocco's Chief Engineer and Director of Public Works, M. Delure, who, in order to dissipate the doubts as to whether Casablanca would be the best location, wrote to Lyautey in 1913:

> Everyone had agreed, to date, to start with the Port Commission, which, in the programme laid out since its return, was absolutely clear in the sense that the only major port envisaged on the Moroccan coast should be established at Casablanca. Nobody, either in this Commission or among the technical experts involved in the studies to date had considered that this initiative was impossible. (cited in Chastel, 2009, 171; see also Hatton, 2009)

According to its advocates, the concentration of the port would indeed entail irrefutable advantages in responding to the demands of the modern economy, as it would enable better and cheaper equipment to be available and the routing and export of products to be simplified. Entry and exit data for port movement are given in chart form (Figure 4.1).

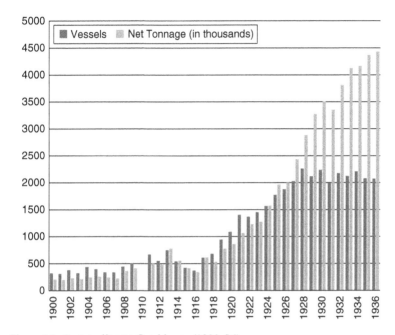

Figure 4.1 Port traffics in Casablanca (1900–36)
Source: Foreign Office, 1908–14; Société, 1933–38; Eyquem, 1933; Protectorat, 1953. Compiled by author.

2.2 Design and Construction of a Major National Port

In previous centuries, the difficulties posed by the Atlantic coast for the construction of ports together with the hostility of the Islamic authorities to outside contact had led the country to be closed for centuries. What was originally known as Anfa became Dar al Baida (Casablanca) in the times of Sidi Mohammed Ben Abdellah, but the modern growth of Casablanca took off with steam ships.

Before the nineteenth century, the monopoly granted to the Five Major Trades (a collective of five large commercial corporations from Madrid) dissuaded shipping companies from setting up. These monopolies started with the Anglo–Moroccan trade treaty (1856), signed by John Drummond Hay and the Sultan; thereafter several companies visited the port of Casablanca and port traffic increased (Miége and Eugène, 1954, cited in Chastel, 2009).

The Atlantic coast of Morocco had a bad reputation for navigation for several reasons. For example, the characteristics of the seabed in this area caused large waves to break in the open sea, giving rise to the formation of a barrier. This made the coast dangerous and anchoring unsafe, unless significant work were undertaken to build a shelter for vessels. On the other hand, Casablanca was impassable during the rainy season, bad weather and high tides. Only barges could take refuge, and even these vessels were not free from risks. Boats, even those of low tonnage, were forced to weigh anchor at roadstead, exposed to the winds and the danger of being driven by the waves onto the rocks, with the ensuing loss of cargo.

But the port of Casablanca is the safest on the coast of West Morocco. It is protected from the sea swell by a kind of dike made up of the reefs of Dar al Baida and the 8 to 20 feet deep anchor points are located only half a mile off-shore. The unfavourable natural conditions did not help. The challenge of building the port was tackled for reasons of economic development, because of the need to have an area protected from the wave action in an essentially hostile maritime environment. As the Director of the Navy's Hydrographic Service published in the *Revue Générale des Sciences* (1912) put it,

> It is impossible to create on the western coast of Morocco a port that ships can use in all weathers; the line of breakers that forms in storms has to be overcome and to envisage piers at depths and over distances that are not technically feasible.

The modern construction of the port started just before the First World War. Casablanca is an example of a port open to any kind of future development given the increase in traffic and technological innovations. Aware that trade would increase, the port designers envisaged good prospects; they also foresaw that technological progress would lead to giant ships that would need corresponding infrastructure in order to berth. Thanks to this vision of the future imbued with realism, this port has continued to develop and its design has enabled it to adapt with extraordinary flexibility to the major transformations that have marked the world of maritime transport. The key infrastructure is the Moulay Youssef quay, which has been termed a masterpiece, an important contribution to the annals of maritime engineering.

We can also consider that its construction was a laboratory and a study on scale models that was experimented on for fifty years, given the unfavourable conditions at Casablanca. Its construction was carried out empirically without any prior technical studies but, paradoxically, it coincides with the 'Hudson formula', discovered forty years later in the 1960s. In 1920, a violent storm moved the 260-ton blocks that made up the base a dozen metres. In 1923, the port was totally inaccessible and remained paralysed for seven months; this event forced the authorities to set up a service to forecast the state of the sea and the approach of lethal waves, as the *Daily Telegraph* published, indicating that this Moroccan port was a pioneer in the field of meteorological oceanography (Ministére, n.d., 13).

In the first place, it is worth pointing out that the port of Casablanca was a barge port until 1923, when the trade quay started to operate, that is, that goods were transferred from boat to barge and thence deposited on the shore, where they were unloaded by hand. The representatives of the traders complained repeatedly, so the Moroccan Administration, under the government of Sultan Moulay Hassan, concerned by the customs' turnover, ordered some improvements to be made, starting with the construction of a small masonry quay, apt for barges. This work, carried out without any prior studies, was given up as useless.

Despite all these difficulties, trade flows became established over time, with a notable level of collaboration between Jewish, Muslim and European traders.

The Moroccan administration considered it necessary to have a safer, more practical port. In 1905, on the initiative of Sultan Mulay Abd el Aziz, a contract was signed with the French company Compagnie Marocaine[2] for the building of a small port for the barges that transported goods from the boat to the shore, where they were unloaded by hand. The Compagnie Marocaine chose the Schneider et Cie et J. Vignes company as its partner, and they, in turn, subcontracted to Gendre Donnadieu, from Marseilles.[3] The modest project was signed by the engineer J. Renaud (1904) and comprised two small quays of between one and two thousand metres, to protect the bay. However, cargo vessels remained moored between 1000 and 1200 metres from the shore, but two small piers were built to protect an area of ten hectares, which allowed barges to reach the quay more easily and the cargo to be handled in calm waters, well protected from the large waves and winter storms.

Works began in 1906 but the initial project was replaced by another one that enabled larger vessels to be accommodated. This project suffered several interruptions until the signing of the Fes Treaty marked a turning point in the history of the port of Casablanca. The political reorganisation required a 'national port', and Casablanca was chosen, backed by the energetic political personality of Marshall Lyautey, the Resident General (the decision was taken in the wake of studies by a commission chaired by M. Gérard, the Inspecteur Général des Ponts et Chaussées (Celce, 1952, 32), and the policy of centralised ports, supported by a series of historical and economic data, triumphed). The new works were adjudicated on 25 March 1913 to the Schneider and Cie, associated with the Compagnie Marocaine and MM. Hersent Frères. Between 1913 and 1934, 2450 metres of the main dike were built, together with the transverse dike and the trade port, although the port was really built according to M. Delure's Plan of 1918. This Plan envisaged a major port in three stages (Vidalenc, 1928; Eyquem, 1933): in the first, a large quay 1300 m long would be built, made with piles and crossing out towards the west. The final result was to reach 1100 m of the main quay, which would be sufficient to allow the section to be executed. By means of this work, a marine surface area of 35 hectares was achieved by 1920, which was sufficient to cope with Casablanca's traffic for some considerable time; the second stage aimed to build a dike 1650 m long, subsequently to be extended by a further 600 m. The third stage envisaged a second bay, extending the main dike to 2250 m, and the building of a transverse dike, extending the bay's surface area to 66 hectares, with a depth of 9.5 m and a length of 2250 m.

On the other hand, the discovery of the phosphate deposits of Khouribga marked a turning point in the port, which enjoyed rapid growth at the same pace as the increase in production of these minerals. At the end of the year, the dike was 1528 metres long, and at that point construction work began on a section of the quay known as the phosphate quay, which grew to 2185 metres in 1928.

From then on, the port and city of Casablanca enjoyed a number of favourable developments such as the economic preponderance that had started in previous decades, acting as the landing point for the French occupying army and so forth. European initiatives, mainly French, but also Italian and Spanish, prevailed. A minority of dynamic traders set up in the city and they exerted an irrefutable political and economic influence. From then on, the port of Casablanca became the trading port for the exceptionally rich hinterland, covering the provinces of Tadla and Chaouia.

The city's growth was an immediate consequence of the construction of the port, as the port preceded urban development and paved the way for the city in just the same way as the implementation of major works or the discovery of minerals in the ground gives rise to the emergence of boom towns in new countries, as can be seen on other continents. The city grew in a disorderly fashion and gave shelter to a heteroclite multitude made up of traders, adventurers and workers.

The major construction work ended in 1933, although a number of supplementary works were carried out up until the Second World War: the construction of the grain docks (for silos), the building of the fishing port and improvements to the phosphates quay (Celce, 1952). The

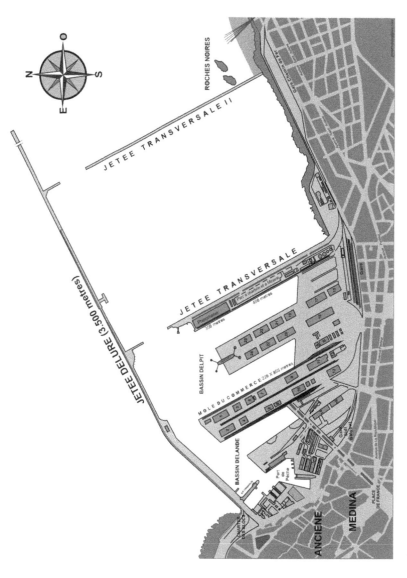

Map 4.1 The Port of Casablanca in 1953

Table 4.2   Expenses on the Port of
Casablanca (1904–32) (in francs)

Year	Francs
1904	2,500,000
1914	50,000,000
1920	220,000,000
1928	148,000,000
1932	195,000,000

Source: Eyquem, 1933, 57.

boats no longer needed the services of the barges as intermediaries as they could unload their goods directly. It was in 1933 that the main quay, known as Jetée Delure in memory of its designer, was inaugurated. From then on, particularly during the Second World War, the sustained growth of the port of Casablanca continued.

The construction of this port entailed a major financial effort, as it absorbed more than 80 per cent of budget allocation to port construction and up until 1932 cost 615.5 million francs, provided in successive loans, as Table 4.2 shows. This table reflects the total expenses incurred in the port of Casablanca up until 1932.

This massive investment was criticised by those in favour of a decentralised port, particularly when the number of boats entering port fell in the wake of the crisis of the 1930s.[4] But the fact remains that, from the years leading up to the Second World War, the construction of the Port of Casablanca played an important role in the country's major economic growth and, after the War, it enjoyed sustained growth, holding its own as Morocco's most important port, as we shall see below.

3   Management of the Port of Casablanca

If we consider the port installations as one more component of infrastructure, it would appear that the port managers gave priority to the economic development of the surrounding area rather than to business criteria as such, that is, maximising profits and balancing the budget. The state, just as in mainland France, allowed autonomous bodies or bodies governed by public law to play a leading role in port management. As was also the case in other colonial ports belonging to the French administration, the administrative dependence on mainland France and its institutions was well known and the Chambers of Commerce and Business Associations played an important role, acting as lobbies.

It is worth remembering that Morocco was a French-Spanish protectorate from 1912 onwards, with a one-off political and administrative status. From that moment on, Casablanca remained under the administration of the local French colonial authorities, although the (Moroccan) *Sherifian* authorities retained some areas of responsibility. The port was, as in mainland France, directly owned by the state; the state was not only in charge of building infrastructure and platforms, but also of the superstructure, the sheds and the cranes.

The port management was in the hands of the Ingenénieur en Chef des Ponts et Chaussées, who was responsible not only for the administration but also for the port installations, assisted by a team of technical experts: the Merchant Marine was represented by two bodies, the Central Service and the Trade Division, whose teams were made up of civil servants, inspectors and controllers. Moreover, we should mention the port's pilots, who had formed an autonomous association, and the tugs, the public health and safety services and the customs administrations. Nevertheless, the state granted the private sector the opportunity to carry out certain activities. The originality of the system adopted in Casablanca lies in the assignation of specific tasks to each institution:

- L'Office Chérifien des Phosphates, a public body created by a Dahir on 7 August 1920 in an attempt to preserve the profits of an essential raw material, the Moroccan phosphates, and prevent said profits from falling into foreign hands. This company was granted the concession of the installations planned for handling phosphates at the quay Casablanca port 1928. The company contributed to the construction and maintenance of the installations.
- The Casablanca Chamber of Commerce and Industry was the concessionary of the docks grain silo, following the example of the ports of Marseille and Bordeaux. Likewise, with the profits obtained it had to contribute to the port infrastructure's maintenance. It is no coincidence that the Chambre de Commerce et Industrie was born at the same time as the modern port's construction, begun in 1913, and that it immediately expressed an interest in the port and the smooth running thereof (Marill, 1952, 21). The Chamber also had a much older and better-known consultative role, and it periodically issued reports on the region's economy; as far as its administrative role was concerned, it was in charge of managing the silos (Marill, 1952).
- In turn, the Société Chérifiene de Remorquage et d'Assistance was exclusively responsible for assisting the shipping companies, specifically in the towing and mooring of boats. The concession contract allowed it to fix its fees in agreement with the port's director.

- The Manutention Marocaine was the most important concessionary, in terms of the functions assigned to it, and the one that presented most differences with other French concessionaries. It had a monopoly on loading and unloading goods, fish, coal, minerals (except for phosphates) and so forth. Before the Protectorate, these activities were in the hands of the (Sherifian) Moroccan government, who handed them over to the colonial administration, who in turn passed them on to the Société d'Entreprise Maritime et Commerciale in 1951. Finally, the monopoly was granted in 1922 to Manutention Marocaine, with local and foreign capital stakeholders (Celce, 1952, 68–70).

However, the necessary coordination between the public service and concessionaries was established, to which end a daily meeting was held after midday, attended by representatives of public works, the Chamber of Commerce, customs, the police, Manutention Marociane,[5] the railway, shipping agents, freight forwarders and the Central Transport Bureau. Its mission was to examine all the operations underway, set the departure time for ships, name the work teams and so forth (Celce, 1952, 95).

The accounts management of the Port of Casablanca was based on the setting up of an appended budget, rather than the principle of one sole budget, justified in this case by the importance of the service in question. This appended budget was based on two procedures. First, it was included in the Protectorate's budget and prepared by the Direction Générale des Finances du Gouvernement, after consulting with the Administrations des Travaux Publics, responsible for running the port;

Figure 4.2   The institutional organisation of the Port of Casablanca
Source: Documentation destinée á la réunion projetée en vue de Pallier l'encombrement de Port de Casablanca, National Archive of Nantes, Morocco Section.

second, it was proposed by the Resident General for approval by the Sultan of Morocco (Celce, 1952, 80). This document included a breakdown of the income, made up of the duties levied by the port, of which approximately 55 per cent corresponded to taxes paid by Manutention Marocaine (although the amount and percentage varied over time) and loading and unloading duties. The taxes levied on the loading and unloading of liquid fuel were relatively significant, as Casablanca progressively became a fuel provider. Part of this income corresponded to the state.

In terms of expenses, the main item corresponded to payments for working material (maintenance of tools and dikes, dredging etc.), constituting between 70 per cent and 80 per cent as they were fundamental for port operations of all kinds. Other items included staff payments, the management quota corresponding to Manutention Marocaine and the rental of real estate and movable goods.

So the management of the port of Casablanca shared some characteristics with the French ports of mainland France such as Marseilles, Strasbourg, Le Havre or Bordeaux, which had the same autonomy regarding concessions to private companies under certain conditions. The infrastructure and superstructure were paid for by the state, who delegated this responsibility to the Chamber of Commerce and Industry of Casablanca, as did its counterpart in Marseille, although the port of Marseille did not enjoy the same level of financial autonomy as the Moroccan port.

But we should not forget the staff, that is, the port community. Here we refer to the group of individuals who work in the port, be they public employees, businessmen or workers, whose work enables the port to act as a working enterprise; they give life to the port. Thus, a port constitutes an integrated whole, where the highly qualified managers are just as important as the workforce which, as in all ports, has to be familiar with a difficult, complicated trade, and must therefore be qualified and have appropriate physical characteristics. Just as in the whole of the French Union, in Casablanca port the staff was made up of employees of public services and private bodies, each different from the other. The Administration des Travaux Publics was responsible for running the port and its agents were among the numerous members of port staff. The Merchant Navy, customs, trade, National Defence, the French Ministry of the Interior, Public Health and concessionaries were all involved in the working of the port and played an active role. To complete the picture we should mention the insurance brokers, the freight forwarders and the shipping agents.

A set of private services also joined the above-mentioned public services: the freight forwarders, of which there were 299 professionally qualified ones in 1950; some 20 agents of insurance companies grouped together to form an association as of 1941, and the maritime brokers, professionally accredited to broker maritime insurance (Croze, 1949). The general characteristic of the public service personnel is that they were civil servants, with some exceptions. The managers were subject to a general statute, but civil servants were not, neither were the officials or employees; there were few local people among the administrative personnel employed.

The tasks of stowage, loading and unloading were services adjudicated by concession to the Manutention Marocaine company, carried out almost exclusively by a local workforce. The number of day-workers could have amounted to 1500 or 2000; it is difficult to set an exact number. Most were loaders and stevedores, as well as crane operators, drivers and tractor drivers.

Finally, as far as the organisation of work is concerned, as in major ports, the operations of stowage, loading and unloading were carried out by teams, or *hands*, of nine or ten men, with the members of the teams working shifts each day. Once the teams had been constituted, they went to the quay, under the direction of a Moroccan, a confident of the Manutention, a well-respected person who carried a cane as a sign of authority. This workforce, recently arrived at the city, maintained a very strong rural spirit, with little sense of class, although the General Work Confederation gained some followers, who only gained the benefit of trades unions rights in 1947 (Celce, 1952, 98).

4   Port Activity

The Port of Casablanca carried out the three economic functions required of major ports. As far as the regional and transit function is concerned, it was the exit and entry point for merchandise from and for its hinterland, mainly Chaouia; likewise, it represented the meeting point between maritime transport and the different land-based means of transport. At the same time, port activity drove forward the industry of transformation of imported products consumed in its hinterland and third, it played a trade role, acting as an *entrepôt*, in that it redistributed the merchandise received to its various destinations. However, Casablanca also played a national role, present from its conception, that is, it acted as the meeting point for the territories located in its near hinterland, both from the Rif and from the Atlas.

The trade function was the most significant; it served both as a marketplace and as a financial centre. In the local context, it had the advantage of having a supply centre for raw material, a vital element for the industry of consumer goods such as food, craftwork and construction material. The former fishing fleet grew considerably thanks to the new port and it serviced the fishing industry fed by the abundant fish from the nearby fishing ground. In military terms, the port was an important part of African defence.

The trade function reflects the port activity, as shipments from the French zone of Morocco were largely transported by sea. Thus, the port traffic tells us both about the characteristics and nature of the economy of the hinterland, as well as the major lines of the country's economic structure, as it encompassed three quarters of national trade, the sea being the main exit point for national produce.

In 1931, the trade movement of the ports of Western Morocco stood at 2613 thousand tons, 92.5 per cent, while land traffic through Oujda, in the north, fell. Therefore, the ports, and Casablanca first and foremost, underpinned the country's economy. Moreover, after the Algeciras treaty, they opened up to international traffic, a question that was facilitated by a permissive customs administration, as we saw above, although, as the ports needed considerable infrastructure, the goods paid 2.5 per cent *ad valorem* (Eyquem, 1933, 30).

Shipping lines from many American and African ports sailed to Casablanca, in this case connecting with other parts of the French Union, particularly with Dakar, as the exit port for the French Sub-Saharan colonial territories. Peanuts and fish products were imported from Dakar and fruit, conserves and material were exported. It was also a stopover point for colonial shipping lines, which connected it to the most important mainland French ports (Marseilles, Bordeaux and others), as well as other European ports, such as London and Southampton, Antwerp and Hamburg, together with Atlantic island ports such as Las Palmas, Madeira or Mindelo, the latter located in Cape Verde.

From the early twentieth century, Casablanca was chosen as a stopover port for important companies. There were six regular French companies and the foreign companies included three English ones and one each from Spain, Italy and Germany. There were also six French companies that used the port as a stopover on an irregular basis, and the foreign companies in this category included two each from the United States and Italy, one Yugoslavian company and a Swedish one. The various companies that visited this port formed part of a network that linked several ports in this part of the Atlantic: the Compagnie Maritime

Belge; the Paquet Company for the Marseilles–Dakar line; the Spanish Transmediterranean line on the Barcelona–Casablanca–Canary Islands route or the Italian General line. Thus, the port gradually became a port of call for ships travelling from Europe to Africa and South America. The French flag accounted for between 46 per cent (1911) and 51 per cent (1931) of visiting vessels, the British flag fell from 20 to 15 per cent and the Spanish flag also fell from 16 to 5.23 per cent; the rest were divided between German and Italian boats, bearing in mind that Morocco enjoyed the freedom to choose which flag to fly, according to section 69 of the Algeciras Treaty (Eyquem, 1933, 68–71).

As of 1912, Casablanca was the most visited port in Morocco, with 670 ships and 502,562 registered tonnes, 42 per cent of the overall shipping movement of the ports of the French zone, while in 1930, 2234 ships entered the port with 3,506,000 tons (73 per cent). Through Casablanca, products sourced at ground level and also underground were exported, as were consumer goods and equipment. This is where agricultural products based on ancestral cereal crops (barley, wheat, corn) were embarked, together with husbandry products, olives, wood, grain and so forth, which were exchanged for other products such as material, tea or sugar. While activity initially focused during the early part of the twentieth century on activities typical of a primitive economy, it evolved towards tertiary sector activities. But it also sustained, to a certain extent, a modern economy, mainly put into practice by the European minority, using modern working methods, as can be seen in the modern factories and in the industries of equipment goods, giving rise to modern towns and means of transport.

The development of the city and port led to the expansion in Casablanca of certain industries that enjoyed particularly favourable conditions, at least for Morocco, of abundant cheap labour, raw material that was easy to transport, and easy provisioning and transport facilities. In 1926, a total of 709 establishments occupied a surface area of 25,000 square metres.[6] But the most important port-related industrial activity was directly derived from the port. The former fishing fleet grew considerably thanks to the activities in the new port and supplied the fishing industry, based on the plentiful fish found in the neighbouring fishing banks (Table 4.3).

The number of workers employed in the fishing industry was 640, of which there were 260 indigenous women. They used 124 boats, 44 of which had engines, according to a census carried out in 1926 by the Service de la Marine Merchante.[7] The port had modern installations with which to deal with the fish brought to port, used by the local fleet

Table 4.3   Fishing activities in Casablanca (1938–52)

Years	No. of factories	Salting and smoking factories	Production in tonnes
1938	14	4	6863
1939	19	–	6805
1940	21	8	5806
1941	21	22	8881
1942	22	13	9081
1943	21	10	2792
1944	19	10	1092
1945	23	222	5642
1946	20	31	4861
1947	28	26	4382
1948	36	11	5117
1949	39	12	4099
1950	32	–	3438
1951	34	–	6413
1952	40	–	4043

Source: Notice sur le Port de Casablanca, 1953, 61.

as well as those belonging to neighbouring and foreign ports. The fish were distributed between the 32 canneries, the salting and drying centres, for local consumption or that of inland cities.

Lastly, Casablanca offered shipping services such as the provision of water, coal and liquid fuel at favourable prices because these products did not have to pay customs duties, as well as ship's chandlery and provisioning. In the 1920s, tourism completed the picture, as the city offered its attractions, from its benign climate to the wide range of art deco buildings, to visitors.

5   Conclusion

The Port of Casablanca is an example of a modern, well-managed port that has enabled the country's potential to be enhanced and to rise in value. It also had its detractors, who mainly questioned the excessive degree of centralism and the level of investment it enjoyed to the detriment of other secondary ports. Similarly, it constitutes a brilliant example of both human actions over nature and of science and technology over adverse elements. By overcoming the difficulties posed by natural elements, it became a major maritime entity, the creation of which required a considerable national financial effort.

Just before the Second World War, Casablanca had become the most important port of Morocco: centralised ports had triumphed in Morocco. It enabled its hinterland, the region of Chaouia, to become richer and in a broader sense served almost all the Moroccan economy. It also made it easier for passengers to travel to an important commercial centre. However, as we mentioned in the introduction, the port is not just building work; we have to take into consideration the management of the administration and those working to ensure that the infrastructure and services ran smoothly.

Notes

1. For example, the Hersent brothers undertook a major campaign for construction in Fedala, where D. Rivet had real estate interests (cited in Kaioua, 1996, 68); El Jadida also offered possibilities, but was finally disregarded (Jmahri, 2008, 34–5).
2. This company was set up in Paris on 18 December 1903, with a share capital of 3,500,000 francs, thanks to the contribution of the Banque de l'Union Parisienne, agreed with Schneider et Cie (De Caquerey, 1952, 10). In fact, the participation of the Compagnie Marocaine was possible thanks to the French government's commitment as it intervened to put an end to the rivalries between the two powerful business groups, Schneider and Paribas. This work provided major profits for the Schneider group (Kaioua, 1996, 60).
3. When the French Protectorate came into force in 1912, French economic groups enjoyed considerable freedom and exercised almost absolute power up until Independence, as some experts have concluded. See, for example, Kaioua (1996, 58). The Compagnie Marocaine 'was a kind of charter company that managed all economic life in Morocco', according to P. Guillen (1965) in 'L'implantation de Schneider au Maroc, les debuts de la compagnie marocaine (1902–1906)', *in Revue d'histoire diplomatique*, cited in Kaioua (1996, 60), d'Angio, 1995, 132, and others.
4. The Senator M. Messimy, criticised the investments, saying they were excessive, bearing in mind that the infrastructure built up until 1932 exceeded the traffic demands (cited in Eyquem, 1933, 145).
5. The Manutention Marocaine company was controlled by the Rothschild group, the Compagnie Génerale Transatlantique and the Hersent group; the equipment was supplied by the Schneider group (Kaioua, 1996, 70).
6. Figures taken from the *Recensement des Industries du Protectorat (Anné 1924)*, official publication (cited in Vidalenc, 1928, 26–9).
7. Comité d'Oceanographie et d'Etudes des Cotes. Comité Local du Marc, no. 2 COEC/TM, Casablanca, 23 February 1949, entitled 'Compte-Rendu Séance du Comité d'Oceanographie et d'Etudes des Cotes de Maroc', 20 (typed), Nantes Diplomatic Archive.

Bibliography

d'Angio, A. (1995) *Schneider & Cie et les travaux publics (1895–1949)* (Paris: École de Chartes).
Bird, J. (1963) *The Major Seaports of the United Kingdom* (London: Hutchison).

Celce, G. (1952) 'Le port de Casablanca et l'économie marocaine', doctoral thesis. Faculté de droit de Paris.

Chastel, R. (2009) *Témoignages et chuchotements. Histoire de Casablanca des origines à 1952* (Rabat: OKAD El Jadida).

Croze, H. (1949) *Le Port de Casablanca. Causerie Faite à la Chambre de Commerce et d'Indusrie de Casablanca*, extrait du *Bulletin de la Chambre de Commerce et d'Industrie de Casablanca*, 280 (Jan.–Feb.).

De Caquerey, G. (1952) 'Porquoi et commet Casablanca eut son port', *Notre Maroc. Revue Bimestriele Ilustreé*, special issue, 'Le Port de Casablanca et la naissance d'une grande Ville', 5–13.

Eyquem, J. (1933) *Les ports de la zone française du Maroc, leur rôle économique* (Alger: V. Heintz).

Foreign Office (1908–14) *Diplomatic and Consular Reports. Morocco: Casablanca* (London: Foreign Office).

Hatton, G. (2009) *Les jeux financiers et économiques du Prtectorat Marocain (1936–1956). Politique publique et investisseurs privés*, 2nd edn (Paris: Publications de la Société Française d'Histoire d'Outre-mer).

Jmahri, M. (2008) *Le Port d'El Jadida. Une histoire méconnue* (Casablanca: Imprimerie Najah El Jadia).

Kaioua, A. (1996) *Casablanca. L'Indusrie et le ville*, Fascicule de Recherche, 30, Urbama. Centre d'Etudes et de Recherches sur l'Urbanisation du Monde Arabe (Tours: Université de Tours).

Laroche, C. (1927) 'The Port of Casablanca', in *Twenty-third Ordinary General Meeting, Société des Ingénieurs Civils de France, British Section* (16 December, London), pp. 1–23.

Marill, H. (1952) 'Le grand port sur lequel veille la Chambre de Commerce et d'Industrie', *Notre Maroc*, special issue titled 'Le Port de Casablanca et la naissance d'une grande ville', June, 19–22.

Martner Peyrelongue, C. (1999) 'El puerto y la vinculación entre lo local y global', *Revista Eure*, 25(75), 103–20.

Miège, J. L., and E. Eugène (1954) *Monographie de Casablanca de 1907 à 1914* (Paris: Le Petit Marocain).

Ministère des Transports du Royaume du Maroc (n.d) *Historique du Port de Casablanca*, available at: www.mtpnet.gov.ma/Vpm (accessed 5 Jan. 2013).

Protectorat de la République Française au Maroc (1953) *Notice sur le Port de Casablanca*.

Royaume du Maroc (1998) *Le Port de Casablanca par l'image, 1907–1987*, Ministère des Travaux Publics de la Formation Professionnelle et de la Formation de Cadres, Impression Multimedia, legal depot, 271/1988.

Société d'études économiques et Statistiques (1933–38) *Bulletin Économique du Maroc* (Rabat: Imprimerie Officielle).

Timoule, A. (1988) *Le Maroc à travers les chroniques maritime. Tome II. La mer dans l'Histoire du Maroc. De Hassan Ier à Hassan* (Casablanca: l'Imprimerie SONIR).

Veltz, O. (1994) 'Jerarquía y redes en la organización de la producción y el territorio', in Benko y Lipietz (ed.), *Las regiones que ganan. Distritos y redes: Los nuevos paradigmas de geografía económica* (Valencia: EdicionsAlfons El Magnánim).

Vidalenc, G. (1928) *Une œuvre française. Le port de Casablanca* (Casablanca: Librairie Faraire).

Weisgerber, F. (1947) *Au seuil du Maroc Moderne* (Rabat: Ed. La Porte).

5
The Port of Dakar: Technological Evolution, Management and Commercial Activity

Daniel Castillo Hidalgo

1   Introduction

This chapter is mainly dedicated to explaining the management model and the process of technological modernisation in the paradigmatic West African colonial port of Dakar (Senegal).[1] Located on the Cape Verde Peninsula, the port of Dakar constituted the main transport infrastructure for the French Empire in West Africa, serving as a port of call and a commercial gateway for French West Africa (FWA). The original harbour before 1910 – when the commercial port was officially inaugurated – was designed to serve as a base for imperial expansion inland, something that the railway connections, the advanced military posts and the extension of the capitalist system through export cash-crop agriculture and wage-earning work would make possible. Hence, the port of Dakar was a key tool in the development of the colonial economic system based on the massive export of cheap raw materials from the inland agricultural and mining regions. In addition, the port served as a port of call for the French vessels operating in West Africa. It generated significant competition with the Canary Islands' ports, which functioned as notable coaling stations for the European steam-lines. However, the distinctive facet of Dakar was its role as a commercial gateway, which included the development of a proper port community where the major imperialist trade companies were present (Bird, 1971). Furthermore, the extension of railway connections from Dakar to Upper Senegal and the Niger made the process of economic concentration in the city-port in the last decades of the nineteenth century easier. The increase in commercial activity associated with the extension of 'legitimate trade' from 1880 and during the years prior to the Great War required important reforms in the port infrastructure as well as in port management. These were two elements of port modernisation required in the light of emerging issues in the transport sectors which required modern and well-equipped infrastructure and efficient port institutions in order to facilitate trade. It is important to bear in mind the configuration of the West African port network during this period because the different ports were interconnected and the success of one port could bring about the demise of others. Hence, the different ports included in this network, such as Las Palmas and Tenerife (Canary Islands), Saint Vincent (Cape Verde), Casablanca (Morocco) or Freetown (Sierra Leone), had specific characteristics with which they competed on the maritime market. Moreover, inter-port competition was an important element to be considered when analysing port infrastructure and management models from a broad perspective. This competition was a fact, even though the colonial policies in West Africa gave rise to strong protectionist measures to preserve the 'motherhood interests' that were essentially the interests of French companies. In this sense, the functions of these ports were varied and ranged from coaling services to major commercial activity, which was a feature of the continental West African ports. In several cases, the leading role was played by the same entrepreneurial agents, who developed an in-depth commercial network in West Africa, as was the case of the British companies of Wilson and Sons, Elder Dempster or the French Compagnie Française d'Afrique Occidentale (CFAO). They created their own commercial Empires in West Africa, supported by the imperial governments interested in developing commercial activity, which led to the imperialist expansion in the region and profits obtained from the African resources for the European powers (Rodney, 1971).

Scholarly literature on ports in West Africa has paid attention to several questions derived from the ports and corresponding infrastructure and their role as privileged connectors with the global markets. Pioneer work was written in the 1950s at the onset of colonial economic liberalisation processes and when scholars' interests were dominated by the increased importance of African resources for the reconstruction of Europe and the capitalist economy. The events of Suez in 1956–57 increased the interest in these studies and several works were written by scholars such as Benjamin Thomas (Thomas, 1957). The second wave of scholarly interest in West African ports occurred in the 1960s, when most African countries achieved their political independence. For Dakar, key research was carried out in the latter years of the decade by Richard Peterec, who analysed the commercial activity of Dakar and its decisive influence on the economy of Senegal and French West Africa (Peterec, 1967). Some years later, university lecturer Assane Seck published an important – and not reprinted – work on the city-port of Dakar, the impact of maritime activity on urban development and the shaping of the economic clustering process (Seck, 1970). However, scholarly production in this field stopped, although other works were written including social features such as port work or entrepreneurial analyses. In this sense, the Nigerian literature advanced thanks to the research started by the university lecturer Babafemi Ogundana and followed up by researchers such as Ayodeji Olukoju, who renewed these studies with approaches from multidisciplinary perspectives, particularly that of economics (Olukoju, 2004). The most recent research on the port of Dakar has been carried out by Jacques Charpy (Charpy, 2007 and 2011), who has researched the initial construction work to the port at Dakar, but a long-term historical analysis of trade or port activity has not been conducted to date. These issues were studied by Castillo Hidalgo in his doctoral thesis (Castillo Hidalgo, 2012a). In this research, long-term commercial activity from 1900 to 1957 has been analysed, bearing in mind the strong competition with the Canary Islands' ports, particularly Las Palmas. Other issues concerning infrastructure and the development of an economic clustering process at Dakar – and other city-ports – are being studied by himself and the Atlantic Studies Group Research of the University of Las Palmas (Castillo Hidalgo, 2012b).

This chapter offers an analysis of the long-term evolution of the infrastructure and the management model at Dakar, looking at the internal and external factors that affected the port's growth. Furthermore, it will explain how Dakar contributed to the extension of industrial capitalism in West Africa through the outstanding role it played as a commercial and transport system centre. The railway running from inland regions to the Atlantic coast linked the distant markets in landlocked Africa to the global markets in Europe and the United States, leading to an increase in both Dakar's trade indicators and the presence of imperialist companies with interests in this profitable trade based on dominion and dependence. Thus, the railway and the vessels' steam were the physical representation of a new economic and political order in West Africa where ports such as Dakar played a key role.

This chapter is divided into four parts. The first part studies Dakar's modernisation processes, focusing on the different internal and external factors that helped to ensure the improvements in port infrastructure from 1857. In that year, the French government started to plan the future project for a commercial port in the Bay of Dakar. These plans are covered at the beginning of this chapter. I explain how the port and its infrastructure changed according to the trade and shipping needs and how it facilitated the decisive introduction of modern industrial elements such as railway connections running right up to the quays or the improvements made in the coaling and fuel services. This integral modernisation of the infrastructure plays a key role in explaining how Senegal and French West Africa entered the global commodities markets through the port of Dakar. This was a complex phenomenon in which the African economic structure was transformed and, consequently, the West African political and social structure. In addition, this section studies the establishment of a civil port institution to manage and regulate the maritime activity at Dakar. This important feature represents the transition from a pre-industrial port to an industrial port with the capacity to serve the economic globalisation process. In this sense, different institutions such as the Port Council or the role played by the Chamber of Commerce will also be analysed in the first part. The second half of this chapter shows the evolution of commercial activity at Dakar between 1900 and 1929. In this section I will set out the range of commodities and goods exchanged in the Senegalese port, paying attention to the degree of specialisation in these commodities and the port's general position in the whole of FWA. Lastly, some concluding remarks are offered.

Finally, some questions about the sources and methodology employed should be clarified. Primary sources from different international records have been used. These include the following: Archives Nationales du Sénégal (hereafter ANS) (Dakar), Archives Nationales Section Outre-Mer (hereafter ANSOM) (Aix-en-Provence) and the Public Record Office (hereafter PRO) (Kew Gardens). Other sources, such as the British Diplomatic and Consular Reports and the records of the Colonial Office, were also important. In terms of methodology, some parameters of economic geography have been used, especially with questions regarding the impact of port infrastructure on urban economies and the formation of agglomeration economies. Some materialist approach concepts and theory have been used when analysing the organisation and evolution of the economic structure developed by the imperialist powers in West Africa that marked the increased dependency of these territories on the European decision-making centres.

2 Dakar, a Colonial Seaport: Modernisation of Port Infrastructures and Port Management

2.1 The Modernisation of a Colonial Port (1857–1929)

The port of Dakar is a clear example of what a colonial seaport in West Africa was like and how it was run. This type of port typically displays outstanding commercial functions reflected by the port activity indicators (see Table 5.3) that dominated port functions. The port of Dakar paved the way for the economic introduction of FWA into the global commodities markets as of the last decades of the nineteenth century, when the slave trade was replaced by 'legitimate trade' comprising the systematic exploitation of the overseas territories' natural resources by imperialist nations. The economic structure designed by the colonial government during this period was characterised by the rise and predominance of Dakar over the regional Senegalese port network and its supremacy over other former commercial centres. Hence other ports, such as St Louis or Rufisque, which had played an important commercial role in the past, were displaced from the main commercial trends by Dakar. This economic clustering process at Dakar was a consequence of the deficient port infrastructures at the two other ports and the specific policies planned by Paris to articulate the economic structure of Senegal and French West Africa for the efficient exploitation of resources (Charpy, 2007 and 2011). The French engineers who designed the modernisation plans for the port of Dakar decided that the economic future of Senegal and FWA would pass through Dakar and its port infrastructure. However, the port in itself did not guarantee the commercial exploitation of the colonial territories; a determined aggressive expansion policy to reach the inner regions in West Africa was also needed.[2] In addition, it was necessary to develop the inland African transport infrastructures in order easily to ship the cash-crop production from the Senegal River, the Upper Volta and the Sine-Saloum regions. Said infrastructures facilitated the economic introduction of these territories into global commodities markets, encouraging African farmers to produce the industrial crops intensively. So, the combination of the railway and port helped to make it easier to transport merchandise, increasing the profits for the Europeans as well as for Africans:

> The population is the same, and it is confidently expected that as in the case of the Dakar–St. Louis Railway, the people will begin to cultivate ground-nuts as soon as the rail affords the means of transport (in the case of the Dakar–St. Louis Railway, the freight of ground-nuts pays the whole of the working expenses everything else being profit).[3]

Thus, colonial investments in infrastructures were concentrated on the port of Dakar, which became the centre of the Senegalese railway network as of 1882 when construction of the Dakar–St Louis railway started, as a consequence of the increased importance of Dakar and its port. In 1883, another railway line was built between Dakar and Rufisque. This latter port had been Senegal's main centre for peanut exports since the middle of the century and it absorbed most of the cash-crop production from the Sine-Saloum. The peanuts were shipped in small steamboats running from Kaolack to Rufisque and then tran-shipped to Dakar. Once the Dakar–Rufisque railway connection was finished, the peanuts were transported by train and the freight costs consequently decreased significantly. In addition, the capitalist system penetrated towards the interior of Senegal thanks to the railway, and the Kayes–Thiès railway line (1903–09) linked Dakar with Upper Senegal, permitting the cash-crop production of Upper Senegal and Niger to be shipped more quickly, and a prolongation of the line reaching Kolikoro and Tombouctou (Mali) was developed after 1908.[4] These railways facilitated the movements of commodities (chiefly oleaginous raw materials) from the producer regions to the port of Dakar, where the major imperialist companies traded profitably. In Map 5.1 the extension of the Senegalese railway network in 1909 and the distinguished role played by Dakar as an import–export node can be observed.

It must be noted that Dakar was the main gateway for Senegal, Mali, West Niger and the South of Mauritania, absorbing most of FWA's com-mercial activity and reaching figures of up to eighty per cent of global external trade. There is no doubt that the colonial seaports in West Africa were the main tools used by the imperial powers to structure an economic system based on the exploitation of the natural and human resources of the overseas territories for the benefit of their industrial and commercial sectors.

However, it is important to point out that all these political projects for the expansion of markets in the colonial territories required modern transport infrastructure that had to be adaptable to the technological demands of the shipping industry, which progressed enormously from the middle of the nineteenth century onwards. The improvements in this infrastructure required a large amount of public capital, resulting in the concentration of investment in Dakar, to the detriment of the old and inadequate ports of Gorée and St Louis. Neither of these ports offered the geographical possibilities for the establishment and develop-ment of a modern industrial port, and space limitations made it impos-sible to establish a port industry that would include workshops, large storage facilities, coal bunkers or shipyards in either of them. These key factors led the French government to decide to establish Senegal's main port at Dakar. In addition, in 1857 the French government agreed a regular stop-over at the Bay of Dakar (Europe–Dakar–Brazil) with

96

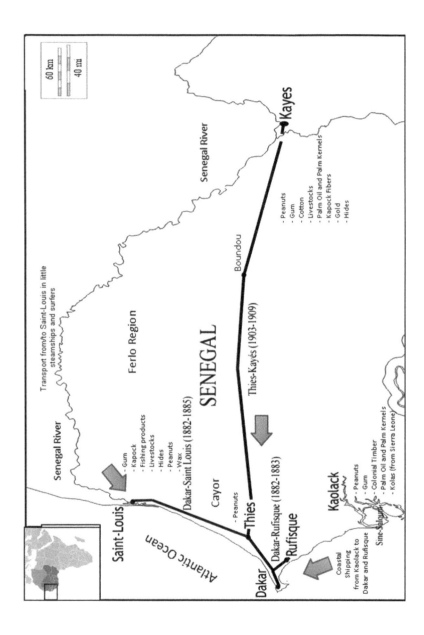

Messageries Impériales, with a view to promoting transport and trade relations between the West African colonies and the mainland French ports, including the route to Brazil, which was growing considerably in economic terms due to the massive capital investments made by European industrialists. This agreement was the definitive factor that sped up the works at Dakar because the French company refused to stop at Dakar until the port infrastructure had been improved and the stop-over and coaling operations could be carried out safely. Hence, they called at Mindelo in the Cape Verde Islands, where some British coaling companies offered competitive port services for shipping lines. The increased competition among the Canary and Cape Verdean ports during a period in which the struggle for Africa began encouraged French administrators to establish a transport programme aimed at improving infrastructure and adapting it to modern demands. It is clear that Dakar was the central point in this modernisation programme.

The Bay of Dakar was the best place to establish a safe port due to its favourable geographical conditions. The decision to choose the Bay of Dakar was a consequence of the different research and studies carried out by the French engineer Émile Pinet-Laprade, who was taken on in Senegal to transform and develop the main infrastructure. He planned the future Senegalese railway network structure centred at Dakar that would permit the development of the interior markets and the increased presence of European agents.[5]

But the establishment of a port of call at Dakar was not only decided on for economic reasons. The French Imperial Navy wanted to establish a safe naval base in West Africa as a safeguard in the struggle against the other imperial powers acting in the region, chiefly Great Britain. The main works began in 1864 with the construction of the South Jetty that was to be at least 200 m long.[6] The main objective of this initial work was to create a safe zone in the bay to ensure that the maritime operations of the vessels calling in at port were safe. In November 1866, the first steamship – *Le Guianne* – reached Dakar from Bordeaux en route to Brazil, and after a decade of troubles between the company and the French government that gave rise to delays, this line was established on a regular basis.

There were very few developments in the port infrastructure at Dakar over the following years, but it became important in the decades of the 1870s and 1880s, when the modern intermodal connections were planned and developed at the Senegalese ports. These were a direct consequence of Freycinet's Plan that, from 1878, projected the modernisation of port infrastructure in France and its overseas territories

(Marnot, 1999, 653). At Dakar, this project entailed the integration of the St Louis–Dakar railway into the port in 1885, the first stage of which had ran as far as Rufisque and was concluded in 1883.[7] These modernisation projects, which affected the port of Dakar, were completed in the first decade of the twentieth century, when the Dakar–Kayes–Thiès–Koulikoro–Tombouctou railway line reaching Upper Senegal and Mali was constructed. The main section of the railway (Kayes–Thiès) was finished in 1909 and it enabled the cash-crop production and other African commodities to be sent quickly to the port of Dakar, which was officially inaugurated in 1910. These works facilitated the introduction of the inland areas into the global commodities markets by means of the connection through Dakar because the African farmers could offer their production to the European middlemen who had settled in the trading posts at the railway stations.

Moreover, the works at the naval base at Dakar (1896–98), where the war vessels of the French Navy could be supplied with coal, water, foodstuffs and war materials, came to an end during the first decade of the twentieth century. These years were characterised by the major works implemented at Dakar to develop its Commercial Port (1902–10). Following the Baudin Plan parameters, which envisaged the improvements to the French Empire's transport infrastructure, the colonial government of FWA designed a major project to develop the commercial port, concentrating commercial activity and intermodal railway connections as well as political predominance. Consequently, in 1904 the FWA federal government negotiated the concession of a loan to develop transport infrastructure in FWA for the sum of 65 million francs with the French Ministry of Colonies.[8]

The works at the port of Dakar absorbed 62 per cent of the total loan (40 million francs). The main works were carried out by the French companies MM. Jammy et Galtier and MM. Hersent, who had also participated in the works of Dakar's port arsenal in 1898.[9] The works at the Bay of Dakar lasted from 1904 to 1910. The project entailed a radical reform including the enlargement of the South Jetty and the creation of a Jetty in the North Zone, closing the port zone and making it safe. It was necessary to dredge the bay in order to reach depths of 12 m and accommodate the bigger modern vessels. Furthermore, two commercial quays were constructed in the South Zone, linked to the railway connections and the embankment areas of the port zone. These embankments were being prepared to develop buildings and spaces for port activity such as warehouses, coal stores, offices and workshops.[10]

Once the works at port were finished, it operated as one of the main commercial bases on the West African coast. However, it did not receive any major improvements until the 1920s. During the First World War, the port served as a naval base for the Allies, replacing the unsafe stop-over ports of St Vincent (Cape Verde) and the Canary Islands' ports. During this war period, the port underwent a considerable increase in calling traffic and the coaling services were improved with the construction of new coal warehouses and coaling infrastructures served by British coaling companies, which dominated the coal markets in West Africa[11] (Table 5.3). It is important to bear in mind the role played at the port of Dakar by Elder Dempster and Wilson and Sons during the war. They both moved their coal stocks from other ports like La Plata (Argentina), St Vincent or Las Palmas to Dakar in order to serve the British Navy in an agreement signed with the French authorities. This agreement aimed to keep the coal stocks in Dakar and Freetown (Sierra Leone) in order to supply the Allied fleet during the war because the coaling stations of the Atlantic islands were being beleaguered by German submarines.[12]

However, the major modernisation projects came in the 1920s as the result of a global economic recovery plan designed by the French Minister of Colonies, Albert Sarraut, in 1921. The Great War had upset the imperial economy and his department designed a recovery plan based on a logical and systematic exploitation of colonial resources that would permit the reconstruction of the motherland's economy. To this end, the French government had to commit considerable public investment to infrastructure (Coquery-Vidrovitch, 1979, 52). Sarraut and the French colonialists thought that the overseas territories –and their peoples – would support the motherland economy and that transport infrastructure was essential, constituting privileged channels with which to bring the colonies into closer contact with mainland French ports.

The colonial government had to allocate considerable expenditure to Dakar's port because the new demands of international shipping required quays adapted to supply fuel. Hence, new fuelling piers were constructed at the deeper North Jetty.[13] During this period many oil companies settled on the West African coast. In the main city-ports, names such as Shell, Vacuum Oil Company or Texaco became familiar. However, the entry of these companies in the protected Senegalese market was blocked until the end of the decade, due to the huge pressure exerted by the Anglo-French companies that controlled this sector.[14]

On the other hand, the colonial authorities installed modern port equipment such as electric cranes to handle large goods including cars, iron bars and engines. However, the main cargo handling work that involved the loading of colonial commodities (bulk goods) was carried out basically using African manpower, which was poorly paid and hence profitable for the port companies. The Sarraut Plan was designed to last a decade, but the events of October 1929 in New York and the subsequent financial crisis brought it to an abrupt end. The demand for West African oil commodities dropped due to the bankruptcy of many European industries that had previously demanded them in large quantities. Hence, the European and American markets cut back massively on their imports of peanuts, palm oil, palm kernels, karité butter and other commodities that were exported through Dakar and the other West African Atlantic ports. This situation affected the African farmers and the economic productive structure in Senegal slumped into a deep crisis that affected the Africans' wages and living conditions (Daumalin, 1992, 198). In addition, the improvements projects at Dakar were cancelled and no significant works were implemented until 1935, when the peanut quays were constructed in the North Zone to make shipment of this commodity easier. These works led to the virtual elimination of Rufisque as a peanut export harbour. As of the second half of the 1930s, the port of Dakar was the main and only port responsible for the export of most FWA goods, replacing Rufisque in this commercial function.

2.2   Port Management at Dakar (1910–29)

The advances in the shipping industry that took place from the middle of the nineteenth century onwards increased global port activity considerably. The role formerly played by ships' officers in matters such as trade or insurance was played by modern economic agents who helped to shape tertiary economies linked to industrial developments and port activity. These agents participated through port companies in maritime activity and included shipping agents, commission agents, insurance brokers and middlemen. The role formerly played by the commanders of the vessels (for example in commercial issues) was now taken care of by new port economic agents such as shipping agents or coaling companies, introducing new elements into port activity.[15] However, these changes did not only occur in the commercial port community. The intensified and complex relationship between the different economic agents acting at the modern ports required the port institutions to improve management and organisation. The historical and economic context required increasingly close coordination between the different port agents from the public and private sectors in order to ensure competitiveness and profits for all parties. Thus, the establishment of civil port institutions in the early decades of the twentieth century in the main nodes was a clear, contemporary answer to the increased demands of shipping and trade.

At Dakar, the Port Authority was created in 1910 and closely linked to the inauguration of the commercial port. Previously, the port had been managed and controlled by the FWA government and the French Navy acting under the surveillance of the Minister of Colonies. In 1910, the port of Dakar became independent from the military ministers, although the French arsenal remained under military control, and operated in coordination with the different imperialist economic agents that made up the Port Council in 1920, as will be explained below.

The port of Dakar was a classic example of a Landlord port during the colonial period (Table 5.1). This mixed management model saw the private and public sectors operating as a whole. In overall terms, their main purposes were to encourage inter-port competitiveness and absorb port traffic from other ports, which in turn affected the number of vessels calling at port (Jansson and Shneerson, 1982). The basic parameters of this port model were fulfilled in Dakar's case, as could be clearly seen in major investments allocated to developing the port infrastructure. The colonial government spent large amounts of capital to develop and improve private companies to carry out commercial functions. The companies paid an annual quota and were taken on to increase inter-port competitiveness, benefiting – at least in theory – the whole of the region through job creation and trade development. These companies exploited concessions in the maritime zone for long periods, obtaining significant returns from the port activity, where they operated from a privileged position as their location generated additional profits.

Thus, the Port Authority of Dakar received income from taxes, concessions and other tariffs levied on exploitation services that served to finance the port budget, decreed as independent from the FWA budget in 1910. This kind of port authority was implemented in France and its overseas territories during the government of Patrice Mac-Mahon (1873–79) as progress in the shipping industry required modern institutions to encourage and speed up maritime activity.

It should be remembered that the colonial administrators did not seriously plan the establishment of a Port Authority at Dakar until the inauguration of the commercial port in 1910. They were most interested in maintaining a regular stock of coal to supply the French Navy and to ensure the supplies for international shipping stopping over at the

Table 5.1   Management model of the Port of Dakar (1910–29)

Item	Management
infrastructure (construction, improvements etc.)	public
port services, exploitation of the port (coaling, shipyards, trade etc.)	private
promotion and inter-port competition	mixed

Source: Castillo Hidalgo (2012a).

port. From April 1884, the French government had assured the regular stock of coal through the French Messageries Maritimes, who purchased it from British coaling companies. The changes in management were most important in the early years of the twentieth century. Military functions were progressively taken over by civil administrators. The Colonial Secretary for Public Works in Senegal played an important role as the person charged with regulating and administrating the activity at the bay until 1910. He organised the lighting system and prepared the emergency protocols, should any wrecks occur in the bay.[16] However, his functions were not sufficient to guarantee the efficient running of the port's commercial activity. In 1910, the president of Dakar's Chamber of Commerce, M. Formeraux, protested to the FWA government saying that the port regulation on trade must be clear and the port administrators should be civil agents linked to economic activity. Formeraux also argued that the Chamber of Commerce should play an active and decisive role in port administration. The demands of the Chamber of Commerce were accepted, but delayed until the creation of the Port Council in 1920. During the 1910s, the war affected the progress of civil institutions at the port because of the strategic role played by Dakar. Until 1920, the port was run directly by the FWA government, which collected port taxes and organised improvement works in line with its own budget.

Eventually, on 18 October 1929, the commercial port of Dakar was definitively separated from the French admiralty and came entirely under the auspices of the FWA government, with the entry of civil administrators and the decisive presence of the Chamber of Commerce. The key figure in the new scheme was the Port Director, named by the FWA Governor. The post was held for a five-year term and the director had authority over the port staff. He had to work in coordination with the Port Council, which was the main port institution created before 1920. Together they planned and managed the strategic policies to be developed at Dakar. Furthermore, the Port Council was a decisive institution for port management. It debated policies, tariffs and planned improvements on the infrastructure, reporting to the FWA government when further funding from the colonial budget was required. Moreover, the Port Council at Dakar acted as an economic lobby because most of its members were representatives of imperial companies. The council included ten agents of the commercial and shipping companies representing the imperial lobby[17] as well as state agents, including the Government Finance Chairman and a representative of the staff named by the Port Director. The council drew up the port's budget and defended the corporate position of the empire's business community.

In the middle of the 1920s, the Port Authority of Dakar divided its structure into two major departments, just as if it were a company divided into different areas. The first of the two was charged with the economic exploitation of the port and it was made up of European expatriate specialists in finance, mechanics and engineering. This department controlled the exploitation of the administrative concessions, collected the taxes and tariffs and controlled the customs at port, operating in conjunction with the customs police and the economic department of the FWA government. In addition, this technical department planned the improvement programmes and prepared the port's maintenance work. On the other hand, the second department of the port of Dakar was charged with the daily maintenance of port infrastructure and included most of the African workers engaged by the port authority. It included the cleaning and health service – created in December 1928 – the port police, the pilots, sailors and day workers. Lastly, in the 1930s the power and water supply at Dakar were under this department's management, working together with the Dakar Town Council, which started to develop the electricity grid in the city.

3 Regional Trade Specialisation: An Analysis of Port Traffics at Dakar (1857–1929)

The commercial port of Dakar played a key role in the Senegalese economy from the latter decades of the nineteenth century, serving as the main gateway for FWA. Before the inauguration of the commercial port in 1910, Dakar was the import centre for Senegal, through which a wide range of goods were imported, ranging from construction materials to build the Senegalese railway network to hardware, cotton clothes, machinery, weapons, alcoholic drinks and others. Hence, the commercial role of Dakar went through at least three phases during the period under review. The first phase began in 1857–66 and was dominated by military functions with little commercial activity, given the healthy status of St Louis and Rufisque, which were then Senegal's trading centres. The first was the former capital and home to the European business community as well as the focal point for Senegal River trade, including the profitable trading of Arabic gum. Rufisque was the peanut export centre, where the European companies organised the export of peanuts and other commodities from the Sine-Saloum region, the main groundnut producer. Apart from the small, depressed commercial centre of Gorée Island, commercial activity was almost non-existent in the Bay of Dakar. This started to change in the 1866 to 1898 period when Dakar emerged over the rest of Senegal's urban centres. During this time, the commercial functions of this city-port had increased considerably as a consequence of the impressive commercial growth in Senegal and FWA, because most external trade passed through its waters (Table 5.2). This period has been known as the Golden Age of trade in West Africa, when imperial companies obtained great profits as a consequence of 'legitimate trade': 'We know that exchanges are made with prodigious profits, and it is no exaggeration to say that the profits obtained from the sale of goods and commodities are not less than 100% [...]. There are excellent business opportunities for everybody.'[18]

This was the result of a number of converging factors. The first was the increased demand for colonial commodities for the European imperial industrial centres, which encouraged the growth and extension of overseas production. In the case of Senegal, the main commodity was peanuts (*arachides*) and their derivatives. The nature of the soil and the rain conditions favoured the expansion of this kind of crop. The introduction of this cash-crop in the 1840s transformed the economic structure of Senegal and introduced it into the global markets of commodities.[19]

As has been said above, the export port of Rufisque accounted for most of the peanut trade until the 1930s. However, most of the vessels calling at Rufisque passed through Dakar in order to take on coal, water or foodstuffs and trade with the port community at Dakar, which had expanded since the 1880s.[20] Hence, Dakar was one of the most important business centres for the imperialist companies in West Africa. At Dakar, the transaction costs started to fall when the main commercial companies began to set up their branches and offices. The same thing happened with the financial and insurance companies linked to commercial activity (Seck, 1970). In addition,

Table 5.2 Import and export trade of French West Africa (1895–1904) (in current British pounds)

Year	Imports	Exports	Total
1895	1,875,300	1,275,783	3,151,094
1896	1,705,034	1,480,795	3,191,629
1897	1,772,839	1,422,506	3,195,345
1898	2,130,736	1,815,264	3,946,000
1899	2,770,135	1,903,757	4,673,892
1900	2,762,465	2,432,108	5,194,573
1901	3,232,587	2,025,935	5,258,522
1902	2,939,640	2,296,791	5,236,431
1903	3,597,934	2,454,971	6,072,905
1904	3,636,836	2,601,555	6,238,091

Source: House of Commons Parliamentary Papers Online. Diplomatic and Consular Reports, No. 3543 (1906).

the port of Dakar developed FWA's commercial activity leading to the introduction of Senegal into the global commodities market, as a result of which its economy was increasingly exposed to the needs of the mainland European ports that further distributed and transhipped the commodities. The port-city took on and brought together the most important urban functions, to the detriment of St Louis, which suffered a progressive economic and political decline and was relegated to a subsidiary position in the Senegalese port hierarchy. Dakar was selected as the node for the Senegalese railway system (1883–1909) and its Chamber of Commerce was established in 1888, replacing the Chambers of Gorée and St Louis as the main entrepreneurial lobby in Senegal. In addition the Banque d'Afrique Occidentale was created in 1901 and its headquarters were located in Dakar, replacing St Louis as Senegal's financial centre.[21] Finally, Dakar was selected as the FWA capital in 1902, bringing together the economic and political power of the whole region.

However, the increased importance of Dakar as the political spearhead for France in West Africa was linked to its growth as a gateway for the region. The improvements made in the port in 1866–98 and the extension of railways towards the interior increased Dakar's import trade due to the massive importing of building materials such as iron, machinery, hardware and cements, among others. Moreover, the third phase of development at Dakar took place between 1900 and 1930. This decisive period saw a strong growth in the port indicators at Dakar, as will be shown below.

In overall terms during the period examined (1900–29) trade at Dakar was characterised by a predominance of the quantity – and value – of imports over exports. The main imports at Dakar were hardware, flour, building materials, cotton clothes, shoes, canned food, liquors, wine and Asian and West African rice. Dakar absorbed the coal imports for Senegal too, because the country's coaling station was established there. Senegal's exports were transported to Dakar by railway, camels or donkeys from the interior and included peanuts, Arabic gum, cotton, ivory, timber, palm oil, palm kernels, gum, livestock, copal gum, kapock fibres and karité butter. Groundnuts constituted the main commodity both in quantity and in overall value exported to the European markets. However, the commercial balance of this trade was unequal and the value of imports was greater than exports, as we can see in Figure 5.1.

It is clear that the port of Dakar is an example of how a West African colonial seaport functioned. Its unbalanced commercial structure and the configuration of the inland transport systems defined a port model serving European interests and introducing these territories into the global economy, albeit from a subordinate position in which they were dependent on the imperial powers.

Table 5.3 shows the main port indicators at Dakar during 1900–29, where we can see the notable increase in commercial activity at Dakar. As far as the figures shown in the table are concerned, it is important

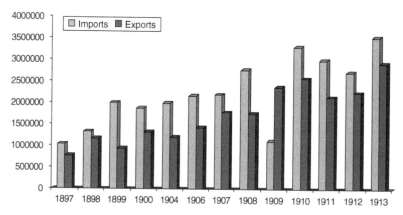

Figure 5.1   Value of external trade of Senegal passing through Dakar (1897–1913) (in British pounds)

Source: House of Commons Parliamentary Papers Online, Diplomatic and Consular Reports, Nos 3883 (1898), 2725 (1900), 3543 (1904–05), 4217 (1908), 5235 (1911–12), 5423 (1910–15).

to take note of the 1914–18 war period, which represented the first major challenge for Dakar and its port community. The impressive rise in the port indicators in 1916–17 corresponds to the massive number of British war and merchant vessels calling at Dakar. This was the result of the German submarine war in the Mid-Atlantic that collapsed commercial traffic in the island coaling ports of the Canary Islands and Mindelo (St Vincent). Hence, the West African continental ports received the attention of both allied admiralties in order to establish safe bases for their fleets. In addition, the British coaling companies Wilson and Sons and Elder Dempster, which controlled the coal market in almost every West African port, agreed with the British and French governments to establish coal stocks in Dakar and Freetown (Sierra Leone) during the war.

The coal for these stocks had to be shipped from Las Palmas, Cape Verde and La Plata, where the German blockage made it almost impossible to keep the Allied trading routes safe.[22] Moreover, the closure of the

Table 5.3   Port indicators at Dakar (1900–29) (bi-annual averages)

Years	Number of vessels entered	Gross Register Tons (t)	Import traffic (t)*	Export traffic (t)	Coal imports (t)	Water supplied (t)
1900–01	n/a	n/a	66,257	12,414	30,654	n/a
1902–03	n/a	n/a	60,382	30,544	22,652	n/a
1904–05	1206	1,424,630	110,205	39,909	76,854	n/a
1906–07	1464	2,096,189	154,260	26,878	94,05	n/a
1908–09	1396	2,414,970	196,539	127,052	104,606	58,152
1910–11	2162	3,671,491	272,589	174,127	184,096	91,803
1912–13	1924	3,669,851	389,999	293,596	295,000	100,930
1914–15	1175	2,173,112	322,180	239,672	216,879	110,756
1916–17	3065	5,457,718	529,975	455,804	465,000	142,860
1918–19	1313	2,339,104	526,068	425,289	362,000	152,115
1920–21	1283	2,678,585	361,508	286,679	526,000	130,655
1922–23	2029	2,467,546	318,511	237,985	349,106**	147,823
1924–25	2184	3,103,266	388,404	283,314	398,657**	195,307
1926–27	2158	3,111,867	448,542	367,594	406,463**	198,339
1928–29	2856	4,456,904	582,695	488,574	552,543**	199,890

*Includes coal imports. **Import and supply of coal aggregated.
Source: for vessels and traffics for 1900: House of Commons Parliamentary Papers Online, Diplomatic and Consular Reports, No. 2725 (1900); for the period 1900–02: Public Record Office, Foreign Office 27/3682; for 1900–15: House of Commons Parliamentary Papers Online, Diplomatic and Consular Reports, No. 5423 (1915); Le Port de Dakar (1918), Grande Imprimerie Africaine, Dakar, 1918; for 1915–29: Morazé, 1936, 607–31; Thomas, 1957, 1–15; Castillo Hidalgo, 2012a, 466.

Suez Canal in 1916 also increased the port traffic in these continental ports in West Africa. The long journeys from Australia, India and the Far East had to sail round Africa in order to reach Europe, and the West African ports were safe coaling bases.

At the end of the war, the port activity at Dakar recovered slowly due to the economic crisis in France. It must be borne in mind that the FWA market was protected and that external trade largely depended on the economic situation in the European Imperial countries. The recovery of the Dutch and German markets affected the Senegalese economy, because they were importers of peanuts and other West African commodities. The loss of the investments made by French capitalists in revolutionary Russia and the consequences of the massacres and desolation of the war affected the industrial tissue in France and had significant repercussions for the overseas territories. As we have explained above, Paris designed a plan to boost its weak economy that involved the decisive exploitation of colonial material and human resources. The government wanted to increase the colonies' productivity in order to help industry on the mainland through the stabilisation of its external trade. It was necessary to improve infrastructure to speed up the export sectors and expand those commercial activities that could compete in the global markets for the benefit of European interests.

In Dakar, the project designed by the French Minister of Colonies, Albert Sarraut, focused on the introduction and development of fuelling services on the commercial quays. The increased demand for these services required considerable expenditure to adapt the quays for larger vessels and the port authority had to find and prepare land on which to install tanks and fuel bunkering services. The port authority had to negotiate with the coal-fuel cartel established at Dakar, which obstructed the entry of new competitors in this local and monopolised market. The new members, Shell and Texas Company, delayed their entry in Dakar until the decade of 1930, when the American and Dutch oil companies began to expand their influence in West Africa. The fuelling services were provided by the companies that controlled the coal market and they had to adapt their staff to the new market demands. The extraordinary growth of this port service (fuel-oil supplies) soared from 12,106 tonnes in 1926 to 110,681 tonnes in 1930.[23] The changes in port services caused in-depth modifications to the labour organisation at Dakar and reduced the number of coal stevedores required to supply the vessels calling at port. It had a major impact on labour relationships at Dakar where the urban African workers were already suffering from deteriorated living conditions.

4 Conclusion

In this chapter, I have shown how the colonial port of Dakar has undergone different modernisation and transformation processes since its creation in the middle of the nineteenth century, as a consequence of the technological advances in transport and the demands of modern shipping, as well as the economic imperialist expansion in West Africa. This modernisation developed different aspects of maritime activity from the port infrastructure itself to the establishment of port institutions charged with regulatory and management tasks. The port of Dakar was an economic cluster where colonial trading activity was encouraged, chiefly after the inauguration of the commercial port in 1910. Hence, the port reflected the progressive introduction of Senegal and the whole of FWA into the new economic dynamics that dominated the overseas territories as of the last decades of the nineteenth century, moving from an economy based on the slave trade to an economic structure dominated by cash-crop export sectors, of which peanuts were the most important crop. The port of Dakar improved its infrastructure and adapted it to serve imperial European interests, increasing the amount and variety of exports from the colonial territories. In addition, the expansion of modern intermodal (railway) connections reached the interior regions where the export crops were grown on a huge scale, benefiting European companies and making African producers dependent to a certain extent on the exterior. Thus, the port was the key element in the introduction of these regions to the global commodities market, affecting their economic, political and social structures.

Notes

1. This chapter forms part of the R&D+I Project of the Spanish Ministry of Science: *Modelos de Gestión de Puertos y la Comunidad Portuaria en el Ámbito Atlántico (siglos XIX y XX)* (HAR2010-17408).
2. ANS. Ports, O. Public Works. Letter from Pinet-Laprade Governor of Senegal to Chausselaup-Laubat, French Minister of Colonies, 14 October 1865.
3. PRO.879/86 (1914).
4. Consular and Diplomatic Reports, No. 3883, French Colonies (1908).
5. ANS. Ports, O. Letter from Chausselaup-Laubat, French Minister of Colonies to the Governor of Senegal, 24 July 1863.
6. ANS. Moniteur du Sénégal, 31 January 1865.
7. PRO.879/86 (1914).
8. ANSOM. 14MIOM/1462, 24 December 1903. See also *Journal Officiel de la République Française*, 20 January 1904. The British archives also include interesting information about these loans. For instance: PRO, Foreign Office

27/3682. Letter from H.G. Mackie, British Consul at Dakar to the Marquis of Landowe, the British Minister of the Foreign Office, 25 January 1904. It must be remarked that since 1900 FWA (and the other French colonial territories) had financial autonomy to develop its own budget.

9. ANSOM. Travaux Publics, Dossier 21, Comité des Travaux Publics des Colonies (1898).

10. It included the offices of the Port Administration, which was also built in this decade. ANSOM, Travaux Publics, Carton 26, Dossier 2, Dossier 8 (1904).

11. There is a remarkable amount of British documentation on this subject: PRO, Ministry of Transports, MT23/564; MT10/1896 (1916). PRO, Admiralty ADM 1/9214 (1917).

12. PRO, Ministry of Transport, MT23/680/1 (1916).

13. *Journal Officiel de l'AOF*, 16 May 1924 and 20 June 1925.

14. *Journal Officiel de l'AOF*, 30 March 1929.

15. It has been described by Suárez Bosa (2003) and González Lebrero (1989).

16. ANSOM, 14MIOM/1455. Report on Port Management at Dakar, 8 March 1904.

17. A modification to the election system for the Council of the Chamber of Commerce was approved on 31 May 1950. The number of representatives increased to 11 instead of the former 10 members. ANS. Chamber of Commerce of Dakar. Section 09, 00485–26/23.

18. Report by M. Maillat, inspector of the *Compagnie Française d'Afrique Occidentale* (CFAO) in 1886. Quoted by Bonin, 1987, 16–17 (translated from French).

19. On the development of monoculture economies in West Africa, see Hopkins, 1973; Brooks, 1975; Moitt, 1989; Ndao, 2009.

20. Approximately 80 per cent of the vessels calling or leaving Rufisque passed through Dakar. PRO, Foreign Office, FO2/629. *Official Bulletin of Senegal and Dependencies*, 1 June 1902.

21. The Banque of Afrique Occidentale (B.A.O) was backed by the Maurel et Prom company and it constituted the evolution of the Banque of Senegal, created in 1853 in St Louis. The main functions of B.A.O were to develop trade in FWA, support loans to traders and farmers and encourage the extension of the monetary economy in the colonies, in the face of the rivalries and the influence of the British Bank of West Africa, created in 1884 by Alfred Lewis Jones, chairman of the British Elder Dempster.

22. PRO, Ministry of Transport, MT23/680/1.

23. ANS, 2G56-93.

Bibliography

Bird, J. (1971) *Seaports and Seaport Terminals* (London: Hutchinson University Library).

Bonin, H. (1987) *C.F.A.O. Cent ans de compétition* (Paris: Economica).

Brooks, G. E. (1975) 'Consequences of the Commercialization of Peanuts in West Africa, 1830–70', *Journal of African History*, 16(1), 29–54.

Castillo Hidalgo, D. (2012a) 'Tendiendo Puentes: Dakar y la configuración de la red portuaria de África Occidental. Evolución y análisis de una comunidad portuaria (1857–1957)', doctoral thesis, University of Las Palmas de Gran Canaria.

Castillo Hidalgo, D. (2012b) 'Buques, ferrocarriles y cacahuetes. Modernización de las infraestructuras en el puerto de Dakar y la introducción de Senegal en los mercados internacionales (1857–1936)', *Transportes, Servicios y Telecomunicaciones*, 23, 140–64.

Charpy, J. (2007) *Dakar. Naissance d´une Métropole* (Dakar: Editions Les Portes du Large).

Charpy, J. (2011) 'Aux origines du port de Dakar', *Outre-Mers*, 99(370/371), 301–17.

Coquery-Vidrovitch, C. (1979) 'Colonisation ou impérialisme: la politique africaine de la France entre les deux guerres', *Le Mouvement Social*, 107, 51–76.

Daumalin, X. (1992) 'Marseille, l'Ouest Africain et la Crise', in M. Courdurie and J. L. Miège (eds), *Marseille Colonial face à la crise de 1929* (Chambre de Commerce et d´Industrie Marseille-Provence), pp. 168–218.

González Lebrero, R. (1989) *El agente consignatario de buques en España* (Barcelona: Librería Bosch).

Hopkins, A. G. (1973) *An Economic History of West Africa* (New York: Columbia University Press).

Jansson, J., and D. Shneerson (1982) *Port Economics* (Cambridge, MA: MIT Press).

Marnot, Bruno (1999) 'La politique des ports maritimes en France de 1860 a 1920', *Histoire, économie et société*, 18(3), 648–52.

Moitt, B. (1989) 'Slavery and Emancipation in Senegal's Peanut Basin: The Nineteenth and Twentieth Centuries', *International Journal of African Historical Studies*, 17(1), 27–50.

Morazé, C. (1936) 'Dakar', *Annales de Géographie*, 45(258), 607–31.

Ndao, M. (2009) *Le ravitaillement de Dakar de 1914 à 1945* (Paris: L´Harmattan-Sénégal).

Olukoju, A. (2004) *The Liverpool of West Africa* (New Jersey: Africa World Press).

Peterec, R. J. (1967) *Dakar and West African Economic Development* (New York: Columbia University Press).

Le Port de Dakar (1918) (Dakar: Grande Imprimerie Africaine).

Rodney, W. (1971) *How Europe Underdeveloped Africa* (Dakar: Pambazuuka Press).

Seck, A. (1970) *Dakar, Métropole Ouest-Africaine* (Dakar: IFAN).

Suárez Bosa, M. (2003) *Llave de la Fortuna. Instituciones y Organización del trabajo en el Puerto de Las Palmas, 1883–1990* (Las Palmas: Fundación Caja Rural).

Thomas, B. E. (1957) 'Railways and Ports in French West Africa', *Economic Geography*, 33(1), 1–15.

6
The Port of Lagos, 1850–1929: The Rise of West Africa's Leading Seaport

Ayodeji Olukoju

1 Introduction

A common feature of the West African coastline is the limited number of natural harbours because of the lack of major indentations. This contrasts sharply with the coastlines of Western Europe and Japan, for example. Hence, only Dakar and Freetown have 'good natural harbours' (White, 1970, 14). Consequently, port development in the region has involved extensive engineering works to create or expand port facilities. This chapter details the development, administration and trade of Lagos (Nigeria) from the mid-nineteenth century to the late 1920s. The period begins with British colonisation between 1850 and 1861, and ends with the onset of the Great Depression of 1929–33. A combination of the institutional, technological, legal and commercial changes wrought by British colonialism, the transition from a local economy based upon the transatlantic slave trade to one driven by the so-called 'legitimate' trade in non-human commodities, the migrations and settlement of return-ees from the African Atlantic Diaspora, urbanisation and port development, and global dynamics propelled the former lagoon port into the leading port-city of West Africa (Olukoju, 2004). By 1880, Lagos had earned the appellation of 'the Liverpool of West Africa', a reference to its pre-eminence in the maritime economy of the region.[1] It was also a clear allusion to its role in cementing the trade and products of the hinterland to the industry of Britain, the mother country. The port was to be the principal conduit of Nigerian maritime trade orientated towards Europe in general and Britain in particular.

The discussion in this chapter draws on original research, primary and secondary source material and the author's sustained engagement with the subject (Hopkins, 1964; Ogundana, 1970, 1976, 1980; Olukoju,

1992a, 1992b, 1994, 2004). In addition to secondary sources, academic books and journal articles, the analysis relies on colonial archival sources of various descriptions, not least official correspondence, Blue Books, Annual Reports, reports of commissions of inquiry, private papers and contemporary newspapers. These sources richly document aspects of the development of the port and its trade, relations between the port and its hinterland, colonial policies and the indigenous people's agency in these developments.

2   The Development of the Port of Lagos, c. 1850–1929

The development of the port of Lagos between 1850 and 1929 can be traced in three broad phases – the period from the establishment of the British colony until 1892, the eve of the declaration of the protectorate of Lagos in 1893, which extended the administrative, political and economic reach of the colony into the Yoruba hinterland; the next, from 1893 until the onset of the First World War; and, finally, the years between 1914 and 1929. These phases witnessed certain landmarks, such as the construction of the railway, the dredging of the harbour and the creation of the Apapa wharf as the railway-linked port outlet of Lagos. The entire period witnessed successive improvements in port facilities, port entrance accessibility, the draught and size of shipping, and the variety, value and volume of seaborne trade.

The period between 1850 and 1892 may be described as the stage of the 'undeveloped' port, when natural conditions prevailed, especially in the entrance to the harbour. As it had been for centuries, Lagos was a lagoon port that was shielded from the open sea by a sandbar, the notoriety of which earned it the nickname of the 'Bugbear of the Bight' by the early sixteenth century (Olukoju, 1992a, 61), when the entrance was described as 'really dangerous' (Ogundana, 1976, 69). The combination of the heavy surf from the Atlantic and the bar, a product of sand propelled by the longshore drift, made direct shipment impossible. Consequently, until 1914, ocean shipping had no direct access to Lagos. Better access to ocean shipping was afforded by nearby lagoon ports at Badary, Lekki and Palma. Recourse was, therefore, made to bar transhipment by surf boats, which added to the cost of shipping and often damaged the cargo. This type of transhipment took place in two stages – surf boats took cargo from the ship lying a few miles off-shore while branch boats then conveyed the cargo across the bar into the harbour. Exports were conveyed to the ocean-going ships in reverse order (Ogundana, 1976, 72).

However, port-working by surf boats was most unreliable as turbulent surf conditions at the harbour entrance at Lagos often prevented the operation of surf boats altogether. Under such conditions, Lagos cargo was transhipped by a second method – adjacent entrance transhipment – via the Forcados river, 128 miles to the east. The calmer waters at Forcados permitted direct handling of cargo between ocean shipping and branch boats. Although transhipment via Forcados took 16 hours, the same length of time that it took for cargo to be handled by transhipment across the Lagos bar, it gave rise to far less damage to or loss of cargo. In 1900, a firm reported only 2.3 per cent loss of cargo via the Forcados route compared to about 10 per cent across the Lagos bar (Ogundana, 1976, 73). Even so, branch boats could only operate across the Lagos bar at high tide during the day given the hazards of night crossing. In all, the cost of transhipment was considerable. By 1892, at the rate of five shillings per ton, it totalled £25,000, 2.5 per cent of the total value of Lagos's trade for the year. If a higher rate of 12s 6d is accurate, cost of transhipment imposed a heavy burden on Lagos maritime trade (Ogundana, 1976, 73). Apart from the problem of the sand bar, the harbour water was shallow, which limited the draught of shipping, even once the access problems had been solved.

Colonial officials in Lagos and London recognised from as early as the 1860s that improvements to the Lagos port entrance were necessary if the port was to achieve its potential. But up until the 1890s, the competing proposals for such improvements did not attract serious attention because the trade of the port could not match the cost of the project. Even when an American company proposed in 1860 the construction of floating breakwaters in return for the revenue from harbour dues for the next 20 years, the offer did not elicit a positive response. But before the end of the century, it was widely accepted that access to the port was contingent upon constant dredging and the construction of breakwaters (Ogundana, 1976, 74). Accordingly, various proposals were considered for the construction of two stone moles to protect the entrance and a third mole (the west training bank) to channel water to scour the entrance. This proposal was submitted by Messrs Coode and Partners of London in 1892 at an initial cost of £830,000 that was revised to £797,000 in 1898. Alternative proposals for a canal and a 720-foot pier to ease port-working were considered in the 1890s (Ogundana, 1976, 76). Apart from considerations of cost, neither offered a better long-term solution to the problem of port-working in Lagos. In particular, they were short-term solutions that could not cope with the anticipated rapid growth of trade and increase in the size and draught of ocean shipping. Still, although the moles project was widely accepted in Lagos as the best long-term solution to the problem of access to the port, its cost was considered somewhat prohibitive. Unlike the scepticism in London, given the well-known penny-pinching attitude of the British Treasury, the local colonial officials in Lagos were convinced that revenue from port charges and trade would repay the loans required to finance harbour works.

The year 1906 was a turning point in the history of port development in Lagos. First, the British government amalgamated its two colonial administrations in Southern Nigeria – the Colony and Protectorate of Lagos, and the Colony of Southern Nigeria. This was in accordance with the policy of making the latter colony share its wealth with the former, thus rendering the amalgamated colonies self-sufficient. The revenue of the combined administration in 1906 was over £1 million, compared to only £200,000 for Lagos alone by the end of the nineteenth century. In the event, it was now possible for the revenue of the enlarged colonial administration to bear the cost of port development at Lagos. In the classical exploitative mould of imperialism, local resources would now be used to develop a facility that was primarily intended as an imperial project in the economic interest of the United Kingdom. Second, it was in 1906 that the government also decided to make Lagos the sole coastal terminus of the western railway, the construction of which started in Lagos in 1895 (Ogundana, 1976, 77).

The western railway line was meant to channel the trade of the hinterland to Lagos. Accordingly, it progressed slowly northwards towards the River Niger, the major artery of internal trade in the Nigerian hinterland. The railway line was crucial to the construction of Lagos port for two major reasons. First, it facilitated the transport of stones from the Aro Quarry some 45 miles to the north for the construction of the moles. Second, the line became a major conveyor of trade in both directions between the port and the hinterland. Again, like other colonial-era infrastructure projects, the railway was intended primarily to facilitate the extraction and export of the natural resources of the port for the benefit of the metropolitan economy.

With the railway facilitating the supply of stone, construction work on the moles project commenced in 1907.[2] Small wharves were first constructed at Iddo and at the east mole site. Stone discharged at Iddo was then conveyed by barges across the harbour to the mole wharf, and from there, rail trucks carried it to the tipping point. Work began at the sites of the east and west moles, and at the west training wall in 1908, 1910 and 1915, respectively.

As can be seen from Table 6.1, steady progress was recorded as stone was deposited in the harbour. There was a slight overlap in the commencement and completion of the three projects. On completion, the two moles and the training bank had a combined length of 3.5 miles built with some 1.8 million tons of stone.

A second major challenge for port development at Lagos was the deepening of the approach channel and the harbour. Between 1877 and 1907, the official bar draught at Lagos fluctuated widely, between the lowest figure of 9 feet 6 inches (December 1899) and the highest of 13 feet (February–March 1889). Whereas the draught was 10–11 feet in 1877, it was 9 feet 9 inches in December 1905 (Olukoju, 1992a, 63). The shallow entrance greatly impeded and imperilled navigation. In 1895 alone, three steamers were wrecked on the Lagos bar and totally disabled. A fourth damaged its sternpost and became a hulk in the harbour. The conditions on the bar were further compounded by adverse weather. Heavy rains from June to August created 'bad bar' conditions and further hampered shipping at Lagos. Accordingly, dredgers were employed to raise the official bar draught. In May 1907, the first dredger, the *Egerton*, was acquired and it commenced work a month later. A second dredger, the *Sandgrouse*, joined it in August 1909. However, the cost of dredging strained the finances of the colony (Olukoju, 1992a, 60–2).

Table 6.1   Progress of Lagos Harbour Works (mole projects) (1908–22)

Year	East mole	West mole	West training bank
1908	988*		
1909	3048		
1910	5571		
1911	7123		
1912	8009	1072	
1913	8813	2111	
1914	10,043	2772	
1915	10,423	3154	413
1916		3581	1322
1917		3814	2026
1918		4226	2516
1919		4716	2562
1920		4952	2772
1921		5073	3186
1922		5175	3292

*In feet.
Source: Data extracted from Table 1 in Ogundana, 1976, 78.

Yet, after an expenditure of nearly £200,000, dredging seemed to have made little difference, as was lamented by a Lagos newspaper, which then recommended the constant use of four or more dredgers during a favourable season in the year to create a deep channel across the bar while a local dredger would subsequently rid the channel of further silting (*Lagos Weekly Record*, 8 October 1910). It appears that this line of action was pursued as consistent dredging did achieve steady improvements in the bar draught, as detailed in Table 6.2. Nevertheless, although the minimum bar draught increased steadily throughout the period, the maximum for 1919 was a foot less than the preceding year.

An immediate consequence of the improvements in the bar draught was the impact on shipping through the port. By August 1913, with the attainment of a 16-foot draught over the bar for seven consecutive months, the long-desired goal of port development at Lagos was achieved: ocean-going shipping could now enter the port for the first time in its history.[3] With Germany's Woermann shipping line blazing the trail, European shipping lines began direct sailings from Europe in February 1914. Consequently, the port of Lagos had become a major outlet for ocean shipping on the Atlantic coast of Africa on the eve of the First World War. Yet as much as half of Lagos's shipments were carried by branch steamers via Forcados, an indication, as a Lagos newspaper noted, that the conditions on the bar were far from perfect, given the occasional shallowness of water on the bar (*Nigerian Pioneer*, 31 July 1914).

Table 6.2 Lagos official bar draught (1907–19) (in feet and inches)

Year	Minimum	Maximum
1907	9′	11′
1908	11′ 6″	13′
1909	12′	14′
1910	13′	15′
1911	11′	16′
1912	9′ 6″	16′ 6″
1913	12′	18′
1914	13′ 6″	19′
1915	13′	17′
1916	15′	19′ 6″
1917	19′ 6″	20′
1918	20′	21′
1919	20′	20′

Source: Adapted from Table 4 in Olukoju, 1992a, 66.

While the foregoing section has detailed engineering works to narrow and deepen the entrance to Lagos harbour, the discussion now shifts to the provision of increased wharfage accommodation for ships in the port. Both issues were interwoven and contingent on the direction of port development policy in Nigeria – whether to limit seaborne trade to a few ports (port concentration) or create multiple outlets (port diffusion) (Ogundana, 1970). Throughout the period from 1850 to 1929, Lagos was the pre-eminent port even as policy oscillated between concentration and diffusion. This arose from the advantages of the port's location vis-à-vis other Nigerian ports: its water and rail transport access to a rich and diversified hinterland, a modernising urban setting and colonial capital-city status (Olukoju, 1996).

That said, the expansion of wharfage involved deciding which of the Lagos wharves would be the terminus of the railway. The consulting engineers had recommended the construction of wharves at a location different from the railway terminus at Iddo, given the prohibitive cost and disruption of the urban setting attendant upon extending the railway across the Lagos township to link a possible site at Wilmot Point on Victoria Island. Consequently, Nigeria's Governor General Frederick Lugard recommended to the Secretary of State for the Colonies in London in 1913 that the wharves be constructed at Apapa on the opposite side of the marina, to which the railway had access. Following approval by London in October 1913, work commenced on the Apapa wharf scheme, which on completion in 1919, had a 180-foot wharf with a depth of 26 feet at low water, achieved by dredging the approach channel. Additional wharves at Iddo and Lagos Island complemented the Apapa wharf (Olukoju, 1992a, 67).

The three wharves handled different components of the external trade of the port (see Table 6.3). The import trade was handled through the Customs wharf (so-called because it grew from the Customs pier constructed in the 1860s) on Lagos Island and Iddo, the former accounting for two-thirds of the traffic. This was essentially because of the extensive private warehouse accommodation owned by importers on Lagos Island. Iddo also handled the bulk of the export trade until Apapa supplanted it as of the 1925/26 financial year. From that year, Apapa wharf captured and controlled all of the export trade, given its rail connections with the hinterland. Indeed, Iddo ceased to handle maritime traffic though it dealt with the local coal traffic (Olukoju, 1992a, 71).

It can be said that by 1919, the most significant port engineering works had been accomplished at Lagos. Yet, though dredging continued to increase the bar draught, which peaked at 25 feet in 1923, depth alone was not the governing factor in navigation across the bar. More important, a contemporary observer noted, was 'the strength and direction of the tides'.[4] Strong tides during the rainy season hampered navigation across the bar by larger vessels which could have taken advantage of the increased depth. It was, therefore, unnecessary to deepen the entrance beyond 25 feet for the rest of the 1920s.

3   Port Administration:
Stakeholders, Coordination of Services, Tariffs and Revenue

A concomitant of port development at Lagos was the political control and financial administration of the port. In terms of control, Nigerian ports up until to 1954 were administered by a multiplicity of port authorities, which engaged in turf wars (Olukoju, 1992b). Given the heavy commitment of government funds to port development, various agencies and departments of government were involved in the administration of Lagos port (Ogundana, 1980, 171–2; Olukoju, 1992b, 158–9). The Marine Department patrolled the entrance to the port and provided technical data on the conditions of the bar. It was responsible for pilotage, storage, the berthing of ships and buoyage (which it took over from Elder Dempster Agencies in 1926). The Harbour Department emerged as the supervisory agency for the port entrance works. In 1922, the Port Engineering Department took over civil engineering maintenance works below the quay face. At the Customs Wharf on Lagos Island, the Public Works Department was involved in the maintenance of port buildings while the Customs itself nominally handled the landing, loading and delivery of cargo. It also collected berthage and harbour dues. The Railway Department took part in port administration from the commencement of railway construction at Iddo in 1895. From then onwards it handled port operations at other rail-linked wharves at Ijora and Apapa. Shipping firms, too, were involved in port administration. Elder Dempster controlled lighterage services and was also responsible for buoyage until the Marine Department took over in 1926 (Olukoju, 2001–02). Inter-departmental rivalry was rife during the pre-1954 period as the various departments protected their narrow interests at the expense of coordinated port-working. The expected synchronisation of railway delivery of cargo with ship sailings coordinated by the Marine Department did not materialise, with adverse effects on shipping turn-around and overall port-working.

 The negative impact of the diffusion of the port authority on trade necessitated the intervention of the business community in Lagos and the United Kingdom, which pressed for remedial action. A report on the Nigerian railway system submitted to the government in 1924 recommended better coordination of port services when Apapa was fully developed and noted the demand by the business community for a Harbour Board (Hammond, 1924, 174). The report generated much debate and elicited opposition, especially from mercantile interests, to perceived railway domination of Nigerian ports. The recommendation for absorption of the Port Engineering Department by the Marine Department was also stoutly resisted. Consequently, the administration of the port of Lagos remained under the control of multiple authorities with dire consequences for the trade and administration of the port. As the colonial governor remarked, the various port authorities, rather than cooperate for the common good, 'put their own [...] interests, as they conceive them, in the forefront and as a consequence they are on many occasions pulling one against the other, public business being hampered and delayed'.[5] This remained the state of affairs until the Nigerian Ports Authority was created in 1955 as the overall coordinating authority for Lagos and other Nigerian ports.

In terms of port revenue, various charges were levied for lighterage, lighting and buoyage, berthage, pilotage and harbour services to off-set part of the cost of transforming the port as stated above (Olukoju, 1994). Until 1917, the rate of harbour dues at Lagos was two shillings six pence per ton of cargo landed or shipped from the port. The rate was doubled to four shillings per first- and second-class passengers, and from six pence to one shilling on others, by an ordinance of December 1918. The rates on cargo were set at £1 per ton of hides and skins, 6s 3d per ton of groundnuts and palm kernels, 5s 6d per ton of palm oil and 4s per ton of tin. Berthage dues were charged from 1917 at the rate of one penny per registered ton for every 40 hours that a vessel spent alongside a government wharf, but warships and similar vessels owned by the British imperial government were exempt.[6] Towage dues were also levied on vessels according to their draught. In 1920, vessels with a draught of 16 feet or below paid £17, and those between 16 and 20 feet were levied £20 while those exceeding 20 feet paid £22 10s. Additional charges were imposed for services on Sundays and public holidays at the rate of £1 10s for any period exceeding 1.5 hours and £3 for longer.[7]

In addition to the aforementioned charges on shipping, port charges were levied by railway authorities. At Iddo, which had a rail link, consignees paid five shillings per ton on their cargo while port charges were borne by the shipping firms. At the Lagos Island Customs wharf, which had no rail links, no handling charges were levied. There, shipping firms included cargo-handling charges in their freight rates (Olukoju, 1994, 114). When added together, the various charges on shipping and port users averaged £60 in 1923.[8] Compared to Cape Town (South Africa), Colombo (Ceylon) and other West African ports, Lagos was said to be 'one of the most expensive in the world – it is undoubtedly an expensive port'.[9]

Yet, a comparison of revenue from the admittedly high and varied charges with the actual cost of constructing and running the port showed that the port was run at a loss. But it was the terminal charges levied by the railways that unduly inflated Lagos port charges. The Director of the Marine Department, therefore, recommended that they should be separated from port charges to reduce overall cost per vessel by 2s 6d.[10] This was not entirely altruistic; it was a dig at the rival Railways Department, which duly defended the terminal charges that it collected. As the matter generated intense debate without resolution, a committee of experts was convened in 1925 to recommend fair charges for the Apapa and Port Harcourt wharves. After extensive consultations, the committee's report was submitted in May 1925 but immediate action was delayed by the late response of the British Chambers of Commerce, whose views were considered indispensable. This further illustrates the extent to which local developments were subordinated to metropolitan official and mercantile considerations.

After extensive consultations, the government introduced new port tariffs in 1926, effective from 1 January 1927 (Olukoju, 1994, 152). First, ships that exceeded 100 tons were required to pay light and buoyage dues of three pence per net registered tonnage and a maximum of five pence if the vessel visited any other Nigerian port. No vessel paid more than once within a 30-day period. Second, ships were also required to pay towage dues for the use of tugs within the port. The rate was £17 10s on ships with draught of 16 feet or less; those with draught between 16 and 20 feet paid £20 and those above twenty feet paid £22 10s. Vessels were charged special rates for services on Sundays and public holidays. Third, anchorage dues of four pence per ton were collected from all vessels (except government vessels of any nationality) for each day longer than a month in port.

Although mercantile stakeholders had been consulted before these charges were levied, there were complaints that towage dues, for example, fell too heavily on small vessels. A notable British firm, John Holt, declared that 'no other port of the world takes the view that small steamers should be penalized because they are small'.[11] This protest and the demand for a fairer tariff regime failed to impress the government, which maintained the rates levied in 1927 until 1932, which is beyond the period considered in this piece.

Meanwhile, as a corollary of the analysis of the administration of the port of Lagos and other Nigerian ports during this period, we shall examine the role of the business community, specifically, chambers of commerce (Hopkins, 1964, 423–54; Hopkins, 1965; Iyanda, 1989; Olukoju, 1995, 2004). First, a distinction should be made between metropolitan and colonial chambers of commerce. In the first category we can find the London, Liverpool and Manchester Chambers of Commerce (that is, the Africa Trade Sections of the chambers), and the Association of West African Merchants (AWAM) as contrasted with the Lagos Chamber of Commerce. Second, it is important to highlight their roles and differential influence on government policy. The metropolitan chambers were far more influential than the colonial chambers, which were essentially appendages of the former.

The Lagos Chamber of Commerce had a chequered history (Hopkins, 1965; Iyanda, 1989). Founded in Lagos in 1888, it collapsed within two years, and its second coming in 1890 also lasted two years. It was finally re-established in 1897 and has survived to date. From inception, it was not an exclusive European body as it had African members until 1903. Africans were re-admitted in the late 1920s and one of them, Peter Thomas, was elected president in 1929. But the Chamber was never an influential body in the administration of the port of Lagos or even the colonial economy of Nigeria. Though local expatriate traders in Lagos represented mercantile interests on the colonial Legislative Council, they always referred important issues to their principals in the metropolitan chambers, who exercised real influence on colonial policy. Yet, the colonial government routinely sought the views of the Lagos Chamber of Commerce on any proposed legislation relating to economic policy, especially shipping and port tariffs, and even everyday issues such as sanitation and urban planning. Although often divided by self-interest on these issues, with regard to taxation and revenue, government and business maintained a symbiotic relationship underpinned by a common objective of exploiting colonial resources in the interest of imperial Britain (Olukoju, 1995).

Considered as a whole, the mercantile community in Lagos consisted of two broad categories – importers and exporters – and three racial groups – Europeans, Asians and Africans. Even among Europeans, there were differences on the basis of nationality, with the British enjoying an advantage over the Germans and French since Nigeria was a British colony. During the First World War, for example, German firms were expelled as 'enemy firms'. British firms, aided by their home and colonial governments, then captured the trade previously handled by the 'enemy firms'. In effect, the business community was not homogeneous, varying in the size of the firms, individual firms' specialisation in various aspects of the import and export trade, the spatial range of their operations and the nationality of the firms. Competition was fierce and cartelisation by the expatriate firms was common, especially during the First World War and in periods of economic depression, such as during the late 1890s. Generally, expatriate firms dominated the export trade but indigenous firms were represented in the import business, though often as agents of the former. It was easier for indigenous traders to raise the capital required to participate in the import business.

4   Maritime Trade and Commercial Enterprise in Lagos

Allusion has been made in the foregoing discussion to the multiplicity of mercantile interests, both indigenous and expatriate, in Lagos. Undoubtedly, their commercial enterprises were tied to the port, both in the shipping and commodity trades. The trade of the port consisted of forest products from its immediate hinterland (Yorubaland). But the extension of the railway to Northern Nigeria in 1912 expanded the range of Lagos exports (Hopkins, 1964, ch. 6; Olukoju, 2004). In effect, until the end of the First World War, Lagos depended on considerable canoe-borne lagoon traffic in palm oil and palm kernels, which constituted more than 70 per cent of its exports up to the First World War. The Ogun River, navigable from Abeokuta, 45 miles north of Lagos, and the lagoon network running east and west of Lagos, provided a natural, ancient artery of trade that underpinned the economy of Lagos. Indeed, the port-city was dependent on the river and lagoon trade for its foodstuff supplies and for the forest produce that it exported.

Lagos had a symbiotic economic and political relationship with the important lagoon markets and settlements of Badagry, Ejinrin and Epe, which covered a distance of some 90 miles in a west–east direction, with Atijere much farther to the east. Up until the First World War, European traders were based in Lagos and depended on African 'middlemen' traders to procure the commodities from the hinterland markets by the lagoon traffic. The river and lagoon trade utilised an efficient canoe transport, which operated water craft ranging from dug outs with a draught of nine inches to canoes that were 72 feet long and 10.5 feet wide.[12] Depending upon the commodities that they carried (cocoa, corn, palm kernels and farina/garri) and the distance covered (Badagry, 48 miles to the west and Ejinrin, 42 miles to the east), canoe operators' rates ranged between three and six pence. As late as 1914, the lagoon traffic yielded 25,000 of the 63,000 tons of palm kernels and 9000 out of 13,000 tons of palm oil exported from Lagos.[13] Table 6.3 details Lagos import and export trade through three wharves between 1919 and 1929.

Three major developments between the 1890s and 1914 altered the composition of Lagos trade (Olukoju, 2004). These were railway construction, the introduction of modern currency and the development of the cocoa industry in the Yoruba hinterland of Lagos. With the extension of the railway northwards across the forest belt towards the River Niger, a greater quantity and variety of produce was conveyed to the port and the railway also facilitated the distribution of foreign imports into wider areas of the hinterland. As indicated above, the railway enabled Apapa wharf, which had a rail link to the hinterland, to displace Iddo and Lagos Island, which had relied heavily on the lagoon traffic. From 1912 onwards, rail-borne commodities from northern Nigeria – groundnuts and cotton – and cocoa from western Nigeria significantly expanded the range of Lagos exports. The imposition of European currency and the de-monetisation of the existing currency – cowries in Lagos and its proximate hinterland – and the introduction of modern banking institutions facilitated trade within the Nigerian colony and between it and foreign markets. British coinage and currency notes coexisted with earlier media of exchange until the 1930s, or even later in other parts of Nigeria. But in Lagos, the adoption of British currency was rapid and had been completed before the First World War. However, the transition was fraught with difficulties, as epitomised by the poor handling of colonial subjects' reservations by the colonial authorities when introducing currency notes between 1916 and 1920 (Olukoju, 1997).

While the export trade of Lagos throughout the period between 1850 and 1929 consisted of forest products and tin from northern Nigeria, imports comprised a wide range of European manufactures (Hopkins, 1964; Olukoju, 2004). Imports reflected the changing tastes and levels of modernisation in Lagos and the hinterland. Already, in addition to resident European officials, missionaries and traders, an emergent class of indigenous Western-educated professionals (lawyers, doctors, journalists and clergymen) and merchants had imbibed Western tastes and values. Accordingly, in addition to items of mass consumption (clothing, kerosene, household utensils, building materials and foodstuffs), luxury items, such as motor cars, were imported in large quantities. The railway facilitated the spread of such imports to a widening hinterland.

Table 6.3 Total annual tonnages of imports and exports (including coal and railway materials) handled at the Iddo, Ijora and Apapa wharves (1919–29)

Year	Exports — Iddo Goods	Exports — Ijora Goods	Exports — Apapa Goods	Imports — Iddo Goods	Imports — Iddo Railway materials	Imports — Iddo Coal	Imports — Ijora Goods	Imports — Ijora Coals	Imports — Apapa Goods	Imports — Apapa Railway materials	Imports — Apapa Coal
1919	85,688	–	3,049	32,696	35,582*	–	–	–	–	–	16,923
1920	88,136	–	16,318	30,183	45,939*	–	–	–	135	384	28,322
1921–22	89,527	–	11,899	28,489	52,849*	–	–	–	114	170	39,694
1922–23	87,040	–	11,436	34,489	42,428*	62,418	–	–	352	13,942	4,074
1923–24	111,258	–	17,125	32,825	80,051	49,807	–	–	58	80	5,236
1924–25	173,921	–	24,772	45,546	6,949	–	–	19,996	37	–	8,747
1925–26	182,609	–	55,786	55,454	7,167	–	2,362**	106,219	–	–	–
1926–27	87,180	–	127,241	62,006	4,121	–	7,886**	100,205	9,574	1,921	–
1927–28	–	–	178,128	1,005	–	–	3,571**	82,960	103,933	31,823	–
1928–29	–	417	201,307	–	–	–	11,457	74,144	111,470	14,134	–

* Railway materials and coal.

** Timber, kerosene etc.

Source: CSO 1/32/97 702 of 25 June 1929, Baddeley to Webb, enc. 2.

The volume and direction of Lagos trade throughout the period from 1880 to 1929 varied with prevailing economic conditions (trade boom or depression), and global and local developments, such as war, anti-colonial revolts, crop failures, locust infestation and epidemics (exemplified by cattle diseases, bubonic plagues and influenza). Otherwise, Britain, the imperial power, generally took the lion's share of the trade. Yet, other countries, especially Germany, were key players in certain sectors of the external trade of the port. For example, German firms dominated the palm kernel export trade of Lagos up to the outbreak of the First World War because they superseded their European rivals in the crushing and processing of the kernels, and in the domestic consumption of the resultant cattle feed. Germany was also a strong competitor in the import trade because it understood and met indigenous peoples' tastes, was able to manufacture such products at a lower cost compared to its British competitors, and dominated the 'trade spirits' business. But the British took over the German share of the kernel and import business when German traders were expelled during the war. Otherwise, the two countries – Britain and Germany – together controlled 96 per cent of the exports and supplied some 87 per cent of the imports into Lagos between 1880 and 1914 (Hopkins, 1964, 383). The exit of the Germans from the shipping and commodity trades merely strengthened the grip of the United Kingdom on the maritime trade of Lagos.

The development of steam shipping in the nineteenth century coincidentally with the transition from the transatlantic slave trade to the export trade in forest products strengthened existing maritime links between West Africa and Europe. This was further bolstered by the acquisition of colonies in West Africa by Britain, France and Germany in the second half of the century. From the 1880s until the outbreak of the First World War, the shipping trade of the port of Lagos was dominated by British, German, Dutch and French shipping lines. Elder Dempster, Woermann Linie, Holland West Afrika Lijn and Chargeurs Reunis provided regular sailings between Europe and West Africa (Davies, 1973; Hopkins, 1988). From the late nineteenth century until the end of our period, these expatriate lines tightened their grip on the shipping business of Lagos and other West African ports by operating under a liner conference, a very effective cartel which kept out any significant competition. However, the First World War displaced Woermann Linie, which could not regain its pre-war position after the war. American and Italian shipping lines also called at the port of Lagos, including the last of the sailing ships of the era. What is significant about the shipping trade of Lagos during the period under review is not merely how shipping services facilitated maritime enterprise, but the way it sustained the predominance of expatriate trading firms, who received secret rebates and preferential freight rates to the exclusion of their indigenous competitors. Shipping thus aided the marginalisation of indigenous enterprise in the maritime economy of Lagos (Olukoju, 1992c). It was also a key element of the machinery of exploitation and transfer of colonial resources to the metropolis.

5 Conclusion

This chapter has examined the development of the port of Lagos, the administration and finances of the port, and its trade and entrepreneurs. It is important to emphasise the context in which these developments took place for a better appreciation of the role of the stakeholders and the peculiar situation of the port. Essentially, the interlocking contexts of the economic and strategic interests of British imperialism, global cycles of trade boom (1906–14, 1918–20) and depression (1880–92, 1920–22), the advantages of the location of Lagos vis-à-vis other ports, the alliance between business and government, and the asymmetrical competition between expatriate and indigenous entrepreneurs were the undercurrents that drove the developments examined in this chapter. Critical to this process was the intervention of British arms and men in colonial conquest and administration, expatriate firms in the trade and transfer of resources, and British engineering expertise in transform-ing the port of Lagos into West Africa's leading seaport. But it was the wealth derived from the exploitation of colonial resources that financed the transformation studied in this chapter.

That said, the rise of Lagos to pre-eminence in West Africa emanated from a long-drawn process that began with the imposition of British rule and its concomitants, and the application of technology to sur-mount the natural disadvantages of the port. Lagos thus epitomises the triumph of human ingenuity over environmental challenges. But the colonial context in which this feat took place meant that whatever material development accrued from it was the outcome of an imper-ial project aimed primarily at harnessing the resources of the colony, including its improved harbour, indigenous labour and enterprise, and forest products, in the interest of the metropolitan economy.

Notes

1. National Archives of Nigeria (NAI), Chief Secretary's Office (CSO) 1/19/45, Boyle to Harcourt, Financial Report for the Year 1910, 2.

2. Details of the issues discussed in this paragraph are available in Ogundana, 1976, 77; and Olukoju, 1992a.
3. NAI CSO 1/19/59, Frederick Lugard to Lewis Harcourt, 18 August 1913.
4. NAI, AR.5/MI, Nigeria: Annual Report on the Marine Department for the year 1923, 2.
5. NAI CSO 26/1 09860, vol. II: 'Scheme for co-ordinating all works in connection with shipping', D. C. Cameron to J. H. Thomas, 12 September 1931.
6. NAI, CSO 26/1 09049, vol. I, Comptroller of Customs to Sec to Government (CSG), 9 March 1923.
7. NAI, CSO 1/32/58, Clifford to Secretary of State for the Colonies, 1 December 1920.
8. NAI, CSO 26/06788, Governor's Address to the Nigerian Council, 1923, 26 February 1923.
9. NAI, CSO 26/09049, vol. I, CSG to Comptroller of Customs, Director of Marine and General Manager of the Railways, 6 April 1923.
10. NAI, CSO 26/09049, vol. I, R. H. W. Hughes to CSG, 24 September 1923.
11. NAI, CSO 26/1/03535, vol. I, 'Pilotage, Towage Services', John Holt to CSG, 13 January 1928.
12. NAI, CSO 26/1 09860, vol. I: Lagos Harbour Survey, Southern Nigeria, Abridged Report by Mr Coode, 24 December 1910, 44.
13. NAI, CSO 1/32/18 853 of 24 September 1915, Lugard to Law, enc: Comptroller of Customs' memorandum, dated 26 August 1915.

Bibliography

Davies, P. N. (1973) *The Trade Makers: Elder Dempster in West Africa, 1852–1972* (London: Allen and Unwin).
Hammond, F. D. (1924) *Report on the Railway System of Nigeria* (London: Crown Agents).
Hopkins, A. G. (1964) 'An Economic History of Lagos, 1880–1914', doctoral thesis. University of London.
Hopkins, A. G. (1965) 'The Lagos Chamber of Commerce, 1888–1903', *Journal of the Historical Society of Nigeria*, 3(2), 241–59.
Hopkins, A. G. (1988) *An Economic History of West Africa* (London: Longman).
Iyanda, O. (ed.) (1989) *The Lagos Chamber of Commerce and Industry and the Nigerian Economy, 1888–1988* (Lagos Chamber of Commerce).
Ogundana, B. (1970) 'Patterns and Problems of Seaport Evolution in Nigeria', in B.S. Hoyle and D. Hilling (eds), *Seaports and Development in Tropical Africa* (London: Macmillan), pp. 167–82.
Ogundana, B. (1976) 'Changing the Capacity of Nigeria's Seaport Entrances', *Odu: Journal of West African Studies*, 14, 69–88.
Ogundana, B. (1980) 'Seaport Development in Colonial Nigeria', in I.A. Akinjogbin and S.O Osoba (eds), *Topics on Nigerian Economic and Social History* (Ile-Ife: University of Ife Press), pp. 159–81.
Olukoju, A. (1992a) 'The Development of the Port of Lagos, 1892–1946', *Journal of Transport History*, 3rd series, 13(1), 59–78.
Olukoju, A. (1992b) 'Background to the Establishment of the Nigerian Ports Authority: The Politics of Port Administration in Nigeria, c.1920–1954', *International Journal of Maritime History*, 4(2), 155–73.

Olukoju, A. (1992c) 'Elder Dempster and the Shipping Trade of Nigeria during the First World War', *Journal of African History*, 33(2), 255–71.

Olukoju, A. (1994) 'The Making of an "Expensive Port": Shipping Lines, Government and Port Tariffs in Lagos, 1917–1949', *International Journal of Maritime History*, 6(1), 141–59.

Olukoju, A. (1995) 'Anatomy of Business–Government Relations: Fiscal Policy and Mercantile Pressure Group Activity in Nigeria, 1916–1933', *African Studies Review*, 38(1), 23–50.

Olukoju, A. (1996) 'Spatial Analysis and Inter-port Competition: Lagos, the Niger and the 'Capture' of the Kano–Tripoli Trade, 1890–1914', *The Great Circle: Journal of the Australian Association for Maritime History*, 18(1), 30–47.

Olukoju, A. (1997) 'Nigeria's Colonial Government, Commercial Banks and the Currency Crisis of 1916–20', *International Journal of African Historical Studies*, 24(2), 277–98.

Olukoju, A. (2001–02) '"Getting Too Great A Grip": European Shipping Lines and British West African Lighterage Services in the 1930s', *Afrika Zamani: Journal of the Association of African Historians*, 9/10, 19–40.

Olukoju, A. (2004) *The Liverpool of West Africa: The Dynamics and Impact of Maritime Trade in Lagos, 1900–1950* (Trenton, NJ: Africa World Press).

White, H.P. (1970) 'The Morphological Development of West African Seaports', in B.S. Hoyle and D. Hilling (eds), *Seaports and Development in Tropical Africa* (London: Macmillan), pp. 11–25.

7
Port of Havana:
The Gateway of Cuba, 1850–1920

Francisco Suárez Viera

1 Introduction

Havana port has been the main Cuban port for the last five centuries. It has also been one of the most, if not the most, important port in the Caribbean-Gulf area. This chapter will analyse its evolution between the late nineteenth century, when important administrative changes took place, and the early twentieth century, when the new Republic initiated a fresh process of port expansion. Our working hypothesis is based on the premise that Havana was a traditional Iberian port that evolved into a port with a nature of its own, as it was subjected to specific factors that drew it away from its original Spanish background.

The second part will set out a historical framework for Havana port, with considerable emphasis on its role as a slave port and its consolidation as an import–export port. The evolution of a port oligarchy and the decisive American influence in Cuba are also dealt with.

The history of Havana's port governance is the subject of the third part. The most important point presented in this part is related to the development of Havana port as an individual institution, according to the Spanish tradition. The fourth part is devoted to the management of port operations. Our aim is to clarify how Havana addressed improvements in services and infrastructure. Docks, railways and warehouses will be analysed, and a short description of the workforce presented. In short, the third part is devoted to those who managed the port while the fourth looks at how the port was managed.

As far as nineteenth-century Cuba is concerned, the huge amount of information generated by the Spanish colonial administration provides a wealth of data for historians. While the original Spanish material constitutes the backbone of the reconstruction of the port management,

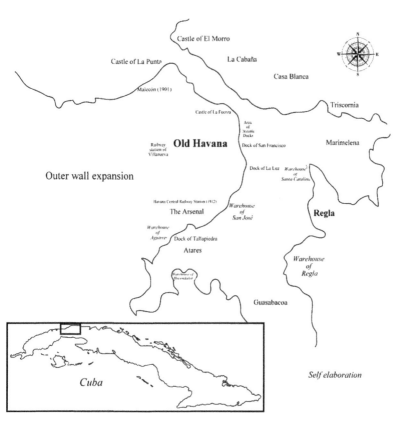

Castle of El Morro

Castle of La Punta

La Cabaña

Casa Blanca

Malecón (1901)

Triscornia

Castle of La Fuerza

Area of transit Docks

Railway station of Villanueva

Old Havana

Dock of San Francisco

Marimelena

Dock of La Luz

Warehouse of Santa Catalina

Outer wall expansion

Havana Central Railway Station (1912)

The Arsenal

Warehouse of San José

Regla

Warehouse of Aguirre

Dock of Tallapiedra

Atares

Warehouse of Hacendados

Warehouse of Regla

Guasabacoa

Cuba

Self elaboration

Map 7.1   Port of Havana, nineteenth century

the data available from the Cuban censuses plays a fundamental role in helping us understand what happened during the early years of the Cuban Republic and the American occupation. This original material will be complemented with works by other authors, on the general theoretical framework of Atlantic History. In this sense, the contribution of Cuban and Spanish authors is crucial.

Extensive and varied works have touched on Havana's city development since the nineteenth century. There are numerous studies on Havana regarding the Indies run (*Carrera de Indias*), the military shipyard known as the Arsenal, city fortifications, railways, sugar and a plethora of related military and *Ancien Régime*[1] subjects. However, only a very few of these works will be referred to in this chapter.

Modern historiography specifically concentrating on Havana port has grown in leaps and bounds, especially over the last ten years, mirroring the growing interest in Caribbean ports. As a consequence, the most important works specifically related to Havana port date from recent years.

2   The End of Slavery and the Rise of Capitalism

2.1   The Spanish Era: The Remnants of an Old World

Havana was born as a hub port (Fuente, 2008), with some characteristics of an *entrepôt*. All the Spanish fleets of the New World converged there before returning to Spain. For two centuries, port activity was dominated by this seasonal arrival of large fleets. The crisis of this model and the expansion of the Cuban export sector led Havana port to act as a local gateway. During the late eighteenth and early nineteenth centuries, the development of Cuba was marked by two contrasting, parallel factors: although industrial technology arrived on the island at an early stage, earlier than most European areas, it did so in a context of increasing slavery in sugar production.

During the nineteenth century, Havana was the main port of entry for both forced and free immigrants into Cuba. In 1850, when slavery had been abolished in other American territories, slaves continued to enter the port. It was in the late part of the century when a large amount of free or indentured European and Asiatic workers entered Cuba. From 1900 onwards, immigration was centralised in the Camp of Triscornia, a centre inspired by Ellis Island in New York (see sec. 4.4 for more details).

The expansion and demise of slavery is directly related to the astounding development of sugar industry in Cuba, in two clearly different phases. The first one comprises up to 1887 (abolition of slavery), when the industry was basically supported by slave work, while the second runs to 1930. The first era was dominated by Spanish capital, investing fundamentally in sugar mills located in the western provinces of Cuba. They were not, however, alien to technology, especially after 1850, when strong obstacles to slave acquisition existed. During the first half of the nineteenth century, Havana had acted as one of the main, if not the leading, slave markets in the world. From 1790 to 1821, as many as 240,747 slaves entered Havana port, of the approximately 300,000 entering the whole of Cuba (Murray, 1980, 18–19). The rhythm of imports remained steady in the following years, with Havana coming to be the operational base of a large fleet of slave ships, to the extent that by 1850 the bulk of slaves leaving West Africa were owned by Havana companies (Eltis, 1987, 159). From 1820 to 1840, an average of 45 slaves vessels departed from Havana each year (British, 1842, 37). Moreover, Havana traders established agents in African ports, such as Ouidah, to facilitate operations (Law, 2004, 173).

However, the golden years of the slave trade were soon to come to an end. Although slavers had settled in Havana, anti-slavery agents were also present in the port, and they exerted strong pressure on Spanish authorities to put an end to trafficking. In 1842, Gerónimo Valdés, the Captain General, enforced the regulations against trafficking, closing six slave markets and rendering the shipping of new slaver vessels difficult (Eltis, 1987, 200). In the following 20 years, profits fell back sharply and many traders went bankrupt (Eltis, 1987, 160–1). This made the acquisition of slaves difficult and expensive.

The business was displaced out of Havana, and later died. While factors in Cuba acted against trafficking, a more complex process, which goes beyond the limits of this chapter, was taking place in Africa itself: the British and other European powers were actively pursuing trafficking along African shores, as is well known, but they were also expanding their empires in the area, disrupting the economic organisation that dominated the eighteenth century, and effectively breaking the connection between the two Atlantic shores.[2]

In spite of these drawbacks to the Havana slave trade, the port continued to grow in importance for two main reasons: on the one hand, sugar and tobacco exports soared. On the other hand, the bulk of Cuban imports entered the country through Havana and was subsequently re-exported. In short, Havana's role as Cuba's gateway controlling exports and imports was reinforced; although its relative importance in exports dropped off after 1900. A parallel process involved a growing complexity in port management, more related to tonnage of ships than to the number of vessels, as Table 7.1 highlights.

Such favourable conditions gave birth to a thriving trading community (Laviña, 2007, 12–23; García Álvarez, 1990; García Álvarez, 2002,

Table 7.1 Shipping traffics at Havana (1827–1906)

Year	Vessels	Tonnage (t)	Vessel/Tons
1827	1053	169,281	160
1857	1974	406,912	206
1900	1468	2,827,295	1925
1906	1622	3,976,176	2451

Source: INE, 2012b; Census Bureau, 1908; Real Hacienda, 1828.

239–42). It is important to consider in detail the oligarchy in Havana. During the early nineteenth century, a clear division within this group could be observed: the Creole oligarchy concentrated its efforts on production; trade was controlled, first by black freedmen and then by immigrants from mainland Spain. This was not so much a precise division, but rather the parallel development of two general tendencies. In any case, the trade oligarchy resided in Havana, the island's main port. During the nineteenth century, this social division vanished when the trading group invested in agriculture, which also enhanced their social prestige.

However, up to 1900, they continued to control Cuban trade, particularly the imported food trade and the export of refined sugar and tobacco (García Álvarez, 2002, 242–53) from their main base in Havana. The importation of food was of crucial importance to Cuba, as its concentration on export crops prevented it from producing enough to feed its population. This situation gave this elite special power, as we shall see in part 3.2 Given the power of the Cuban oligarchy on port decisions and on port management, to which they could get direct access through the constitution of the Port Works Board, it is important to consider the extent to which Havana port development was the result of geographic or purely economic factors, or of a conscious effort by Havana's elite group. In spite of the fact that the oligarchy generally supported Spanish policy, the clash between the Spanish Navy and the Board of Trade over the military dock of San Fernando highlights a growing tension among the most powerful social sectors and the Cuban administration (see sec. 4.1). Such tension is a well-known precondition of reforms, or revolutions, and it may have played a role in the loss of the legitimacy of Spanish domination, when slavery was on the verge of collapse.

2.2   The Post-Independence Years: Rampage Capitalism

If, before 1900, Havana controlled the bulk of Cuban exports, the trading elite of the capital subsequently lost that monopoly. The cause of this process can be explained by the American occupation of 1898–1902, after the long struggle between Cubans and Spaniards, and especially by the increasing participation of American capital in sugar production. The process had begun just during the Spanish era, in fact, in 1850 around 50 per cent of sugar was exported to the United States, and as much as 80 per cent by 1880 (Naranjo Orovio, 2009, 78). This contrasted with the traditional trade of Havana, which was aimed at Europe. The bulk of these exports, controlled by the Havana oligarchy, took place through Havana port, and to a lesser extent through other ports such as Matanzas. In short, by the end of the century, production and distribution was still mostly in the hands of Cubans and Spaniards, but Americans began to be involved in the business.

This situation changed during the American occupation. First, thanks to Military Order 62, those communal lands and properties not properly delimited were reorganised, that is, expropriated, and then sold in the free market, allowing American capital to enter into sugar industry on a huge scale (Rodríguez Díaz, 2004, 176). Second, American investment in the central and eastern areas of Cuba triggered a colossal development of sugar production that far outdid any level achieved by the Spanish in the western provinces of Cuba (Santamaría, 2001, 13–51). On this occasion, the basis of the sugar industry was the free workforce, originating in large numbers from Europe, the Canary Islands, Haiti and Jamaica. The introduction of the most modern industrial sugar mills (*centrales* in Spanish) serviced by private rails and ports, allowed direct shipping from the mill to American markets. This led first to a decentralisation of the entry of immigrants, who went directly to production areas and second to a significant decline in the importance of Havana as an export port, as Table 7.2 highlights.[3]

Moreover, the American market displaced other areas as the main supplier of the Cuban market, disrupting the hegemony of trade in the Antilles area. It could be considered that a first step in this American offensive took place in 1890, when the United States promulgated the MacKinley Tariff. Subsequently, a tariff conflict erupted between Spain and the United States with disastrous consequences (Navarro García, 1998, 195). As Table 7.3 shows, American companies succeeded in their offensive, which not only affected Spain, whose trade totally collapsed, but also decreased the share of other European powers, especially that of the United Kingdom, which had enjoyed a good position in previous years. In the case of Spain, Cuba was a captive market for the Spanish,

Table 7.2   Exports of ports by province (1899–1919)

	1899	1907	1919
Pinar del Río	0	0	1.2
La Habana	61.1	40.2	17.1
Matanzas	15.1	18.4	20.8
Santa Clara	15.9	21.1	19.1
Camagüey	0.5	2.3	20
Oriente	7.4	18	21.8

Source: Census Bureau, 1908; Dirección General del Censo, 1920.

protected by very high duties. This situation enabled mainland Spain's industry, especially the textile sector, the most important one, to grow and profit for a century (Soto Carmona, 1989, 89). The Spanish defeat of 1898 generated shock waves in both the economy and the psyche of Spain.

By 1906, direct American inversions in Cuba amounted to 150 million dollars, still lagging behind the sum of 200 million that corresponded to Britain. The British investment was heavily concentrated in railways and ports, as the case of the Baring family and the presence of British companies such as the Cuban Central Railways Limited highlights (Cayuela Fernández, 1998, 416). Over the next years, American investment grew to control 60 per cent of Cuban sugar production (García Molina, 2005, 17), becoming the major investors in the island with 1195 million dollars, far surpassing any other rival (Dye, 1998, 56–64). The United Kingdom, the leading world supplier of coal, lost the Cuban market: while in 1845, the British supplied more than 90 per cent of coal (Real Hacienda, 1846, 74), in 1905 the situation had been totally reversed, as the United States exported 565,613 tons of coal to Cuban ports, while the British only supplied 9848 tons (Foreign Office, 1906, 5). In sum, a certain degree of competence existed among the United States and the United Kingdom (Hull, 2013), a struggle that was solved in favour of the Americans. This was a further step in the separation of Havana from the eastern shore of the Atlantic, as it became increasingly involved in the New World orbit, in the sphere of American imperialism.

Furthermore, the American shipping companies took advantage of their favourable position in the port. For most of the nineteenth century, American ships enjoyed a privileged position in Cuban trade, but after the occupation, they were able to displace Spanish, and to a lesser extent British, competitors. By 1919 the weight of US shipping companies in Havana was crucial: out of 60 foreign companies working in the port, 44 of them were American, most of whom were closely

Table 7.3   Cuba: imports by partner in percentage (1894–1919)

	1894	1900	1907	1913	1919
United States	32.6	43.7	49.1	53.7	76.1
Spain	43.7	14.6	9.1	7.2	4.4
United Kingdom	14.2	15.7	14.7	11.5	2.4
Germany	1.6	4.5	7.3	6.9	0
France	1.7	4.9	5.8	5.2	2.7
Other	6.2	16.6	14	15.5	14.4

Source: Foreign Office, 1901; Census Bureau, 1908; Dirección General del Censo, 1920.

related to West Indies shipping (Dirección General del Censo, 1920, 217). As examples, we could name the following: Atlantic Chartering Co., Caribbean Steamship Co., Earn Line S. S. Co., New Orleans & South American Line, Philip Shore, South Atlantic Maritime Corp., United Fruit Company and many others located in the eastern and southern United States.

In spite of this considerable influence, Havana port did not follow the American port model. In order to understand this paradox, it should be understood that Cuba constitutes an oddity of history. It remained a colony at a time when its neighbours had enjoyed nearly a hundred years of independence. When the country was on the edge of securing full independence, it fell into the hands of a new colonial power. But, unlike those African areas analysed elsewhere in this volume, this power was not European, and by contrast with the case of African cities, Havana and Cuba in general formed part of a European tradition. As a consequence, the Americans found themselves in the midst of a well-constituted modern society. So their footprint, although very important, was not as decisive as the European impact in African ports. This was largely due to the robustness of the institutions set up in the Spanish era.

3 Port Administration

3.1 The Spanish Public Institutions

Cuba was run by Spain in a similar, although not identical way to ports in mainland Spain. It is clear that the figure of the Captain General,[4] with its power and subjugated institutions, had no parallel in mainland Spain. As a matter of fact, Spain's policy during its final years of dominion over the island was somewhat erratic and centralisation alternated with processes of independence. During the second half of the century, on the basis of the administration described above, the Spanish introduced some changes in port management that sometimes led to a somewhat chaotic state of affairs. The creation of the Overseas Ministry (Ministerio de Ultramar) in 1863 reduced the power of the Captain General, subsequently considered a delegate of the Ministry in Cuba. Thus, the late nineteenth century saw a growing influx of legislation from ministries in mainland Spain. Furthermore, the Captain General was more often called General Governor (Gobernador General), emphasising the supreme nature of his civil power, or even Superior Civil Governor (Gobernador Superior Civil).

By 1850, on a daily basis the structure of Havana port administration was run as follows: the Captain General was the supreme figure, and his orders were executed by the most important person in daily port activity, the Harbourmaster.[5] This figure is of crucial importance: from 1793, he organised the daily activity in the port, and was also the Head of the military harbour. The Royal Exchequer (Real Hacienda) was also heavily involved in daily activities through its Customs section (Aduana, created in 1802), because of its tax collection activities and the fight against smuggling.

Port infrastructure maintenance and expansion experienced a complex administrative evolution. In 1854, the Cuban Public Works Direction (Dirección de Obras Públicas de Cuba) was created. This institution, under the Governor's power, replaced the former Board of Development in tasks relating to port infrastructure, among other things. The Administration Council of Cuba (Consejo de Administración), created in 1861, also inherited a small part of the Board of Development's activity. Its role was merely consultative, although it did issue important advice on port problems.

Initially, the Public Works Direction was almost exactly the same as its predecessor, and it also suffered a chaotic reorganisation process that led to a stagnation of its activity. The Direction was downgraded to Subdirection in 1862, a lower echelon than its original status, under the auspices of the Board of Administration (Dirección de Administración), a section of the civil government. Surprisingly, this change enabled far better performance in the public works (Subdirección, 1866, 8–23) and for the following years up to the end of Spanish domination, in 1898, the Subdirection carried out extensive work on port infrastructure.

To make things even more confusing, the constitution in 1878 of the six classic Cuban provinces, which put them on an equal footing with mainland Spain, was accompanied by the limited power of the Provincial Deputations (Diputaciones Provinciales) over ports. They had responsibilities in financial matters, and also in port maintenance (Sanger, 1900, 55), mostly in areas of lesser importance. Further study would help to clarify this point.

If the introduction of the Harbourmaster was a milestone in the birth of the port as an independent entity, a further and crucial step in that direction took place in late nineteenth century: the Havana Port Works Board was created in 1884, following orders from the Overseas Ministry providing the institution with detailed regulations (Junta de Obras, 1884, 3). The members of this crucial institution were representatives of the main port institutions, such as the Harbourmaster, and also representatives of the main Cuban political and economic institutions (see note below for further details).[6] The Board was financed by Havana town council and Havana provincial deputation.

The Port Works Board was in charge of administering the funds invested in Havana's port infrastructure, organising the works and port maintenance. In addition, the Junta played an advisory role, either on its own initiative or if required by the government. As such, its members were not interested in commercial affairs, and they insisted that the power of decision lay in the hands of the government, that the Port Works Board only managed decisions and proposed changes (Paradela y Gestal, 1885, 7). This premise is debatable, firstly because the Port Works Board was not an institution founded on equal social representation, but on power of interests. In any case, in 1889, the Overseas Ministry ordered a reorganisation of the Cuban Port Works Board, while the following year the Ministry stipulated that Cuban ports should be organised under the same law as those of mainland Spain.

In Spain, the Port Works Boards were created during the same period, and were to be the main port institutions. Subsequently, during the late twentieth century, the Spanish Port Works Boards became the Port Authorities: public, independent and fully individualised institutions. The evolution of the Cuban Port Work Board over the years, and the development of the present Havana Port Authority (Autoridad Portuaria de La Habana) would appear to play a crucial role in the understanding of Havana's port governance during twentieth century.

3.2 The Institutions of the Bourgeoisie

The creation of the Port Works Board symbolised the final triumph of the Cuban oligarchy in their efforts to enter directly into the public management of Havana port. This fact should be addressed in the wider context of the reorganisation of the Cuban bourgeoisie, which took place in the second half of the nineteenth century. In 1878, the import traders of Havana, who usually met around the docks, created the Market of Groceries (Lonja de Víveres), an institution specifically focused on people working in trade. The importance of this group derives from the fact that Havana was first and foremost the entrance point to Cuba. Among the imported products, given that Cuban agriculture focused heavily on export crops, food was the most important item. In 1900, total food imported into Havana port amounted to 2,875,520 pounds, or 30.4 per cent of all imports (Foreign Office, 1901, 37). The importance of the Market of Groceries grew to such an extent that it influenced food trade around the Caribbean area (Pérez Lavielle, 1957, 44–6).

The main institution that grouped the Havana elite was the Commercial, Industrial and Shipping Chamber of Havana (Cámara de Comercio, Industria y Navegación de La Habana), founded in 1888. A decade before, in 1877, the Board of Trade (Junta de Comercio) had been created, an important institution that acted as a bourgeoisie lobby. The Chamber of Havana was an improved version of that previous institution, with support from Spanish public authorities. In 1887, the Overseas Ministry had instructed the members on how to organise the new institution: the Chamber should be formed by three practically independent sections, covering aspects of the city's activities; one of these was shipping, to include everybody concerned with the bussiness[7] (Cámara de Comercio, 1888, 33). The Chamber was given the privilege of being consulted on any aspect of shipping, navigation and tariffs, among other subjects. As a result, it played an important role in many activities within the Cuban economy, such as the creation of the Bank of Cuba, or the establishment of trade agreements with the United States of America (Pérez Lavielle, 1957, 44–6). By 1906, the Chamber of Havana had become the sole Chamber of Cuba (Santiago de Cuba had previously had its own independent chamber).

Neither of these two institutions had direct influence on public port administration, but they are important for an understanding of the growing institutional power of Cuban bourgeoisie, which had an effect on Havana port.

3.3   Some Notes on American and Cuban Administration

In any case, private initiatives in the port were closely monitored by Spanish authorities. While the state regulated the private properties linked to the harbour, the widespread presence of privately owned docks in Havana, as was the case of Regla, and the further expansion of private ports in the rest of Cuba is an oddity. In spite of the fact that the Spanish controlled the expansion of private docks and ports, it is true that both expanded more intensely under American rule.

Initially, the extent of American innovations in port administration is not easy to determine. It is true that during the American military rule, headed by General J. R. Brooke, public works were reorganised under the Cuban Secretariat for Agriculture, Commerce, Industry and Public Works (Secretaría de Agricultura, Comercio, Industria y Obras Públicas). This large institution was divided when the new Republic was founded. Given that Brooke was in command of Cuba during that time, he was ultimately responsible for the port, and exerted his power through military orders of crucial importance. During the second American occupation, in 1907, ad hoc Boards were set up in order to improve the port of Havana. Ports related to sugar mills popped up all over Cuba, although not in Havana.

The Public Works Secretariat (Secretaría de Obras Públicas) implemented the bulk of the very extensive port infrastructure development that took place after 1902. It also carried out significant maintenance work. The Cuban state directly controlled the public docks, half of which were in Havana (only ten public docks existed in the rest of Cuba). It is also well known that the State continued to grant concessions to private companies operating in the port (Census Bureau, 1908, 77–83). The bulk of institutions analysed in previous pages continued to work after 1902 with few changes.

3.4 Classification of Havana Port

It is clear that Havana port initially grew in line with the strong Iberian legal administrative tradition. The port was never out of public hands. If we consider the existence of three major European port ownership models, according to the classical British classification: the municipal model of Northern Europe, the state model of Southern Europe and the private model of the British Isles (Trujillo and Nombela, 1999, 14), the port of Havana corresponds to the second of these. As for private Cuban ports, they were closer to the British model, in which ports are not controlled or conditioned by the government, or publicly financed (Carvalho, 2007, 18–20). But this could not be applied to Havana port, given the existence and absolute authority of the Harbourmaster. The existence of private dock-warehouses in the port, though regulated by the public authority, is the most singular characteristic of Havana, which moves this port away from its earlier Spanish tradition. In sec. 4.3 this aspect will be analysed in detail.

It can be said that the Port of Havana, as a separate entity covering the whole of Havana Bay, was born in 1793, when the Harbourmaster was appointed as the supreme authority and coordinator of activities inside the port. The exchequer took on a large role in port daily work, since it controlled smuggling and taxes. The successive Cuban Development or Public Works institutions were to carry out the vast undertaking of port infrastructure. This triad can be considered to have been the basis of Havana port management. In, the latter nineteenth century, in response to the increasing complexity of port administration, the rise of the Port Works Board introduced a degree of coordination between the main figures involved in port governance and development.

In terms of Port Management models, following the model adopted by the World Bank and many authors (World Bank, 2007, 16–19), it is not easy to classify Havana within these models. For example: the military dock, which worked with civil traffic, could be considered a service port. The rest of the public docks, the nucleus of the port, could be considered in line with landlord port characteristics, since the public authority owned the infrastructure and organised the activity, but was not in charge of providing services. Port management is clarified in the next section.

4   Port Management: Infrastructure, Services and Transports

4.1   Docks, Services and Workers

By 1800, the bulk of Havana docks were located in Old Havana, in what some authors call the inner port. The potential of the port to expand was limited by the existing city walls and several castles in the area. However, the wall was gradually demolished, as were some of the castles. The first measure indicating an increase in port infrastructure was the creation of the customs building, in the centre of the port. This is considered to be a turning point in port history (Sorhegui, 2008, 11). Over the next forty years, multiple docks were built in the central and southern area of Old Havana, where, close to Regla, the Marimelena dock connected the southern side of the bay with Old Havana. Meanwhile, in 1845 *El Morro*'s lighthouse finally became operative.

In order to provide ships with appropriate repair services, seven careen companies were founded in Regla and Casa Blanca, on the southern and eastern sides of Havana bay respectively. At least two docks at Casa Blanca and Triscornia had stood on the east side since the eighteenth century, though the steep shore prevented further expansion. The eastern area underwent a major transformation in the middle of the century, when a floating dock, made in New York, was assembled there by Salvador Samá and others, who also built new careener docks in the area. In 1872, the floating dock was expanded to a length of 90 metres (Sorhegui, 2008, 19). Despite the difficulties posed by the swampy nature of the terrain, true industrial expansion took place decades later when the southern shore of Atarés cove saw the settlement of the Almacén de Hacendados warehouse in 1855. By the late nineteenth century, the Havana bay port area spread over 5 kilometres of waterfront.

In 1885, the Port Works Board prepared an overview of Havana port's infrastructure and problems (Paradela y Gestal, 1885, 11–13). Its main points can be summarised as follows: with an approximate annual traffic of 4000 ships (up from 2000 in the mid-century), incoming vessels had to wait to unload, while the surveillance of commodities was very difficult. We will now describe the port from the northeast to the southwest.

The first and most important section was made up of five docks of just 500 metres length, designated to serve Oceanic routes, under the names of Villalba, Aduana, Carpinetti, Voluminoso and San Francisco, measuring 132, 69, 90, 45 and 164 metres respectively. These docks were backed by 4500 square metres of sheds, acting as temporary storage for cargo operations. In these sheds, goods were registered by customs officers, and later sent to company agents. This set-up, however, did not work in practice, because there were not enough officers and the volume of traffic was too high. As a consequence, cargo remained in the temporary sheds for long periods of time. Meanwhile, the sheds were used as improvised markets. Agents complained about this serious offence, adding that boats could not operate due to the shortage of space for unloading, leading port activity effectively to grind to a halt, in spite of the apparent frenetic activity everywhere. The problem was not one of mooring lines, claimed the Port Works Board report, but rather of warehouses.

The second section was composed of a single dock, named San Fernando (commonly, 'La Machina'). The dock was owned by the Navy, and could also serve civil purposes, so it was here that passengers' luggage was inspected; consequently the Port Works Board's report considered it to be a passenger dock. The military crane handled goods, a fact that led to important consequences. In the mid- to late nineteenth century, 'La Machina', a 32-metre-high military crane, once used for ship building in the heyday of the Arsenal, provided services to outgoing goods and incoming ships, thereby giving rise to rivalry with private crane services in 1882 (Guimerá and Monge, 2003, 213). The conflict involved the Spanish Navy on the one side, and an alliance of private companies, grouped together in the Board of Trade and backed by local authorities on the other. The latter argued that San Fernando dock, which was public despite being owned by the navy, obstructed port development, thereby blocking through transit, because the navy imposed limitations on the traffic of goods and people through its docks. They called for the dock to be deemed civil instead of military. The navy counter-argued that the cause of this false accusation lay in private interests, which hankered after control of the service that the Spanish Navy provided to ships. Spain backed the navy and the dock continued under the auspices of the military, but the problem remained latent, and was not solved by Spain (Guimerá and Monge, 2003, 28).

The third section was described as follows: three small docks for cabotage, the navigation to and from other Cuban ports; the docks were public, although handed over as a concession to a private business. The dock named La Luz and one other worked with the Almacenes de Regla and Ferrocarril de la Bahía companies, linking the two shores of Havana bay. Furthermore, the state-owned Paula dock, served and was maintained by the Port Works Board itself.

In the fourth section, there were several docks and warehouses of Almacenes de Depósito de La Habana, previously known as Almacenes de San José. According to the Port Works Board, their location could be considered to be the best in Havana bay. Then, to the southwest, there was the Arsenal as well as a military Hospital with its own dock.

The fifth and last section was composed of multiple privately owned docks, including Tallapiedra dock, where the Almacenes de Aguirre were located, and opposite them, on the southern side of Atarés cove, the large Almacenes de Hacendados.

This was the situation in 1885. As late as 1907, ships had to anchor in the bay to wait for boats to carry their cargo to the public docks, leading the new Republic to carry out work in Havana bay. Port authorities over the years had to deal with the problem of the bay silting up. If in the 1860s, the removal of 240,840 cubic metres from the seabed was considered a major, albeit insufficient, piece of work, between 1910 and 1919, the independent Cuban republic moved 3,600,000 cubic metres of mud, throwing 396,000 of these into the inner, swampy areas of the bay. Moreover, in order to obtain a uniform seabed 11 metres deep, they blasted 644,000 cubic metres of rock. These tasks were mainly carried by private companies (Dirección General, 1920, 194).

4.2   Transport in the Port Area

During the early years of the nineteenth century, crossing Havana bay could be a hazardous feat. The man in charge of taking people across was called Rentero, and he charged each passenger half a real. The product of all the crossings amounted to 50,000 *pesos fuertes*[8] per biennium. Seven boats worked on the crossing between Marimelena on the southern side, and Old Havana. Subsequently, a new dock, Ventas, was built in the south. The boats were small and unsafe, and contemporary accounts record frequent accidents. In 1807, the Harbourmaster reformed the service, introducing regulations and placing military personnel in charge of supervision. The service was later covered by an expanded fleet of 83 boats, manned by experienced seamen, a group that founded a specialised guild of its own (Andueza, 1841, 167–8).

As of 1847, the Compañía de Vapores de la Bahía de La Habana provided steamship services all around the harbour with tugboats and ferries (Compañía de Vapores, 1847, 1), replacing or alongside old-style boats. The company subsequently expanded its services by building a railway line connecting docks in Regla with coal mines in Guanabacoa to supply its docks. However, the coal in the mines ran out very quickly, and the line was converted into a passenger service.

Steam ships progressively linked Havana with the other Cuban ports (Moyano Bazzani, 1991, 38–41). In 1819, the *Neptuno* began its route connecting Havana with Matanzas harbour. The ship was owned by Juan de O'Farrill, a private entrepreneur who enjoyed a state concession. The service of cabotage was soon expanded to cover all of the island's main ports. By 1850, ten steam ship lines were operating in Cuba, four of which departed from Havana port. Paddle steamers connected Havana with tobacco production areas.

Land transport access to the port changed over the years. In the early nineteenth century, Miguel Tacón y Rosique, the Captain General, was opposed to locating the public railway station close to Havana docks. As a consequence, private carriers introduced the goods into the port with as many as 700,000 sugar boxes yearly, nearly 2000 a day, crossing the city, thereby created an apparently thriving atmosphere, despite the inefficiency inherent in the business (Cantero y Anderson, 2005, 123). However, private and public docks around the bay (and not in Old Havana) were served by railways, something that helped the port bay to develop. These railways were owned by private companies that had obtained government concessions to build and exploit them, as per the established regulations.

The most significant line, managed by the Ferrocarriles de la Bahía de La Habana company, connected Regla (where the famous private warehouse was located) and the sugar production areas all the way up to Matanzas from 1858 onwards. The entrepreneur in charge of the company that built the line was also the owner of the huge warehouse at Regla. Likewise, Almacenes de Hacendados had a rail link, while the first Havana railway station (called Villanueva) was located too far inland to be able to serve the old port docks. In 1912, the Havana Central Railway Station was created on the land where the old Arsenal was built, just south of the Old Havana wall perimeter. Thus, the old inner port was finally directly linked to the Cuban railway system. In the meantime, the most powerful entrepreneurs solved their storage and transport problems in the bay.

4.3   The Havana Private Dock Warehouses: Regla

Havana has a long tradition of public warehouses: after 1558, when the Castle of the Royal Force was built, the Crown used to store treasures inside the fortress. By 1589, the growing importance of Havana's trade led to an increase in storage capacity: close to El Morro castle, on the eastern shore of the bay, a new public warehouse was built in the Casa Blanca area. It was the General Storage of America (Depósito General de América), a pompous name that highlighted the importance of Havana in the Spanish management of its empire (Gómez Colón, 1851, 101). However, in the long run, public warehouses played an irrelevant role in the port.

Apart from these public actors, privately owned docks also operated in the bay. In spite of the fact that they grew up mostly on the outskirts of the main port areas, private docks and warehouses in the bay were to become one of the most important factors in harbour development. Two different factors help us to understand how the Havana storage system thrived as an oddity: on the one hand, the difficult transport system, on the other, the lack of space around the port, constricted by defensive walls. In these circumstances storage in Havana occupied cellars owned by local inhabitants up until the mid-nineteenth century (Sorhegui, 2008, 19), a factor that limited the possibilities for port expansion. In due time, British style dock-warehouses, generally known as *almacenes de depósito*, were built to replace the hitherto rather haphazard storage facilities in Old Havana.

As far as the handling of commodities is concerned, a stock corporation headed by Eduardo Fesser, an Andalusian trader, built the Almacenes Generales de Regla in 1843, with an initial capital of $150,000. The first warehouse was in fact a dock-warehouse built according to the British port system, with its private cranes, warehouses, workers and docks. The warehouse was a large, eight-shed structure, with a storage capacity of 50,000 sugar boxes. It expanded further in the following years, yet was still not big enough to handle the huge amount of merchandise received. In order to fulfil the demand, Fesser commissioned a New York architect, James Bogardus to design a new warehouse and Bogardus supervised the construction of the new cast iron building in 1874. *Santa Catalina* warehouse, named after its location on the Santa Catalina peninsula, a little to the north of Regla, was the largest in the world (López Dénis, 2007, 62). The building was so large and well communicated that the Spanish converted it into a military hospital during the war, in 1896. It was destroyed by a hurricane in 1906.

Meanwhile, the timber-made dock was improved to accommodate a 560-metre-long berth. The most important characteristic of this *almacén* was that dock and warehouse were next to one another, saving a huge amount of money on transport. Almacén de Regla offered accommodation for a total amount of 3 *reales* for sugar boxes, including the weighing, repair and delivery of boxes. In Havana, the same service cost 7–8 *reales*. The Almacén changed hands a number of times, but prospered steadily. At first, in 1845, probably because of the novelty, the Almacén could only handle 46,848 sugar boxes. Ten years later, it handled 700,000 boxes, and had the capacity to handle half the Cuban sugar production. By 1857, the company was worth 1,500,000 *pesos* (Cantero y Anderson, 2005, 125). In what could be considered a show of collusive capitalism in Cuba, Eduardo Fesser directed the public railway link between Havana and Matanzas, which terminated right in front of the gates of his own warehouse.

The growth of other warehouse companies followed a similar pattern although on a smaller scale. We have stated above that the Overseas Ministry increasingly influenced the Cuban port system. The private docks and warehouses were an example of this involvement: in 1866, a new Ministry regulation organised docks in Cuba, and considered the privately owned docks and warehouse as mere concessions. The concessions were to revert to public hands in 99 years. However, the private businesses were not happy with this measure. The Almacenes de San José company, a dock-warehouse owner company in Havana port that later became named Almacenes de Depósito de La Habana argued that such legislation could only favour negligence by private corporations that were to enjoy the concessions, and also that the railway companies had permanent concessions, so port companies were discriminated against. Consequently, the private company suggested that the legislation should be changed to reflect permanent concessions for port companies, with a 5 per cent annual charge based on the value of the land. The State Council (Consejo de Estado), a high-level legal institution of the Spanish government in Madrid, ruled in favour of the private corporation (Ministerio, 1868, 15–16).

The number of private warehouse-docks around the bay in Havana grew to five in 1885: Almacenes de Regla, Almacenes de los Hacendados, Banco y almacenes de Santa Catalina, Almacenes de Depósito de La Habana (formerly Almacenes de San José) and Almacén de Aguirre. As stated in the transport section, the first three were linked to the

Cuban railway system, the last two in 1912. In later years, the private warehouse-dock model was expanded to other port areas of Cuba. Since the late nineteenth century, but especially during the first two decades of the twentieth century, sugar mills in Cuba developed their own, private ports, called *embarcadero* or *subpuerto* (Santamaría, 2001, 476). The Spanish administration regulated the expansion of these ports, considering them concessions, as in the case of the Dumois family in the port of Banes, but the number of *subpuertos* was boosted by American companies. This process introduced a new type of port that distanced the Cuban port system from its Spanish origin.

4.4   Immigrants and Workers

The most remarkable initiative during the American occupation was executed on the eastern shore of Havana harbour entrance, probably the most distinguishable footprint left by the United States in the port. In 1900, in order to centralise entry into Cuba, the Americans founded an immigration centre in Triscornia, clearly a calque of New York's Ellis Island Immigrant Station. The new Cuban republic continued with the initiative and expanded it: the dock was reformed; six large sheds were built, four for men and two for women, each with 100 beds. Beside these installations, a hospital was built to isolate sick people entering the city. Immigrants had to pay 20 cents to live there; otherwise, they had to work in Triscornia for free. They were only allowed out when businessmen called them to work. The Immigration Commission (Comisión de Inmigración) was in charge of its organisation (Naranjo Orovio, 2010, 77).

Immigration and socioeconomic changes affected the Havana labour force. During the late eighteenth and early nineteenth centuries, a high proportion of Havana workers were black, specifically freedmen or free-born blacks. They were particularly prevalent in some sectors: stevedores, foremen and boatmen, the latter serving the inner port routes. The Spanish government promoted this distribution of labour by race (García, 2002, 167), although the racial divisions became more blurred over the nineteenth century.

Port labourers could be divided into private and public workforces: the bulk of operations were carried out by private hired personnel, while administrative and policy work was done by public agents. However, as the Spanish Navy formed part of the civil service, public personnel were also involved in operational tasks.

Employees of Havana bay developed an *esprit de corps*. During the late nineteenth and early twentieth century, the workers joined together in associations that were the predecessors of more modern trade unions, each according to his specific harbour task – so haulers joined their union, temporary warehouse hands theirs, and so on. These unions were usually named guilds (*gremios*), and they were similar to Ancien Régime organisations, or old Spanish maritime *cofradías* (maritime guilds). This was the case until 1919, when they all joined together in the Havana Bay Federation[9] (Federación de la Bahía de la Habana), a federation of the different guilds operating in the area, each related solely to Havana harbour (Sánchez Cobos, 2008, 296). These guilds and associations grew and became increasingly powerful, with a tendency to anarchist ideology, as also occurred in many Spanish ports. The unification of Havana port labourers took place in parallel with that of private businesses in Havana Bay.

5 Conclusion

Havana port underwent a long and complex development from the mid-nineteenth century onwards.

The Cuban economic boom during the nineteenth century and the end of slave traffic, linked to industrial capitalist expansion, posed significant challenges for the management of Havana port. The first was to improve its infrastructure, a huge task carried out by successive boards. Although not all of Havana's port's requirements were fully met, the port certainly showed a strong tendency to introduce modern technology to improve transport and working performance. Proof of this can be seen in the fact that the first Cuban steam ships and railways were actually the first in the Caribbean and, somewhat further afield, the first in Spain. A decisive milestone for Havana was the occupation by the United States, which redesigned the international links of Cuba: the area of Havana port operations became less transatlantic and more inter-American.

The Royal Ordinance that empowered the Harbourmaster in Havana marked an early turning point for the birth of the port as an entity, but entrepreneurship played an increasingly important role in the shaping of the port during the nineteenth century. In this sense, the fact that private interests finally entered direct port management with the creation of the Port Works Board in 1884 is probably a reflection of a long-lasting struggle between public and private interests, something not unusual on a worldwide scale in the age of capitalism. What was really unusual, in the Iberian port tradition, was the huge initial growth of private infrastructure in the port, as in the case of Regla's warehouse highlights, where public authority was limited to taxes and security.

Notes

1. Spanish historiography uses the term Ancien Régime as a synonym of Early Modern Age political and social aspects. This is the meaning used in this chapter.
2. The relation among the end of slavery and the beginning of legitimate trade in Africa, linked to colonial expansion, is a matter of intense debate among experts. Some works can be suggested, such as Miers and Roberts, 1988 and Law, 1995.
3. Table 7.2 shows only exports by ports, not quantity of exports produced in the province: for a contrary example, Pinar del Río exported a large amount of tobacco to world markets, although not directly through its small ports but ultimately through nearby Havana.
4. Being Captain General, he was the supreme military commander. Being Governor of Havana, he was the supreme civil power in the western half of Cuba. In the eastern half, there was another civil governor in Santiago de Cuba. During the latter years of Spanish domination, there was only one governor for the whole of Cuba, located in Havana, who also was Captain General. For further information, see Sánchez-Arcilla Bernal, 1997.
5. The Harbourmaster's extensive prerogatives are described in Tratado V, Título VII of Ordenanzas Generales de la Armada Naval, published in 1793 by the Spanish Crown. The establishment in Havana of this institution is closely related to the fact that since 1724 a military arsenal operated in the port. For further information about the arsenal, see Ortega Pereyra, 2005; Kueth and Serrano, 2007.
6. The members of the Board of Works were: the Governor of Havana province, a representative of Hacienda, the Vice President of the Provincial Deputation, one member thereof, two representatives of Havana town council, two representatives of the Board of Agriculture, Industry and Commerce, the Chief Engineer of the Province, the Harbourmaster, three traders and ship-owners and the Engineering Director of port works.
7. According to the Chamber's regulations of 1888 the following could be included: ship companies, ship-owners, consignees, agents of ship insurances, shipbuilders and captains of the high seas.
8. The *peso fuerte*, also named Spanish dollar and *real de a ocho*, was equivalent to 23.36 silver grams. During the late eighteenth and early nineteenth centuries, it was considered the official currency of the United States, together with the American dollar.
9. The federation was made up of the following guilds: Gremio de Estibadores y Jornaleros de la Bahía de La Habana, Gremio de Lancheros y sus anexos de la Bahía de La Habana, Gremio de Braceros y sus anexos de la Bahía de La Habana, Gremio de Braceros y sus anexos de Almacenes de Regla, Unión de Chalaneros de la Bahía de La Habana, Gremio de Carpinteros de Rivera de Regla, Gremio de Calafates de Regla y Unión de Dependientes de Almacenes al por mayor.

Bibliography

Andueza, J.M. de (1841) *Isla de Cuba pintoresca* (Madrid: Ignacio Boix).

British and Foreign Anti-Slavery Society (1842) *Third Annual Report* (London: printed for the society).

Cámara de Comercio, Industria y Navegación de La Habana (1888) *Reglamento de la Cámara de Comercio, Industria y Navegación de La Habana* (La Habana: Litografía e Imprenta La Habanera).

Cantero y Anderson, J. G. (2005) *Los Ingenios de la Isla de Cuba* (Madrid: CSIC [1857]).

Carvalho, M. L. N. Cantarino de (2007) *Performance Evaluation of the Portuguese Seaports: Evaluation in the European Context* (Lisboa: Instituto Superior Técnico, Universidad de Lisboa).

Cayuela Fernández, J. G. (1998) *Un siglo de España: centenario 1898–1998* (Cuenca: Ediciones de la Universidad de Castilla-La Mancha).

Census Bureau (1908) *Censo de la República de Cuba. Bajo la administración provisional de Estados Unidos, 1907* (Washington: United States Census Bureau).

Compañía de Vapores de la Bahía de La Habana (1847) *Reglamento de la Compañía de Vapores de la bahía de La Habana* (La Habana: Compañía de Vapores de la B.H.).

Dirección General del Censo (1920) *Censo de la República de Cuba, 1919* (La Habana: Dirección General del Censo).

Dye, A. (1998) *Cuban Sugar in the Age of Mass Production: Technology and the Economics of the Sugar Central, 1899–1929* (Stanford University Press).

Eltis, D. (1987) *Economic Growth and the Ending of the Transatlantic Slave Trade* (Oxford University Press).

España (1793) *Ordenanzas Generales de la Armada Naval* (Madrid: Imprenta Real).

Foreign Office (1901) *Diplomatic and Consular Reports, No.2674: United States. Trade and Commerce of the Island of Cuba* (London: Foreign Office).

Foreign Office (1906) *Diplomatic and Consular Reports. Cuba. Report for the Year 1905 on the Trade and Commerce of the Island of Cuba, N: 3738* (London: Foreign Office).

Fuente, A. de la (2008) *Havana and the Atlantic in the Sixteenth Century* (Chapel Hill: University of North Carolina Press).

García, G. (2002) 'Negros y Mulatos en una ciudad portuaria. La Habana, 1760–1800', in B. García Díaz and S. Guerra Vilaboy (eds), *La Habana/Veracruz, Veracruz/La Habana. Las dos orillas* (La Habana: Universidad Veracruzana), pp. 165–75.

García Álvarez, A. (1990) *La gran burguesía comercial en Cuba, 1899–1920* (La Habana: Editorial de Ciencias Sociales).

García Álvarez, A. (2002) 'El equilibrio entre los comerciantes y la oligarquía habanera', in B. García Díaz and S. Guerra Vilaboy (eds), *La Habana/Veracruz, Veracruz/La Habana. Las dos orillas* (La Habana: Universidad Veracruzana), pp. 239–55.

García Molina, J. M. (2005) *La economía cubana desde el siglo XVI al XX: del colonialismo al socialismo con mercado* (México: United Nations).

Gómez Colón, J. M. (1851) *Memoria sobre la conservación del puerto de La Habana* (Santiago de Cuba: Impr. de M.A. Martínez).

Guimerá, A., and F., Monge (2000) *La Habana, puerto colonial: (Siglos XVIII y XIX)* (Madrid: Fundación Portuaria).

Guimerá, A., and F. Monge (2003) 'Puerto Colonial y obras marítimas: la polémica sobre La Machina de La Habana (1882)', in M. Guicharnaud-Tollis (ed.), *Caraïbes. Éléments pour une histoire des ports* (Paris: L'Harmattan), pp. 195–217.

Hull, C. (2013) *British Diplomacy and US Hegemony in Cuba, 1898–1964* (Basingstoke: Palgrave Macmillan).

INE (2012a) *Fondo Documental. Anuario Estadístico 1859–1860. Isla de Cuba: Presupuesto general de ingresos de la Isla de Cuba para 1859*, available at: www.ine.es/inebaseweb (accessed Dec. 2012).

INE (2012b) *Fondo Documental. Anuario Estadístico 1859–1860. Isla de Cuba: Resumen General de los Derechos de Importación*, available at: www.ine.es/inebaseweb (accessed Dec. 2012).

Junta de Obras del Puerto de La Habana (1884) *Disposiciones orgánicas y reglamento porvisional de la Junta de Obras del Puerto de La Habana* (La Habana: Junta de Obras del P.H.).

Kueth, A. J., and J. M. Serrano (2007) 'El Astillero de La Habana y Trafalgar', *Revista de Indias*, 67(241), 763–76.

Laviña, J. (2007) *Cuba: plantación y adoctrinamiento* (Santa Cruz de Tenerife: Ediciones Idea).

Law, R. (2004) *Ouidah: The Social History of a West African 'Slaving' Port 1727–1892* (Athens: Ohio University Press).

Law, R. (ed.) (1995) *From Slave Trade to 'Legitime' Commerce: The Commercial Transition in Nineteenth-century West Africa* (Cambridge University Press).

López Dénis, A. (2007) *Disease and Society in Colonial Cuba, 1790–1840* (Los Angeles: University of California).

Miers, S., and R. Roberts (1988) *The End of Slavery in Africa* (London: University of Wisconsin Press).

Ministerio de Gracia y Justicia (1868) *Colección Legislativa de España. Segundo Semestre de 1868. Tomo C* (Madrid: Ministerio de Gracia y Justicia).

Moyano Bazzani, E. L. (1991) *La Nueva frontera del azúcar: el ferrocarril y la economía cubana del siglo XX* (Madrid: CSIC).

Murray, D. (1980) *Odious Commerce: Britain, Spain and the Abolition of the Cuban Slave Trade* (Cambridge University Press).

Naranjo Orovio, C. (ed.) (2009) *Historia de Cuba* (Madrid: CSIC).

Naranjo Orovio, C. (2010) *Las migraciones de España a Iberoamérica desde la Independencia* (Madrid: CSIC).

Navarro García, L. (1998) *Las guerras de España en Cuba* (Madrid: Ediciones Encuentro).

Ortega Pereyra, O. (2005) 'El Real Arsenal de La Habana', in M. García Rodríguez (ed.), *Cuba y sus puertos. Siglos XV al XXI* (La Habana: Grupo de Trabajo Estatal Bahía Habana), pp. 16–21.

Paradela y Gestal, F. (1885) *Anteproyecto de las obras de ensanche y mejora del litoral del Puerto de La Habana* (La Habana: Junta de Obras del Puerto de La Habana).

Pérez Lavielle, G. (1957) 'Las corporaciones económicas brindan valioso aporte al auge de Cuba', *Diario de la Marina*, 15 September, 44–6.

Real Hacienda de la Isla de Cuba. Administración General de Rentas Marítimas (1828) *Balanza mercantil de La Habana correspondiente al año de 1827* (La Habana: Imprenta de la Real Hacienda).

Real Hacienda de la Isla de Cuba. Administración General de Rentas Marítimas (1846) *Balanza General del Comercio en la Isla de Cuba en 1845* (La Habana: Imprenta del Gobierno y de la Real Hacienda).

Rodríguez Díaz, M. del R. (2004) 'Independencia con sabor amargo: la intervención y los inicios del gobierno militar estadounidense en Cuba, 1899', *Tzintzun. Revista de Estudios Históricos*, 40, 161–82.

Ruiz Gómez, S. (1880) *Examen crítico de los ingresos y gastos de la Isla de Cuba para el año de 1878–79* (París: Imprenta Hispano-Americana).

Sánchez-Arcilla Bernal, J. (1997) 'Apuntes para el estudio de la Capitanía General de Cuba en el siglo XIX', in D. Ramos and E. de Diego (eds), *Cuba, Puerto Rico y Filipinas en la perspectiva del 98* (Madrid: Editorial Complutense), pp. 163–214.

Sánchez Cobos, A. (2008) *Sembrando ideales. Anarquistas españoles en Cuba (1902–1925)* (Madrid: CSIC).

Sanger, J. P. (1900) *Census of Cuba, Taken under the Direction of the War Department* (Washington: War Department).

Santamaría, A. (2001) *Sin Azúcar no hay país: la industria azucarera y la economía cubana 1919–1939* (Sevilla: Secretariado de Comunicaciones de la Universidad de Sevilla).

Sorhegui, A. (2007) *La Habana en el Mediterráneo americano* (La Habana: Imagen Contemporánea).

Sorhegui, A. (2008) 'La transcendencia de la legislación, en la evolución del Puerto de La Habana (1520–1880)', *IX Congreso Internacional de la Asociación Española de Historia Económica, Sesión B-9*, Murcia: Universidad de Murcia, available at: www.um.es/ixcongresoaehe/pdfB9 (accessed 30 Nov. 2012).

Soto Carmona, A. (1989) *El trabajo industrial en la España contemporánea (1874–1936)* (Barcelona: Editorial Anthropos).

Subdirección de Obras Públicas de Cuba (1866) *Memoria sobre el progreso de las obras públicas en la Isla de Cuba. Desde 1° de Enero de 1859 a fin de Junio de 1865* (La Habana: Subdirección de Obras Públicas).

Thomas, H. (2004) *Cuba: La Lucha por la libertad* (Barcelona: Debate).

Trujillo, L., and G. Nombela (1999) *Privatization and Regulation of the Seaport Industry* (Washington: World Bank Institute).

World Bank (2007) *Port Reform Toolkit: Module 3. Alternative Port Management Structures and Ownership Models* (Washington: World Bank).

Zamora y Coronado, J. M. (1840) *Registro de legislación ultramarina y ordenanza general de 1803. Para intendentes y empleados de Hacienda en Indias* (Madrid: Imp. Del Gobierno y Capitanía General por S.M.).

Zamora y Coronado, J. M. (1844) *Biblioteca de Legislación Ultramarina* (Madrid: Imprenta de Alegría y Carlain).

8
Port of La Guaira: From Public to Private Management

Catalina Banko

1 Introduction

Any analysis of the development of Venezuela's foreign trade, including in this particular case of the port of La Guaira, offers a wide range of potential issues worthy of attention. Clearly, we need to trace the role of the port back to the time of the collapse of the colonial regime and acknowledge the way in which the removal of legal restrictions led to a first dramatic increase in trade. Subsequently, when maritime transport began to use vessels of greater tonnage, there was clearly an urgent need for innovation and investments to improve the port facilities in order to accommodate these larger vessels. La Guaira was of particular importance for the increasing commercial activity because it was the port which served the commercial centre of Caracas, the capital of the Republic, its largest city and, at the same time, focal point for the economic activity of a hinterland embracing the valleys of Aragua, the valleys of Tuy, Guarenas and Guatire. Given the crucial role played by the port in Venezuela's commercial life, there was a natural interest in introducing improvements in its infrastructure capable of facilitating the flow of goods, reducing delays and lowering the costs of distribution. Despite this interest, budget restrictions limited the necessary transformations during the nineteenth century until, in 1885, the government decided to grant a concession for the management of the port to an English company. Thus responsibility for the management of the port passed from the finance ministry to the private sector, into the hands of a firm under foreign control.

The central purpose of this chapter is precisely to study the changes in the administration of the port with its transfer from public to private hands. The English company maintained control of the port administration until 1936, when it was nationalised by decree during the initial stages of the López Contreras government, at a time when the state began to assume a more active role in the administration of the country. In my research, I have paid particular attention to identifying and characterising the main actors in the life of the port of La Guaira, in particular those related to its economic activity. I examine the networks established with its hinterland and the specific activities of the most prominent commercial firms. At the same time, I explore the ways in which these activities were affected by the legislation designed to regulate the activity of the port and by the innovations in the port's institutional structure.

Apart from the relevant secondary sources, my research has relied heavily on the annual reports of the Finance Ministry and of the Public Works Ministry, together with documentation available in the archive of the Foreign Affairs Ministry. Although this coverage provides a wide range of relevant information, the statistics available from official sources are insufficient to enable elaboration of detailed time series, not even for the most basic trade movements such as total imports and exports.

2   Infrastructure and Port Administration

2.1   First Attempts at Modernisation

Some improvements in infrastructure were introduced during the eighteenth century. Piers had to be repaired constantly, as they were not able to resist the relentless violence of the waves, which also prevented visiting vessels from coming too close to the coast. Whereas Puerto Cabello had a peaceful cove where vessels could anchor without any potential danger, weather conditions constantly gave rise to delays in La Guaira. Ships had to anchor at a certain distance from the shore, and take advantage of a sandy bed which allowed the anchor a firmer grip. Despite these difficulties, significant volumes of cocoa, tobacco and indigo were handled in the docks. Between 1793 and 1797 the port accounted for 94.3 per cent of the exports of the Captaincy General of Venezuela. Of the goods sent abroad during the same period, cocoa represented 62.2 per cent of the total, followed by indigo 20.9 per cent and tobacco 10.3 per cent. At that time, coffee exports were still insignificant (Nunes Días, 1971, 460).

La Guaira and Caracas had been closely related since colonial times as a result of intense commercial traffic. However, La Guaira suffered not only from the inconvenience for the ships of strong winds and dangerous ocean currents, but also from the separation from Caracas by an elevated mountain range with peaks reaching some 6000 feet. During colonial times, communication between La Guaira and Caracas took place by way of mountain trails. In 1845 a road was built that wagons could use. It was the first of its type in the country and reduced both the time needed for deliveries and the corresponding costs.

Thomas Walter, a recognised American engineer, was given a contract in the early 1840s to build a 'cutwater' or breakwater, a sort of jetty to tame the violence of the waves as they approached the shore. The job was concluded in 1846, but in the following years this expensive investment was lost as it proved incapable of resisting the most violent waves. As a result, the old system of loading and unloading with small boats had to be restored.

2.2   Transformations in the Mid-nineteenth Century

In the mid-nineteenth century, the interest in extending the existing commercial circuits was stimulated by the establishment of a regular service between La Guaira and Puerto Cabello, covered by the 'Compañia del Paquete de Vapor' from 1854 onwards.

In terms of communication, extraordinary progress was made as the result of the installation of a telegraph. In 1855, a Spanish businessman, Manuel Montufar, and Francisco Aranda, Secretary for the Interior, Justice and Foreign Affairs, signed a contract for the establishment of an electro-magnetic line of communication between Caracas and La Guaira. In this way, a telegraph service was started in Venezuela, and later on was extended to Puerto Cabello, Valencia and La Victoria, bringing obvious benefits for trade.

During the long period of Antonio Guzman Blanco's hegemony (1870–88), Venezuela experienced significant changes in terms of the reorganisation of public finances, the modernisation of the political-administrative apparatus and the promotion of material progress. Special attention was given to investments in railways, gold mining, asphalt, gas lighting, telegraph, electricity and an underwater cable. Some road construction made greater communication possible between productive areas and ports, with a favourable impact on agricultural production. Furthermore, toll taxes together with all the other taxes on fruits, goods and animals that limited their movement from one place to another in the country, were eliminated in 1873, as they were regarded as responsible for an excessive increase in prices. The toll collection was substituted by a general transit tax levied by the central administration, with the express objective of financing the construction of roads and improved traffic conditions.

Despite the obvious importance of a fast and agile system of transportation between Caracas and La Guaira, it was only in October 1880 that a contract was signed with the American William Pile for the construction of a railway between the two. The railroad was inaugurated in the context of the celebration of the centenary of Simon Bolivar's birth in 1883. Maria Elena Gonzalez Deluca points out that the work was concluded in the span of two years, with a route over 33 kilometres in length 'crossing fifteen bridges and viaducts, eight tunnels and numerous embankments'. Naturally, the railway proved an important stimulus to the commercial houses located in the area. As a result of the considerable volume of imports required by the Republic's capital, the freight transported by rail from the port to Caracas was four times greater than that which left Caracas destined for the port (González Deluca, 1991, 222–40).

The modernisation of the port infrastructure in La Guaira was a very slow process, not only because of the scarcity of investment funds but also as a result of technological obstacles in the attempt to prevent the violence of the waves from destroying the docks. In 1874, a project was assigned to the engineer Daniel Dibles, although it did not include the construction of a new cutwater to neutralise the strong ocean currents and the violence of the waves (Arcila Farías, 1974, 328).

2.3 The Port Community of La Guaira

From the 1830s onwards, many commercial enterprises of foreign origin installed their company headquarters in La Guaira, while other companies generally acted as their agents in Caracas. The rapid prosperity of the commercial enterprises was reflected in their capacity to provide advances and loans to estate owners, who could not count on the existence of specialised credit institutions. These enterprises also acted as money receivers and performed foreign exchange transactions. Thus, import and export merchants became key actors in the 'port community' of La Guaira (Suárez Bosa, 2003, 19).

The most powerful group of traders was dedicated to imports and exports, providing a direct link between Venezuela and the world market. Links of solidarity were rapidly forged between the members of this business sector. In response to situations that could represent investment risks, they would send documents to national or local authorities demanding redress in the case of measures they considered harmful to their interests, or request the enactment of laws favourable to their commercial activities (Banko, 1990, 356–7). At the same time, these firms also functioned as representatives of international shipping lines, and of transportation firms and insurance companies.

The stevedores formed another increasingly important core group in port life. They came together in the so-called 'Caleta' of La Guaira. Even though studies on this subject have not accounted for this phenomenon, we can undoubtedly affirm that the guild of stevedores constitutes one of the first modalities of labour organisation in Venezuela. Their tasks included the loading and unloading of goods, together with the storage and transfer of commodities. This kind of work naturally required a substantial number of labourers at the time of the arrival or departure of ships, a propitious circumstance for exerting pressure regarding wage demands or other claims. One example is the incident recorded in La Guaira in 1846 when there was a protest by dock workers who reacted violently to the aggressions suffered by a Spanish sailor on an American ship (Banko, 1990). Beyond the anecdotal interest of the incident, in a society in which regulated paid employment was as yet not common, and in which the slavery system still survived, this event indicates that the port labourers had proved their capacity for mobilisation.[1]

Another essential part of life in the port was the Maritime Customs Office, whose officials belonged to the Ministry of Finance, and which was in charge of administrating imports and exports, as well as collecting the corresponding tariffs or taxes. Detailed legislation regulated the characteristics of vessels, crews, the use of flags, port forwarding for imports and exports, and navigation operations. In spite of registering the strongest commercial movement in the country, the Maritime Customs Office had only a small cadre of finance officials. It was headed by an administrator, accompanied by some controllers and one officer in charge of checking freight weight. In 1834, a total of approximately 11 employees worked in the Office. This number did not vary much until the 1870s when foreign trade had increased notably, calling for the creation of more specialised posts, such as: cashiers, liquidators, bookkeepers, interpreters, payroll and record copyists, and an officer for statistics. At the same time, military guard members were incorporated, made up of a variable number of corporals and guards whose chief was a commander (Ministerio de Hacienda, 1830–75).

During the decades between the beginning of the Republic and 1885, the activities of the port were controlled by the Ministry of Finance, which was in charge of the entire administration and the completion of infrastructure works for the improvement of its services.

2.4 The Privatisation of Port Services in La Guaira

A radical change in the management model took place during the period of Antonio Guzman Blanco's hegemony. On 21 May 1885 a contract was signed in Europe with the English entrepreneurs Punchart, Mc Jaggart and Lowther & Co. for the construction and conservation of a harbour in La Guaira. The contract, which involved the conferment of exclusive exploitation rights for 99 years, was approved by Congress on 27 June of that year. The company was called The La Guaira Harbour Corporation, but was better known as the Cutwater Company and later as the Port Corporation. The Venezuelan government had a representative on the board of directors, N. G. Burch, Venezuela's consul in London. The company's capital amounted to 600,000 pounds sterling, 20 per cent of which belonged to the Venezuelan nation and the rest to the English partners (Castillo de López, 1998, 31–40).

Among the privileges conferred on the company, the following stand out: customs duty exemptions for materials and machines needed for the operation of the port, exemption from national, state or municipal taxes during the term of the contract, and the guarantee of a 7 per cent annual return (Rojo, 2000, 26–7).

The company on the other hand was committed to the construction of warehouses and the building of railroads with locomotives and wagons in order to mobilise both passengers and freight from the docks to customs and from there to the ships. They also had to install machinery for loading and unloading, and provide pipes to supply water to the ships. On the extreme northern end of the cutwater they were required to locate a beacon (Rojo, 2000, 27–9).

In 1889 the opening of the maritime customs service was decreed, once the first harbour section and the cutwater had been completed. Thus, the Port Corporation was in charge of loading and unloading, the storage and transport of goods, imports and exports and also of coastal traffic operations. The company assumed the management functions of port services, which at the same time came under the supervision of maritime customs officers responsible for collecting tariffs. The work of the British company was subordinated to the regulations of the port police and the instructions of the harbourmaster regarding the order and the regularity of services. Official rules issued in 1889 ordered that the Caleta of La Guaira should be eliminated and their labourers seek employment in the service of the corporation or in the commercial enterprises for the transport of goods. This last clause was not fulfilled since the Caleta continued to function in the following decades. The use of the first section of the port and of the cutwater was also regulated, as was everything related to fees for the transfer of passengers and goods.

The contract signed in 1885 experienced various setbacks. Like the railway concessions, it included the privilege of a guaranteed 7 per cent annual yield on the investment, thus generating substantial obligations for the future (Castillo de López, 1998, 24–30). However, due to the delays in the works, the firm waived the guarantee of 7 per cent while, at the same time, the amount the government had to pay for port services for its own imports was halved.

The operations of the English company led to strong opposition among the merchants in La Guaira, especially against the higher charges for port services. In 1894, the Caracas Chamber of Commerce, founded in the same year, requested the reduction of tariffs, because the high costs did not correspond to the services provided. The business sector of La Guaira and Caracas could not compete with the lower trade costs of Puerto Cabello. The problem provoked such strong ill-feeling that the Chamber of Commerce denied the British firm affiliation in the following year, on account of the damage it caused to commercial transactions (González Deluca, 1994, 29, 69).

Towards the end of the century, most of the projected works had been concluded, notably a seawall 625 metres long and 45 feet deep, and three docks. One of the latter was endowed with a 12-ton fixed steam crane and mobile platforms. There were also five storehouses for receiving and dispatching goods: three for imports, one for exports and one for coastal traffic. Additionally, 27 railroad connections were installed, directed toward the piers and towards the Caracas–La Guaira railroad (Rojo, 2000, 28–30).

3   The Port of La Guaira in the National Trade Dynamics

3.1   Commodity Exports

From 1830 onwards, a significant increase in the global demand for raw materials and an expansion of farmland was recorded. Thanks to the stimulus provided by coffee prices as of 1830, this product moved into first place in the exports table, whereas cocoa lost ground, in spite of its comparative advantages due to its high quality and weak competition in the international market. In 1831–32 coffee represented 34 per cent of exports, and it reached 37 per cent in 1836–37.

In the first half of the nineteenth century, the port of La Guaira still preserved its traditional first place in foreign trade, a position that it had enjoyed since the colonial period due to its proximity to Caracas, the country's political and administrative centre. Exportable raw materials were transported to the capital from the surrounding Valleys of Aragua, Valleys of the Tuy, Guarenas and Guatire. Businesses in Caracas would specialise in the distribution of goods that entered by way of La Guaira and also in the storage of raw materials waiting to be dispatched to the port. Moreover, different fruits were received at the port directly from Barlovento and Central coastal region, to be shipped to foreign countries.

In 1832–33, La Guaira consisted of 64 per cent of national imports, Puerto Cabello 17 per cent, and Maracaibo only 6 per cent. In terms of exports in the same financial year, 45 per cent of the country's total were shipped from La Guaira, 30 per cent through Puerto Cabello, and 8 per cent through Maracaibo. The data reveal the immense attraction of La Guaira, which offered excellent opportunities for business. At the same time, Puerto Cabello was increasingly gaining importance due to its close connections with inland productive centres, and its advantages in terms of the loading and unloading of merchandise.

During the 1830s, a great deal of Venezuelan foreign trade was channelled through the islands of Saint Thomas, Curacao and Trinidad, Danish, Dutch and British colonies respectively. These commercial centres in the Antilles fulfilled the role of intermediaries between Venezuela and the European nations. This continued until the mid-1840s when direct traffic began to prevail as a result of steam-driven navigation.

Import operations were based on the following process: ships would arrive in La Guaira consigned to a specific company that had headquarters there and which was responsible for the corresponding contract. At the same time, goods were consigned to specific traders who could be located in La Guaira or in other urban centres, especially in Caracas. It was often also possible to find the names of merchants located in Puerto Cabello as consignees, when the ship continued its journey to that port, after having unloaded part of its cargo in La Guaira. The distribution of goods in Caracas and in the inland cities was generally in the hands of agents of the big companies of La Guaira (Ministerio de Hacienda, 1840–60).

In the case of raw material exports, this process would begin with money 'advances' granted to farmers by 'fruit consignees' or by agents of houses in La Guaira. Those advances would be given to cover basic production costs, mainly those involved in harvesting. The consignees or agents would then receive the fruit that was subsequently dispatched to La Guaira, where it was stored by exporters and embarked onto vessels, consigned under the name of the latter to the foreign ports stipulated in the contracts.

In La Guaira, in close connection with the valleys of Aragua, the Valleys of Tuy, Guarenas, Guatire and the Central Coast, the predominance of English capitalists could be observed. Many of these investors abandoned the country during the 1840s, as British foreign policy was reoriented to favour traders linked to their own colonies. When the English traders moved away, German houses acquired greater prominence. Another decisive factor in the ascent of the Germans was their ability to adapt to the transformations in international trade, and to the transition from indirect traffic through Saint Thomas to direct relations with Europe. At the same time, the Germans absorbed a high percentage of the increase in British imports from Liverpool and almost all imports from Hamburg and Bremen.

A panoramic overview of foreign trade trends reveals that within the span of nearly two decades remarkable growth took place, subject nonetheless to the constant fluctuations of the world market, such as the crisis between 1847 and 1848. Exports composed mainly of coffee and cocoa, registered a fall of 34 per cent between 1840–41 and 1849–50, as a consequence of the crisis that erupted in Europe in 1847. Imports experienced a decline of 63 per cent between 1840–41 and 1848–49 on account of global economic imbalances. The United States, England, Germany and Denmark were the main countries of origin of goods imported by Venezuela.

3.2   The Expansion in Production and Trade

From the mid-nineteenth century onwards, a process of reorganisation of the public administration was undertaken. In 1863 the Ministry of Development was created and, in the following year, a Ministry of Public Credit, the latter separated from the branch of finance, and designed to attend to everything related to internal and external national debt, amortisation, loans and the accounting of credit bureaus. Matters relating to tax collection, customs accounting, national properties and the expenditure budget corresponded to the Finance Ministry. Among these changes in the administrative structure, two fundamental aspects can be appreciated: on the one hand, the fostering of public works through the Ministry of Development and various commissions created for that purpose; and, on the other, the concern to be up-to-date with debt payments through the Ministry of Public Credit. From the 1860s onwards, one can observe a growing interest in new fields of investment on the part of European capital. Examples of this can be seen in the loans of 1862 and 1864, in addition to railroad and mining projects. In those days of extraordinary and vertiginous expansion in international trade, investment in banking and industry was also evident. As a result, an intricate web of financial networks was woven that would expand from Europe to the American continent.

Within this global economic scenario, some positive signs began to appear in Venezuela, thanks to the increased demand for coffee which, in turn, facilitated the expansion of farming on the foothills of the mountains and increasing production in the valleys of the coastal mountain range. As a result of these changes, Puerto Cabello established its primacy as the main port for Venezuelan exports, taking advantage of an agricultural frontier which extended the port's hinterland towards the Llanos plains and the State of Lara.

At the same time, Maracaibo was becoming the centre of a complex commercial network which would embrace the coast surrounding Maracaibo Lake, extending as far as Táchira and Cúcuta.[2] In this context, La Guaira started to lose ground, while Puerto Cabello and Maracaibo increased their export share. Nonetheless, La Guaira has maintained its traditional predominance in the import trade, a predominance that has survived to the present. In the financial year 1869–70, coffee represented approximately 56 per cent of exports, while gold accounted for 9 per cent and cocoa barely 7 per cent (Ministerio de Hacienda, 1863–70).

As for the distribution of exports between the three main ports of the country, we can indicate the following trends: in 1884–85 coffee exports from Maracaibo represented 29 per cent, a figure that rose to 30 per cent in 1893–94. During those same years, in Puerto Cabello, coffee exports stood at 29 per cent of the national total. By way of contrast, the proportion exported through La Guaira diminished from 26 per cent in 1884–85 to 24 per cent in 1893–94 (Ministerio de Hacienda, 1884–94).

4   The English Corporation in the First Decades of the Twentieth Century

4.1   Conflicts with Employers, Workers and Government

The early twentieth century was a time of many political and economic problems. On the one hand, there was a deep global crisis that brought down the prices of fruit exports; on the other hand, internal struggles were accentuated and claims for debt payments were lodged on behalf of foreign nations.

In the case of the Corporation, in 1903, its manager, Herbert Walter Prince, lodged a claim for the payment of 184,004.10 bolívares (7168 pounds sterling), for different obligations which the government had assumed between 1896 and that year. During this period, the Company had loaded and unloaded merchandise, delivered coal, and repaired warships at the government's request without having received the corresponding payments. This problem was immediately resolved when, on 30 July 1903, Francisco Arroyo Parejo, in the name of the government, announced to the Joint Venezuelan–British Commission that the claim was justified and that, as a result, the debts would be honoured by the Republic (AHRE, 1903, 89–95).

In 1908, the Caleta of La Guaira began a prolonged strike demanding wage increases. This conflict generated serious problems in port operations. The government acted as a mediator and eventually wage increases were won. But the workers' demands were accompanied by a government demand for a reduction of tariffs, regarded as damaging to trade interests.

After the contraction in world trade due to the First World War, there was a significant increase in exports in 1919, as international demand recovered. Taking advantage precisely of this increased commercial activity in the port, a major conflict erupted as workers went on strike demanding wage increases. In the following year, the Association of Workers of the Corporation of the Port of La Guaira was founded.

Arguing that the increased wages granted in 1919 had involved greater costs, the Corporation decided to raise tariffs for both imports and exports while, at the same time, beginning to calculate payments by volume rather than by weight, as had previously been the practice. This policy provoked a strong reaction from the business sector. Maria Elena González Deluca asserts in this regard that 'the measure was criticized as a trade tax, untimely when the government had reduced export rights, and when, in other countries, there was a tendency to reduce port charges' (1994, 204).

The pretensions of the Corporation provoked a legal dispute with the Ministry of Public Works in representation of the national government. The latter rejected any increase in rates or even modifications in the method of applying charges, without first negotiating an agreement with the corresponding authorities (Ministerio de Obras Públicas, 1920).

In the face of constant conflicts provoked by the high rates and the persistent discontent of the labour force, the idea of selling the concession began to circulate. In 1923, President Juan Vicente Gomez was informed that an American company was interested in acquiring the concession. However, the English firm announced that they would prefer to sell to the government, rather than to an American enterprise. That same year, a formal sale offer was made for Bs. 25,000,000 equivalent to one million pounds sterling. This transaction did not materialise (Ministerio de Fomento, 1924).

Because of the elevated costs imposed by the port facilities on the commercial firms of La Guaira, the port gradually lost its capacity to compete with Puerto Cabello, where it was not necessary to pay 3 bolívares per 100 kg, both for imports and exports, as was the case in La Guaira. The repercussions of this problem became evident with the fall in cocoa exports in La Guaira. Between 1919 and 1923, two thirds of the Barlovento cocoa was exported from La Guaira, whereas in 1925 and 1926 almost half of its production was channelled to Puerto Cabello, which was much further away and naturally involved greater transportation costs in getting the product to the port (González Deluca, 1994, 153).

4.2   The Nationalisation of the Port

After Juan Vicente Gomez's death in December 1935, a period of profound economic and social changes began. In the programme of February 1936, in the presidential term of Eleazar Lopez Contreras, several policies were introduced with a view to modernising the productive system. To this end, it was considered necessary to undertake infrastructure works in different areas, with the objective of contributing to the growth of the national economy.

In 1936, Venezuela had not yet recovered from the impact of the world economic crisis and the dramatic reduction in the export values of agricultural commodities. This problem was aggravated by the prevailing level of port tariffs and coincided with the urgent need to modernise the already obsolete facilities. In the light of this situation, the government announced its intention to nationalise the port of La Guaira. This project enjoyed the immediate support of labour organisations and of the Caracas Chamber of Commerce, since the latter had repeatedly protested against the high tariffs imposed by the English company (González Deluca, 1994, 264).

The presidential decree, published in *Gaceta Oficial* 19.125 on 1 December 1936, contemplated the nationalisation of the docks, the reconstruction and improvement of the ports, the revision of tariffs and taxes and the establishment of free port areas, all of which were regarded as necessary to ensure the development of the Venezuelan economy. In order to complete the transaction with the corporation of the port, an additional credit of 22 million bolívares was approved. The sale was finally negotiated in 1938 for the sum of 17,531,877 bolívares, for which the government acquired the dependencies of the corporation and nationalised the port services of La Guaira. The Ministry of Public Works (Ministerio de Obras Públicas) took over the administration of the port facilities, while everything related to services was assigned to the Finance Ministry (Ministerio de Hacienda).

5   Conclusion

By the mid-nineteenth century, La Guaira had lost its traditional preponderance in export trade, but continued to retain the highest percentage of imports thanks to the fact that the most important demographic concentration was located in Caracas and its surrounding areas. The increase in the demand for imported goods was associated with new needs derived from the modernisation process in certain urban areas and the construction of public works, together with the dynamism of an economy stimulated by the presence of foreign investment.

In these circumstances, the need to modernise the port infrastructure in La Guaira was imperative, to ensure that the demands of a constantly expanding commercial sector could be adequately addressed. In order to ensure sufficient investment in the port, the government decided to grant a concession to a British firm for its management. However, although technological advances were introduced for the transportation of goods and to facilitate the access of ships, in general the English company's management of the port was characterised by its inefficiency. One of the major problems was the application of high rates that increased the costs for entrepreneurs and therefore reduced the competitiveness of exports made through La Guaira.

On the other hand, the action of the Corporation was a permanent source of conflicts, not only with the workers' union but also with discontented commercial enterprises, and the government was forced to intervene in order to resolve differences or to prevent the application of arbitrary decisions by the company.

The dictatorship of Juan Vicente Gomez, accommodating to foreign capital, did not contemplate the nationalisation of the company. This measure was taken when a new stage in the economic and social process of the country was initiated in 1936, tending to strengthen the productive system, within an environment in which the state was regarded as a key factor in guiding the country's economic development.

Table 8.1 Trade passing through La Guaira (1890–1936)

Year	Imports	Exports	Coastal traffic
1890	69,423,476	15,022,890	31,782,943
1891	96,181,185	17,092,793	37,021,779
1892	68,637,550	19,086,413	26,401,559
1893	85,548,132	13,204,959	22,821,257
1895	60,816,453	18,400,211	–
1896	57,129,140	18,256,985	36,082,826
1897	59,818,394	13,036,244	25,577,987
1898	43,968,233	19,288,513	24,673,839
1900	40,106,184	17,773,277	21,790,835
1904	56,198,403	21,185,032	10,248,256
1905	50,810,060	12,265,207	29,414,496
1906	45,937,967	15,279,270	28,082,379
1907	33,742,329	18,400,252	38,692,747
1908	30,521,206	13,924,712	44,054,716
1909	32,352,000	–	–
1910	34,751,613	16,937,312	29,836,424
1911	46,545,452	15,887,387	29,563,698
1912	60,041,102	14,034,347	31,769,092
1913	57,358,638	18,288,035	40,469,527
1914	49,700,291	19,629,387	41,168,440
1915	41,007,931	22,463,990	41,111,291
1916	46,533,446	18,132,366	48,685,865
1917	40,347,202	24,729,993	58,886,399
1918	25,384,102	26,186,573	55,446,869
1919	38,843,559	30,632,331	64,195,867
1920	62,292,164	19,688,959	68,938,199
1921	33,535,510	22,047,115	53,964,247
1922	42,591,440	18,678,726	55,922,197
1923	49,002,697	20,903,472	61,317,251
1924	70,081,526	17,491,905	54,412,609
1925	94,257,345	22,679,063	62,068,428
1926	147,850,578	14,587,131	67,001,810
1927	114,627,305	13,886,184	71,712,209
1928	131,551,580	11,351,370	81,354,143
1929	133,360,240	17,364,237	84,175,195
1930	145,646,164	11,028,164	72,183,374
1931	127,518,904	15,111,412	71,977,754
1932	102,453,959	11,613,388	77,793,958
1933	76,290,026	10,520,121	65,832,306
1934	57,694,781	13,024,338	62,447,037
1935	74,289,483	17,557,303	59,940,672
1936	119,634,652	14,223,535	73,327,464

Source: Ministerio de Obras Públicas, 1890–1936. There is no information for 1894 or 1899.

Table 8.2   Income, expenses and profits of the Corporación del Puerto de La Guaira (1914–37) (in bolívares)

Year	Income	Expenses	Profits
1914	1,790,261.60	793,765.28	996,496.32
1915	1,650,021.95	717,499.90	932,522.05
1916	1,781,925.65	777,984.48	1,003,941.17
1917	1,870,648.02	926,974.92	943,673.10
1918	1,738,228.38	815,933.01	922,295.03
1919	2,361,995.11	1,113,295.75	1,248,659.36
1920	2,856,018.23	1,481,356.79	1,374,661.44
1921	1,884,050.21	1,259,171.64	624,878.57
1922	2,055,507.58	1,314,323.57	741,184.01
1923	2,352,965.45	1,338,299.54	1,014,665.91
1924	2,654,524.84	1,486,814.42	1,167,710.42
1925	3,236,445.60	1,790,549.77	1,446,895.73
1926	4,266,498.06	2,470,502.84	1,795,995.22
1927	3,820,881.38	2,053,162.50	1,767,718.88
1928	4,065,201.26	2,313,482.70	1,751,718.56
1929	4,656,387.61	2,716,116.96	1,940,270.65
1930	4,544,657.10	2,604,568.94	1,940,088.16
1931	4,070,916.57	2,211,586.63	1,859,329.94
1932	3,417,127.96	2,028,643.77	1,388,484.19
1933	2,852,267.72	1,569,031.26	1,283,236.46
1934	2,876,079.75	1,551,094.08	1,324,985.67
1935	3,067,826.90	1,418,088.73	1,649,738.17
1936	3,994,185.58	2,056,906.27	1,937,289.31
1937	2,583,511.57	1,782,217.59	801,293.98

Source: Rojo, 2000, 64–9.

Notes

1. Slavery was abolished in Venezuela in 1854 during the presidency of Jose Gregorio Monagas.
2. Cúcuta is a city in the Santander Department of Colombia, located close to the border with Venezuela.

Bibliography

Álvarez, M. (1963) *Comercio y comerciantes y sus proyecciones en la independencia venezolana* (Caracas: Tipografía Vargas).

Archivo Histórico del Ministerio de Relaciones Exteriores: Gran Bretaña – Comisión Mixta Venezolano – Británica – Joint Venezuelan – British Commission (AHRE) (1903) *La Guayra Harbour Corporation Memorial* (Caracas, documentary source).

Arcila Farías, E. (1974) *Centenario del Ministerio de Obras Públicas* (Caracas: MOP).

Banko, C. (1990) *El capital comercial en La Guaira y Caracas 1821–1848* (Caracas: Academia Nacional de la Historia).

Cardozo Galué, G. (1991) *Maracaibo y su región histórica. El circuito agroexportador 1830–1960* (Maracaibo: Universidad del Zulia).

Carrillo Batalla, T. E. (1974) *Historia de las finanzas públicas en Venezuela*, 12 vols (Caracas: Banco Central de Venezuela).

Cartay, R. (1988) *Historia económica de Venezuela 1830–1900* (Valencia: Vadell Hnos).

Castillo de López, H. (1998) *La nacionalización del puerto de La Guaira (Los Teques)* (Edo. Miranda: Fondo Editorial ALEM).

Dupouy, W. (1965) 'Los alemanes en el Diario de Sir Robert Ker Porter', *Boletín de la Asociación Cultural Humboldt*, 2, 24–37.

Espínola Benítez, E. (2006) 'Los comerciantes alemanes en Maracaibo 1900–1930', *Paradigma*, 27(1), 349–63.

Ferrigni Varela, Y. (1999) *La crisis del régimen económico colonial en Venezuela 1770–1830* (Caracas: Banco Central de Venezuela).

Floyd, M. (1988) *Guzmán Blanco* (Caracas: Instituto Autónomo Biblioteca Nacional).

Gerstl, O. (1977) *Memorias e Historias* (Caracas: Fundación John Boulton).

González Deluca, M. E. (1991) *Negocios y política en tiempos de Guzmán Blanco* (Caracas: Universidad Central de Venezuela).

González Deluca, M. E. (1994) *Los comerciantes de Caracas* (Caracas: Cámara de Comercio de Caracas).

Harwich Vallenilla, N. (1997) 'Casas de comercio extranjeras', in *Diccionario de Historia de Venezuela* (Caracas: Fundación Polar), pp. 728–31.

Leyes y Decretos de Venezuela 1830–1840 y 1870–1873 (1982) (Caracas: Academia de Ciencias Políticas y Sociales).

Ministerio de Fomento (1924) *Memoria* (Caracas).

Ministerio de Hacienda (1830–1936) *Memoria* (Caracas).

Ministerio de Obras Públicas (1890–1936) *Memoria* (Caracas).

Ministerio de Obras Públicas (1920) *Controversia entre el Ministerio de Obras Públicas y la Corporación del puerto de La Guaira* (Caracas: Litografía del Comercio).

Nunes Díaz, M. (1971) *El Real Consulado de Caracas 1793–1810* (Caracas: Academia Nacional de la Historia).

Pacheco, Y. (2003) 'Comercio y casas comerciales en Puerto Cabello 1870–1940', doctoral thesis. Universidad Católica Andrés Bello.

Pérez Vila, M. et al. (1992) *Política y economía en Venezuela* (Caracas: Fundación John Boulton).

Rodríguez Gallad, I. (1988) 'Perfil de la economía venezolana durante el régimen gomecista', in *Juan Vicente Gómez y su época* (Caracas: Monte Ávila Editores), pp. 81–108.

Rojo, Z. (2000) *El puerto de La Guaira. Una inversión extranjera 1885–1937* (Mérida: Archivo Arquidiocesano de Mérida).

Suárez Bosa, M. (2003) *Llave de la fortuna. Instituciones y organización del trabajo en el puerto de Las Palmas* (Las Palmas: Caja Rural de Canarias).

Walter, R. (1985) *Los alemanes en Venezuela. Desde Colón hasta Guzmán Blanco* (Caracas: Asociación Cultural Humboldt).

9
The Emergence of Santos as a Coffee Port, 1869–1914

Cezar Honorato and Luiz Cláudio Ribeiro

1 Introduction

This chapter seeks to explore the configuration of Santos, the core of the main coffee exporter port in Brazil, in the context of the capitalist modernisation of coffee production, railroads and port operations. The perspective adopted is that of the main logistics and transformation of the Port of Santos and its place as a major export corridor in the world economy.

The port, in the city of Santos, in São Paulo, is today Brazil's main port. Its area of economic influence concentrates more than 50 per cent of gross domestic product (GDP) and its hinterland mostly covers the states of São Paulo, Minas Gerais, Goiás, Mato Grosso and Mato Grosso do Sul. About 90 per cent of industrial basis of São Paulo is located less than 200 kilometres from the port.

The Santos port complex accounts for over a quarter of the movement of the Brazilian trade balance and the list of exported goods includes important products such as sugar, soybeans, containerised cargo, coffee, corn, wheat, salt, citrus pulp, orange juice, paper, cars, alcohol and other bulk liquids. In 2007, the Port of Santos was considered the 39th largest in the world for container handling by the British publication *Container Management*, and was the busiest in Latin America. The system of land access to the port is formed by the Anchieta and Imigrantes highways and the Ferroban and MRS railroads (Fontana, 2009, 441).

The history of the city of Santos is interwoven with the very process of exploration and colonisation of Brazil. In 1531, the expedition of Martim Afonso de Souza chose the sheltered bay, home to the estuary of the small Bertioga River, for its first occupation. In 1546, the hamlet was elevated to village of Port of Santos, and subsequently, Customs were settled there in 1550.

During the next three and a half centuries, the Port of Santos was indistinguishable from other small colonial ports. However, when the São Paulo Railway became operative, linking the plateau to the city of São Paulo in 1867, there was a significant increase in the handling at port of the production of sugar, cotton and coffee, which slowly began to occupy the interior of São Paulo.

Import and export firms, houses of commerce, shipping companies and a whole range of economic activities directly linked to foreign trade settled in the city, bringing to light the difficulties of operating a colonial port that formed part of the global economy. The situation in Santos, as can be seen in the following document dating from 1867, was a common one in other colonial ports:

> the vessels offshore were more than a hundred metres away from the old piers, connected to them by simple wooden bridges where slaves and other workers transited, carrying all commodities on their backs, including thousands of sacks of coffee per that were exported through Santos every year [...] (Gitahy, 1992, 24)

As explored in our previous work,

> Under Decree No. 1746 of 1869, the Brazilian Empire began to treat the ports in a different way than they had done previously. First, the public services of port exploration were opened up to concession through public tenders for interested individuals, leaving the Government to approve projects and other work practices as well as service prices. Foreign capital could be accepted provided that there were representatives in Brazil. (Honorato et al., 2012)

The operator could, in accordance with the above-mentioned decree, expropriate private lands and those small existing improvements carried out by previous owners whose lands were expropriated when the port was built, although this provision is inconsistent with Decree No. 4105 of 1865, which recognised the privileges of the former owners of wooden piers and other betterments in the coastal regions.

That is, to recognise the rights of pier-workers, owners of warehouses and all other operators of the pre-existing port activity (some of which have been installed since the colonial period), Decree No. 4105 of 1865 recognised former privileges by preventing the implantation of a modernisation capitalist type in the industry, making a 'industrial port revolution' in Brazil (Honorato et al., 2012).

However, the major impact on the city and its port structure was directly linked to the expansion of coffee plantations in the interior of São Paulo, so Santos would become the natural gateway for the export of this product to the international market. This chapter demonstrates that Santos was not the biggest exporting port during the Brazilian Empire. Rather, only after its modernisation in the early Republican period in 1889, it gradually became the largest exporting port specialising in coffee shipments. We can see that in this chapter, where we present data showing its fundamental importance as an exporter of the most important product of the Brazilian economy in those days, accounting for the largest share of Companhia Docas de Santos's revenue in exportation and in the trade agenda of Brazil.

We will analyse the changes in the colonial Port of Santos, which had been modernised to meet the need to ship coffee production in São Paulo. Thus, for the research sources and methodologies used, it should be noted that the period we have studied in Brazil is considered as pre-statistical, given that the country did not have any official data collection and treatment systems. The body responsible for statistics in Brazil, the Instituto Brasileiro de Geografia e Estatística (IBGE), was created in the 1940s and produced few historical statistics. Moreover, part of the statistics of Companhia Docas de Santos and other institutions (Associação Comercial de Santos, for example) has been lost over time, which makes putting together large statistical series very complicated. To overcome these difficulties, we have sought diverse sources such as the Ministry of Finance, the Companhia Docas de Santos and the National Department of Coffee (Departamento Nacional do Café).

When we came across conflicts or information gaps, we turned to scientific studies recognised for their accuracy in tract information. To complete the gaps in statistical information we have used documents of the time, which have also served as important memory repositories. Likewise, we have used legislation, particularly to elucidate the process of the emergence and development of the Companhia Docas de Santos and its management process. Finally, we have conducted a thorough survey of the most recent academic work on the subject of the essay.

2   A Historical Summary of the Background of the Brazilian Empire (Nineteenth Century)

The situation in Brazil and, moreover, the whole of colonial America until the turn of the eighteenth and nineteenth centuries with respect to the ports is quite similar. Colonial exclusivism was the key element in Portuguese, as well as Spanish domination in America. In this case, non-Portuguese ships were banned from disembarking and trading directly with the colony. Although there were legal exceptions, such as those covered by Portugal–UK treaties, the ships of other nationalities were forbidden from trading in Brazil until 1808.

By determining this exclusive right, the so-called colonial pact was constituted, by means of which Brazilian products could only be legally shipped to Portugal or marketed by Portuguese traders and then distributed in Europe. Likewise, imported products could only reach the Brazilian ports by the mediation of Lisbon's merchants.

It should be noted that, because of the slave trade, there was a direct relationship between Brazil and Africa, mostly sustained by colonial merchants, which, in theory, did not involve money, but the exchange of products with African ports under Portuguese domination. What was called the colonial port was a bay protected from winds and large waves where the ships weighed anchor. Using small rowing boats, cargo and workers were transported to a small wooden bridge or pier that stuck out into the sea. The load was then carried by hand to a small, makeshift warehouse. A key element in the definition of what we call a colonial port is that all the loading, unloading and storage work of the vessel was performed by slaves. In any case, the whole operation was based on slave labour.

The arrival of the Portuguese Court to Brazil to escape from the Napoleonic Wars brought with it a new reality. The landing of the Portuguese royal family in Rio de Janeiro in 1808 while Portugal was under the military rule of France inevitably sparked the disruption of the colonial exclusive to avoid the paralysis of the local economy and also to meet the demands of English diplomacy interested in maintaining direct relations with Brazil, without the intermediation of Portugal. The total disruption of the colonial pact occurred with the change in Brazil's *status* from colony to the united kingdom of Portugal and the Algarve, in 1815, and finally to its independence in 1822.

The process of the independence of Brazil created a unique model for the rest of Latin America: a parliamentary constitutional monarchy. This was largely due to the fact that it was the heir to the Portuguese crown who led the break with Portugal, and was subsequently acclaimed emperor of Brazil, D. Pedro I. After an extremely tumultuous period in national politics, the parliament was not able to contain the regional uprisings, and in 1831 the emperor abdicated in favour of his son, who was only 5 years old. Crowned emperor of Brazil in 1840, D. Pedro II maintained unity and ruled with a bipartisan parliamentary cabinet.

In this context, the monarchy was overthrown only in 1889 by a republican military movement.

The reign of Emperor Pedro II is extremely rich in analytical terms, considering that although it retained the structure derived from the colonial period in terms of the plantations, monoculture and slavery – especially the latter – it was also marked by a degree of modernisation in the country.

On the economic front, the rise of coffee after the 1830s as the main export product of Brazil allowed public finances, the national treasury, and domestic and foreign private investment to recover, with the British playing a key role in banking, import and export and navigation, especially in railway construction articulating zones producing agricultural exports (sugar, tobacco, cocoa and especially coffee) and the existing ports.

The case of the railroad is noteworthy; it had enabled the expansion of coffee production into the valley of the river Paraíba (northeast of the province of São Paulo, southeastern province of Rio de Janeiro) and to the west of São Paulo. It eased the flow of production to the colonial-type port still existing in Santos, considerably reducing the cost of exporting through the Port of Rio de Janeiro and largely replacing the transport of products by troops of donkeys, which was very costly and time-consuming.

The construction of the Santos–Jundiaí railroad, known as the *Inglezinha* as it had been financed by British capital, promoted the expansion of coffee production in the inland areas of the province of Sao Paulo. However, the structure of the Port of Santos would remain exactly the same from the colonial period, as described above, and the same situation was observed in other ports, including that of Rio de Janeiro, located in the country's capital city. Since the arrival of the Portuguese Court in 1808, the Brazilian ports had traded directly with other countries. Some kind of modernisation in Brazilian ports could therefore be expected. Our research indicates that the existence of a social structure based on slavery, the maintaining of the privileges of the former owners of wooden piers and warehouses, the high cost of the investment required, the problems with the legislation that decreed the Empire exempt from making investments and only guaranteed profits, was clearly the major obstacle to the modernisation of the port industry throughout the nineteenth century.

The main attempt to reverse this situation occurred with the elaboration of the law of 1869 that, following the same principles of law that had granted the right for railroads to operate and had attracted foreign and native capitalists, was not effective in the case of ports. That is why the case of the Port of Santos is emblematic: it was the first private port to be built in the nineteenth century. This is because, fundamentally, it was fuelled by the export of coffee from the region with the largest production in the country, to foreign markets with expanding demand for this product in Europe and North America.

Moreover, taking advantage of the crisis context of the Empire and the beginning of the republican regime, operators managed several victories, especially the end of the privileges for the former owners of wooden piers and warehouses, the monopolisation of the entire dock area and the interconnection with the railway Santos–Jundiai. This meant mounting the first major logistics corridor for export by a native private group in the history of Brazil.

3 The Matter of Coffee in Brazil

Brazil's entry into capitalist production in the nineteenth century owes much to the cultivation of *Coffea arabica*, a plant native to the highlands of Ethiopia, which grows in rainforests with temperatures between 5 and 30 degrees. The culture of coffee plantations began in Brazil at the same time as in Mexico, Colombia, Venezuela, Costa Rica, Cuba and El Salvador, where it was planted under various alternative methods of cultivation (Camargo and Telles, 1953).

In Brazil, in order to benefit from the growing demand, farmers initially chose a project in which slave labour played the key role of providing manpower and guaranteeing loans for planting. Soon after the country's independence (1822) there were plenty of fertile fields in the region of Rio de Janeiro which could be obtained for free and, in these tracts of virgin forest, coffee plantations were established, first under the regime of black slavery, and as of the 1880s, with the increasing use of free manpower provided by white immigrants, especially Italians, who occupied the west of São Paulo, Minas Gerais and Espírito Santo.

The slaves accounted for about 70 per cent of the value of a farm.[1] According to Martins,

The slave played a dual role in the economy of the farm. On one hand, being a source of work, he was a prime factor of production. For this reason, he also constituted, on the other hand, the condition that enabled the farmer to obtain from capitalists (money lenders), commissioners (intermediaries in the marketing of coffee) or banks, the capital that was necessary to fund the expansion of his farms [...].

The slave was firstly subjugated as part of the farmer's capital [...] and was subsequently further subordinated to obtain commercial capital through loans, so that farmers could set in motion their economic enterprises, including the opening of new farms and acquisition of equipment. (Martins, 1981, 26)

Under these conditions, the state provided credit in order to support the occupation of farmland in southeastern Brazil. The financial system, linked to the gold standard, was based on state funding through public revenues obtained by commercial movement. Thus, a relationship of mutual dependence between the state and export sectors of agricultural products was forged in Brazilian political-economic society because farmers used the payments received for their products, expressed in *mil-réis* (valued against the pound-gold), to buy more slaves to further expand their farming activities.

'Brazil is coffee, and coffee is gold', they said.[2] The expression of this dependence was reflected, in the financial world, by the issuing bonds of gold backed by the Treasury, whose variation was measured against the pound, priced by the gold standard. In the case of coffee the farmer was usually paid, on delivering to the commissioner, in bonds. The circulation of these papers, from the moment traders bought on the market until the arrival at the farm, was the currency of exchange in the complex coffee system.

The establishment of Brazilian society in the Second Empire and the dawn of the Republic (1889 until 1930) depended on the relationship between the size of the coffee crop and its value in gold, which was then paid in pounds sterling. Therefore, the Brazilian government, through the circulation of public bonds, financed the economic structure of the slave system, with Treasury backing to pay the profits made by the slaver.[3]

So, while society supplied industrial products imported by paying fees to the state, it, in turn, was based on the revenues of growing coffee exports. At the end of the nineteenth century, exported coffee was primarily responsible for the largest amount of gold, priced in pounds, that financed the Brazilian monarchical state.

Following this trend, as of the decades of 1860 and 1870, the planting areas expanded and coffee exports jumped from 2,666,835 sacks in 1866 to 3,878,382 sacks in 1875. Ten years later, exports had risen again to 6,015,036 sacks,[4] most of which was sent to the United States, as we can see in Table 9.1. Therefore, with guaranteed access to productive fields, manpower and markets, the demands of world trade could be met under the existing socioeconomic conditions. These factors made it possible for the coffee plantations in the provinces of São Paulo, Minas Gerais and Espírito Santo to expand after 1870, and for these regions to become integrated with capitalist consumption and market production through the building of railways, roads and ports for navigation.

It also led to the concentration of manpower on coffee plantations despite the change in slave prices. This concentration of slave labour in the southeast grew and tended to retain a huge amount of capital in the export sector, which also occurred in the productive areas of exportable agricultural goods, as in the case of sugar and tobacco, in the provinces of Bahia and Pernambuco. In the coffee industry, the provinces of Minas Gerais, São Paulo and Rio de Janeiro employed a total of 521,102 slaves in 1875.[5] A decade later, the number of slaves reached 728,112. Thus, the southeast represented 60.65 per cent of the total slave manpower in the country in 1885.[6]

Given the export market, coffee production since 1870 had expanded on a large scale into the best forest areas of São Paulo where there was *terra roxa*, through the middle and lower valley of the river Paraíba, Rio de Janeiro, areas in the south of Minas Gerais and *zona da mata*, and the valleys of rivers Benevente, Novo and Itapemirim in the province of Espírito Santo.

Given the rudimentary techniques used, which were also related to low prices, Brazilian coffee was sold as the 'coffee of the poor' in the United States and Europe. But motivated by instant profits and the abundance of agricultural lands, farmers were not concerned with the details of cultivation methods employed and became the largest producers, flooding world markets with harvests of low-quality coffee. In turn, Europe re-exported blends of poor-quality coffee of any origin with Brazilian coffee under labels such as of 'Brazilian Coffee', 'Rio' or

Table 9.1 Participation of Brazilian production in world coffee production (1820–89)

Years	Participation
1820/29	18.18%
1830/39	29.70%
1840/49	40.00%
1859/59	52.09%
1860/69	49.07%
1870/79	49.09%
1880/89	56.63%

Source: Martins, 1990, 39.

'Santos'. This low quality and poor image of Brazilian coffee were also associated with the horror of black slavery practised in the country.

In 1875, São Paulo had a stock of 106 million coffee plants. Between 1876 and 1883, this number doubled to 211 million. The high profits made the expansion of the stock of coffee plant between 1886 and 1897 to 465 million possible. Compared to 106 million in 1876, this figure represents an increase of 343 per cent (Cano, 1984). In 1920, the volume of plants had reached a total of 824 million and in 1930 it had surpassed the one million barrier, reaching 1188 million (Costa, Hernandes and Lima, 1990).

Earlier in this article, we looked at the plight of Brazilian colonial ports in the first decade of the nineteenth century, and we observed that they fitted the description of a 'colonial port' as described by previous authors (Honorato et al., 2012). It is worth remembering that the improvement of Brazilian ports had concerned colonial authorities since 1816.[7] However, only in the 1840s was there a clear interest in improving ports – 1841, São Luis, 1845, Salvador, 1855, Rio Grande and so forth – sponsored by the Empire that, with its battered finances in the early 1860s, made little progress in improving the port's structure.[8]

> Under Decree No. 1746 of 1869, the Brazilian Empire began to treat the ports in a different way than they had done previously. First, the public services of port exploration through public bidding of interested individuals was opened up to concession, leaving the Government to approve projects and other work practices as well as service prices. Foreign capital could be accepted provided that there were representatives in Brazil. (Honorato et al., 2012)

In the case of Santos, in 1872 the Earl of Estrela and Francisco Praxedes de Andrade Pertence decided to propose to the London firm of Caza Knuzles & Foster the establishment of a company in the city to carry out port improvements. To this end, a project was approved in the following year. However, this project did not go ahead and in 1879 the engineer Milnor Roberts was hired to develop a new project due to insistent requests from the Commercial Association of Santos (Honorato, 1996).

Indeed, as the initiative had also not been successful and the crisis of coffee shipments in Santos had deteriorated each season, the Town Hall of São Paulo passed a law in 1881 giving the state government the right to explore and improve the Port of Santos. Due to financial and technical difficulties in the works by the state government, the imperial government cancelled the concession in 1886 and published a new edict urging entrepreneurs to participate in the concession.

Finally, on 12 July 1888, the result of the controversial bid was published, giving José Pinto de Oliveira, Cândido Gaffrée, Eduardo Palassim Guinle and others the right to implement the improvements and to operate the Port of Santos. Gaffrée, Guinle & Co. was immediately set up.

Decree No. 9979 of 1888 of the Brazilian Empire should be understood as an attempt to demonstrate a modern and entrepreneurial facet, particularly for the elites of São Paulo who had begun to act as the dynamic core of the national economy in the wake of coffee expansion. In this context, the imperial concession for the works in the Port of Santos[9] comprised the construction of

> a quay and embankment between the end of the old bridge of the railroad and Braz Cubas street; the establishment of a dual railroad of one meter and sixty centimetres (1.60m) of gauge for the facility of cranes and freight wagons and the construction of warehouses for safekeeping of goods.[10]

The quay, originally offered in a public tender, measured 866 metres and corresponded to a port model type of piers or bridges much like the system of wooden piers that were still commonplace at the time. In Saboia and Silva's report – on which the competition was based – the engineer had indicated that the best technical solution for the case of Santos, due to the presence of steam ships and steamers, would be the dock straight.

The defence of the argument is clear: 'On a dock straight, the unloading of steamers can be made from all hatches and cranes, as the transportation of goods whether carts, wagons, tramway or railroad, may quickly and without any trampling get close of the ships' (Lobo, 1936, 24). The report was intended to bring port service in line with capitalist production, streamlining the work of stowage, loading and unloading in an attempt to reduce storage time and waiting on the quay and to ensure integration with the railroad. For the implementation of a linear quay, the concession was very limited, small even, although the concessionaires knew this when the tender was made public.

Based on the technical report above and claiming the need to rectify the meandering coastline to maintain the required depth, the Gaffrée, Guinle & Co. sought authorisation from the imperial government to extend the quay under construction a further 122 metres, giving a total of 988 linear metres reaching the Valongo (Lobo, 1936, 24). They were not only able to convince the government but also acquired the right to 'Build in the cove of Valongo, a dike for the repairs of ships and other vessels [...]. The concessionaires will be entitled to charge for the services of the dike: the stop-over of ships and other vessels.'[11]

Besides working towards monopolising the entire area that could be transformed into dock, Gaffrée, Guinle & Co. managed to expand into the naval reform sector, a move justified by the lack of any such service in the city (Lobo, 1936, 26). During the term of the Provisional Republican Government, Gaffrée, Guinle & Co. scored one of its biggest victories:

> Marshal Manoel da Fonseca, Head of the Provisional Government formed by the Army and Navy, on behalf of the Nation, resolves, upholding the representations made by the Town Hall of Santos, in São Paulo, to authorize the Company of Construction of Improvements in the Port of Santos to extend the dock, from Customs to the place called Paquetá the usufruct of the facilities for ninety years from this date, all in accordance with Decree No. 9979 of July 12, 1888, No. 10277 of July 30, 1889, and in accordance with the clauses in this ruling [...][12]

The above-mentioned Decree No. 966/1890 granted Gaffrée, Guinle & Co. over 988 linear metres of land close to the sea to be turned into quay, beyond the 884 linear metres set in the competitive bid. So, the operator now had the right to operate a quay of 1872 linear metres of extension[13] – besides assuring the term of ninety years, the maximum time allowed under Brazilian law for the operation of public services. Not satisfied with this result, Companhia Docas de Santos, the successor to Gaffrée, Guinle & Co., continued to fight for the expansion of its services seeking the monopolisation of the entire set of activities related to the Port of Santos.

The small portion of the quay, once it had been solemnly inaugurated, could not cope with the increasing amount of cargo shipped by Santos. Companhia Docas de Santos was able to make the federal government aware that the solution would be to expand the concession area. Possibly for this reason, the president, given the appeal of the concessionaire, adjusted the initial contract to authorise the extension of the quay from Paquetá to Outeirinhos, increasing the capital up to 14,627,194$707[14] and set a new deadline for the conclusion of the work

> The Vice President of the United States of Brazil, given the need to solve, in the shortest time possible, the crisis that currently affects

the service of loading and unloading of goods from the port of Santos, São Paulo, and considering the current state of the exchange rate and rising wages, as well as the inevitable increase in spending that leads to very fast execution of works, resolves to adjust the contract referred to in Decree No. 9979 of July, 12, 1888 with Company of Construction of Improvements in the Port of Santos [...] the company is authorized to extend the quay from Paquetá to the place called Outeirinhos [...] To complete the construction of the section between Paquetá and Outeirinhos, a period of five years is granted, from November 7, 1895, the date that the construction shall be entirely completed.[15]

With this decision, the federal government extended the control of the port by over 2848 metres, with the operator adjudicated 4720 linear metres. It was, at that time, the only possible area that could be turned into a port zone. In practice, both the maintenance of the old wooden pier structure and the emergence of another company were impossible.

Thus, the monopoly port in Santos was established! Although the parliamentary debates and official documents of the Empire condemn the monopolisation of public services in the same region, as expressed from the Decree No. 1746 of 13 October 1869, which regulated the concessions of the improvement works in the port, and subsequently Decree No. 9.979/88, which granted the improvements in the Port of Santos to Gaffrée, Guinle & Co., concessionaires retained, under the original legal status, preferential right to execute all those works that become necessary in the Port of Santos during the concession period.[16]

However, as we have seen, new works were contracted out to Gaffrée, Guinle & Co. to expand the Port of Santos, without a competitive tender, and involving an area of land five times larger than the original agreement, thereby transforming the Port of Santos into a de facto monopoly of Companhia Docas de Santos. Finally, the government decisions allowed the construction of a space for port activities in the capitalist mould, monopolised by a single business group.[17]

4 The Storage Industry

The progress of Companhia Docas de Santos in the storage industry should be understood in two ways. At first, it was to build warehouses inside the 'premises' of the company, that is, between the wharf and the street, justified as an 'operational need' of port traffic. In the second case, it was to build warehouses on land adjacent to the port, a fully commercial area, dealing with the former owners of the storage market, particularly coffee.

While in the original agreement, derived from Decree No. 9979/1888, the building of sheds or barns was envisaged,[18] the operator asked the federal government to replace this requirement with the right to build a bonded warehouse that would give 'shelter, in the warehouses, to the goods that transited through the dock and could deteriorate, getting these goods free of charge storage when removed within 48 hours'.[19] In fact, the building of warehouses and the increase in the pier's handling capacity represented the strategy of traders of Santos to press the provisional government to improve the loading and unloading system. In the words of one chronicler, 'The dock, for lack of warehouses, lived crammed with goods, whose burdens invaded the Xavier da Silveira street and there they were under the sun and outdoors, inciting some individuals to turn to robbery' (Sobrinho, 1953, 401).

Due to the crisis, the Commercial Association of Santos invited Rui Barbosa, the Finance Minister of the provisional government, to visit the town in search of solutions to the problem. As requested by the Minister to the Town Hall, a committee was set up to study the issue, and it ruled as follows:

> The most convenient way to carry out these works, not only in the short term, but also with all the safety assurance and proper execution, having been carefully thought, was to be regulated per unit price, with the current company of the port of Santos in charge of executing them, overseen by the current fiscal expert from the same company. (Sobrinho, 1953, 401)

The opinion of the municipal commission served the interests of the concessionaire by enabling it to expand storage, still dominated by traditional sectors. The manifestation of displeasure of the former owners of warehouses did not achieve much, as the economic insertion of Brazil into international capitalism required the rationalisation of services and lower costs of port operations. On 29 January 1892, through Act No. 33, the Minister of Agriculture, Commerce and Public Works authorised the inspector of the 5th District of the Ports of the Navy to 'allow the temporary opening of the stretch of 260 metres of dock, as required by the operators and builders of the port improvement works at Santos, provided all the contract provisions were fulfilled'.[20]

Decree No. 943 of 15 July 1892 authorised the building of warehouse no. 2 within the range of the quay[21] that had already been extended by

20 metres in comparison with the original contract[22] that the company needed, and was approved by the government for the construction of other warehouses.[23] Decree No. 1069 of 5 October 1892 approved the budget of five other warehouses to attend the Port of Santos to be built on the stretch between Navy Yard and the riprap that preceded the bridge of the São Paulo Railway Company.[24]

With the justifications of the fiscal interests of the government and concern for long-distance trade, the Minister of Industry, Transportation and Public Works authorised Companhia Docas de Santos to build a special warehouse for flammable and corrosive materials called allamoa,[25] as well as a warehouse designed to receive coal, which was completed in April 1899.[26]

Throughout the first decade of the twentieth century, Companhia Docas de Santos further expanded its participation in the storage sector, with 23 warehouses built in 1909 in the wharf area, and no fewer than 12 external warehouses, and enjoying tax breaks and advantages in the expropriation of areas in which it was interested.[27] Thus, consolidation of the Companhia Docas de Santos resulted largely from the joint efforts between the company and the state with the ultimate goal of establishing a capitalist port system based on rivalry for the monopolisation of the loading and unloading of goods as well as for warehouses, transport, ship repair, supply of electricity and other related factors.

The sprawling growth of the Companhia Docas de Santos in the city routine earned it the nickname 'Octopus'.[28] Once it had achieved the monopoly of the port, the 'Octopus' sought to expand its areas of activities in parallel with the loading and unloading of goods, such as warehouses, for example. Another aspect to be considered is that in so doing, Companhia Docas de Santos could integrate the rail system of São Paulo Railways Co. with its own rail system and use cranes to ship goods quickly, thereby permanently weakening the old carters who worked on the waterfront Port of Santos.

A similar process occurred with the transportation of goods from warehouses to the ships, and vice versa, with the mounting, by Companhia Docas de Santos, of a proper railway system after the authorisation of the Ministry of Industry, Transportation and Public Works. This was in order

to establish, as soon as possible, in the port street, adjacent to the back end of the warehouses already built by that company, a railroad, similar to the one existing in the quay area, in order to put an end to the irregularity in traffic loading and unloading along the exclusive track from the coast [...][29]

Shortly thereafter, on 24 June 1902, under Decree No. 4756, Companhia Docas de Santos was authorised to extend the rail line from Outeirinhos to Forte Augusto to 'ease' the transport of goods from the warehouse to the dock. Considering the limitations of historical sources, it is very difficult, if not impossible, to quantify the extent of the Companhia Docas de Santos's railway. However, the company report stated that, only in 1911, 4678 metres of railway tracks were run, plus four deviations and eight rail crossings.[30]

The sprawling expansion of Companhia Docas de Santos also made its presence felt in the sector of electric power production. As of 1894 the Ministry of Industry, Transportation and Public Works, concerned about tax evasion, the robbery of goods and the reduction of operating-time charges, had authorised the Companhia Docas de Santos to install an illumination system, by electric light, throughout the area of the quay in order to allow the unloading at night as required by customs service.[31] This authorisation occurred just one year after the inauguration of the first public illumination service in Brazil and South America, in the city of Campos, Rio de Janeiro, from a thermal power plant (Centro da Memoria, 1993, 58). In the same year, 1883, the first hydroelectric dam was installed in Ribeirão do Inferno, a tributary of Jequitinhonha River in Diamantina, Minas Gerais (Centro da Memoria, 1988, 30).

In 1901, the president, given the requirement of Companhia Docas de Santos, granted the authorisation to use the hydraulic energy of Jurubatuba River and its tributaries, turning it into light and electric power, in the workshops and the dock.[32] Under Decree No. 4235 of 11 November of the same year, President Campos Salles responded to another request from the company, allowing it to use the Jurubatuba River or another, if it would give better results, and expanded

the authorization granted by the second article of Decree No. 4088, July 22, this year, permitting the *Companhia Docas de Santos* to use hydraulic energy from rivers, as proven appropriate by their studies for the production of electric power and light, for the workshops and the dock in charge of that company.[33]

With the submission of studies from *Companhia Docas de Santos* that acknowledged the Itatinga River as the best for electricity production, the federal government, in 1906, authorised its use.[34]

As far as the conclusion of the works in the dock is concerned, the Union Budget Act of 1897, approved by Congress, defined a further five-year extension from 7 November 1895 for the delivery of the stretch up to Paquetá, a term fixed in the contract. The new opening date was set for 7 November 1900 for that part of the dock and, in 1905, for the stretch between Paquetá and Outeirinhos.[35] On 15 October 1900, shortly after the expiry of the new deadline, President Campos Salles, extended for two more years – until 7 November 1902 – the conclusion of the stretch up to Paquetá.[36]

As the deadline for the conclusion of the entire length of the dock, including the section Paquetá–Outeirinhos, was linked to the delivery of the first part, the deadline for conclusion of the full stretch was automatically extended to 7 November 1907. On 3 July 1906, President Rodrigues Alves and his Minister of Industry, Transportation and Public Works authorised a new five-year extension for the delivery of traffic for the Paquetá–Outeirinhos stretch, setting the final date as 7 November 1909 to deliver the whole dock and 7 November 1912 for the corresponding embankment.[37]

Finally, on 6 November 1909, the eve of the due date, the opening ceremony of the whole dock was held, leaving the embankment section for two years later. At the dawn of the second decade of the last century, Companhia Docas de Santos had, by virtue of its relations with the government in both the Republic and Empire, monopolised the entire port, including the transportation of goods, loading and unloading, warehouses, and had even advanced in the field of electricity in Santos thanks to the facilitation of the government for the fulfilment of contractual clauses.

We should not forget that Companhia Docas de Santos was the leading Brazilian company – the largest in the country in the early twentieth century – in the port sector, composed of Brazilian shareholders whose capital originated in the service sector, particularly trade, and was headquartered in Rio de Janeiro. And that, by contrast with what traditional historiography has emphasised, did not include any shareholders from São Paulo or even those related to the production and marketing of coffee. The lack of a central administration of Brazilian ports during the study period should also be highlighted, with the administration of each port defined by the operator and ratified by the central government.

5   The Port of Santos and the Exportation of Coffee

The building of a port infrastructure consistent with the expansion of the agricultural frontier of coffee in Sao Paulo, starting from the old plantations in the valley of Paraíba do SulRiver and expanding to the plateau region and the new west with its fields of excellent quality, slaves, free migrants and European immigrants in abundance, was the essential complement to boost the coffee economy of Brazil in the last decades of the nineteenth century. Moreover, the construction of numerous railways to the new coffee regions, to transport the coffee crops to the Port of Santos, enabled the former colonial economy to be surpassed. On the other hand, coffee farms themselves, although continuing to use slave labour until the abolition of slavery, were also modernised with the technological boost afforded by the introduction of modern coffee processing machines that allowed them to apply economies of scale while embarking the product better and more quickly. This also enabled them to do without slave labour and to be less dependent on the climatic conditions in the preparation of the product.[38]

The result of the integrated modernisation of the coffee crop, combining improved grain and reduced storage time and transportation to the port, gradually made Santos the main seaport of the Brazilian economy from the 1890s.

As we have explained and can see in Figure 9.1, there was a growing demand to build a modern infrastructure in the Port of Santos, particularly in relation to other Brazilian ports in the decades that preceded the

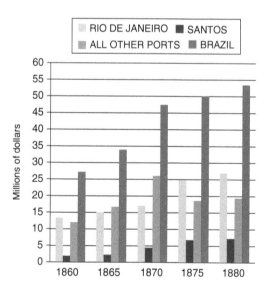

Figure 9.1   Brazilian exports by ports (1860–80) (in US dollars)
Source: Honorato, 1995, 16.

construction of the docks, that is, between 1860 and 1880, as occupation in the interior regions of São Paulo became more intensive. This increase led to a sudden increase in demand through the enlargement of the transport and port services to attend the coffee-crop and other economic sectors that had also grown.

The graph reflecting Brazilian exports 1860–80 (Figure 9.1) allows us to highlight some aspects. First and foremost, in the two decades prior to its modernisation until 1880, the Port of Santos – although very important – was still no competition for the Port of Rio de Janeiro because coffee production – the main export – in the province of Rio de Janeiro and its surrounding areas still exceeded the production of São Paulo. Second, Santos had not been modernised, a process that only took place after 1888, and Rio de Janeiro, although also an archaic port, could embark more goods than any other port in the country. Another important aspect to be taken into consideration is that the existing customs controls at the Port of Rio de Janeiro were much more efficient than in other regions.

In terms of percentages, the data indicates that in 1860, shipment through Santos represented only 7.6 per cent of Brazilian exports, a figure that increased to 9 per cent in 1870 and in 1880 represented 14 per cent of national exports of all products. In fact, during this period, the Port of Rio de Janeiro, also a colonial port, had historically concentrated the largest portion of foreign trade and the city had accumulated the administration of the port services with the corresponding bureaucratic-administrative activities as the capital of the Empire of Brazil. Moreover, planting coffee on a commercial scale had begun early in the territory of Rio de Janeiro itself, even before the Independence of Brazil, and proved that initial exports were satisfied with the existing equipment for shipment at the port.

Information from 1818 indicates that, in this year, Rio de Janeiro exported 89,649 60kg sacks of coffee and thereafter the volume contin-ued to grow, by an annual average of 221,500 sacks, reaching 444,478 sacks in 1828. This represented a jump of 445.8 per cent in the amount exported in just a decade. This increase, in addition to revealing the good acceptance of coffee on the European and North American markets, also demonstrates that coffee had gained the approval of Brazilians, as domestic consumption jumped from 65,000 in 1819 to 445,000 sacks in 1828.[39]

Thus, the successful path of the coffee trade was traced and the con-figuration of the Port of Rio de Janeiro became increasingly associated with the shipment of this product during the first half of the nineteenth century until the 1870s when the provinces of São Paulo, Bahia, Minas Gerais and Espírito Santo also opted for the cultivation of coffee, the last two concentrating their exports in Rio de Janeiro, giving rise to the largest trade volume in the country.

This growth was subject to the availability of virgin fields and workers, for which there was growing demand from the expanding farms in the valley of the Paraíba River. It is curious to see that, even in the 1870s, the whole production of São Paulo (447,580 sacks) reached the average recorded by Rio de Janeiro 50 years previously. That year, however, Rio de Janeiro exported 1,832,947 sacks; but São Paulo had revealed itself as a potential competitor to the other producing regions and its profit was closely linked to Santos. Indeed, the prediction that coffee production in São Paulo would increase was confirmed every year since Rio's exports had stagnated, from the 1870s, growing by less than the figures observed in the next province. In fact, while the average exports growth for Rio de Janeiro had grown 109.8 per cent in that decade, the average production in São Paulo grew by more than twice as much, peaking at 232.8 per cent (2,012,746 sacks) in the same period.

As such, by 1880 Rio de Janeiro's exports reached 60.92 per cent of the volume of coffee exported by Brazil, while Santos exported some 32.90 per cent of the total, leaving other ports, such as Vitória and 'Bahia' combined, with only 8.2 per cent of the overall total. Ten years later, between 1889 and 1890, the Port of Rio de Janeiro had changed positions with the Port of Santos, with the former responsible for 32.65 per cent (1,509,271 sacks) and the former accounting for 44.17 per cent (2,041,503 sacks) of all the coffee exported by Brazil, estimated at 4622 million sacks in a 'broke' year because of a declining crop that consequently increased the product's international prices.

All these data justify the renewed expansion concessions to Companhia Docas de Santos for the building of a quay and warehouses along the waterfront. If we take into account that exports in the Port of Santos accompanied the expansion of coffee plantations in São Paulo and that they also gave rise to the formation of stock companies for investment in the building and operation of transportation services by railways (Ribeiro, 1995), we can see that São Paulo experienced a 'joint movement' in the relationship between society and the coffee economy in line with the major changes (the change from a monarchist regime to a republican government, the use of slave labour and its subsequent abolition, undeveloped techniques to a new infrastructure) that had occurred in Brazil, and was preparing to be the axis of political and economic changes to come.

In fact, coffee crops increased every year and both in terms of external demand and domestic consumption left no doubt as to the urgent need to build the Port of Santos based on capitalist operations and management. In the 1890s, for example, when the transformation of the port began to take place, coffee production had increased both in São Paulo and Brazil, as did the amount of coffee shipped through Santos which achieved an average growth of 58.05 per cent, reaching 4,195,696 sacks per year, while Rio de Janeiro accounted for only 19.18 per cent (1,337,418 sacks) of the national average, which rose to 7,222,656 sacks annually.

In the following decade, and until the beginning of the First World War (1914), the growth in Brazilian exports was even greater. In this period, Brazil exported 10 million sacks of coffee, making an average of 12,492,818 sacks in the period. Of this amount, the Port of Santos was responsible for the export of 71.14 per cent on average per year (8,878,203 sacks), while the Port of Rio de Janeiro, despite adding in the production of part of that of Espírito Santo and Minas Gerais, thereby recovering a portion of the volume exported in the previous decade, represented only around 24.30 per cent of Brazil's annual exports between 1900 and 1914, representing a total of £307,464,000 in the period. Table 9.2 shows the share of the states in the percentage of Brazilian coffee production.

Referring to the role of the Port of Santos in the coffee export performance of São Paulo, one of the greatest business leaders of the period, the Companhia Docas de Santos's president, Guilherme Guinle, states that the growth of the state economy and the resulting momentum it experienced at the end of the Empire and the Republic were fully explained by the expansion of global markets and the exploitation of the coffee trade

Table 9.2   Coffee production by Brazilian states (1900–15) (sacks of 60 kg)

Years	States			
	Sao Paulo	Minas Gerais	Espirito Santo	Rio de Janeiro
1900–01	8,932,000	3,137,000	n/d	*1,264,000
1906–07	15,392,000	3,328,000	748.000	** 739,000
1908–09	9,533,000	2,786,000	461.000	† 739,000
1909–10	12,124,000	1,993,000	408.000	* 746,000
1914–15	9,207,000	3,676,000	968.000	1,180,000

*average for period   ** average for 1904–05   † average for 1908–09
Source: Ministério da Fazenda, 1934, 12.

to attract revenues in pounds. The farms of São Paulo and the Port of Santos had adapted in time to provide this jump for Brazilian economy:

> In recent times, the facts already ensured to indicate that the fast and safe exportable production and shipping were inter-dependent making it necessary for shipping and, in particular, the system port to increase the volume of goods and to ensure the return on invested capital, then the opposite proportion is also true. All events, although their origins may appear to lie in disconnected causes, must have necessarily a basic causality. In the case of the development of the port of Santos and the consequent growth of São Paulo's economy, what would be this powerful cause? It is right to say that coffee has been and remains a privileged commodity imposed on world consumption [...]. Just as coffee is a fundamental activity and under-pins the wealth of São Paulo, without which we would not have the industries that we have [...]. Coffee is the major product the port of Santos, regarded as the headquarters of a company that operates the port services; it is a product that guarantees the security of the capital invested in the dock and allows reasonable rates to be applied to those products that are imported. (Ministério da Fazenda, 1934)

In fact, Guinle was right because when we compare the trade between Brazil and some of the major world markets for the period 1901–14, and look at the volume and value of goods traded by Brazil, we see that with Germany, in 1901, exports totalled £6,014,842 against £2,012,651 spent on imports, giving a surplus in Brazil's favour of £4,002,191. In the following years, the value of exports declined while imports increased, which brought the trade balance for Brazil down until in 1912 the value of exports (£10,684,814) nearly equalled that of imports (£10,909,070). In the following years (1913 and 1914), preceding the First World War, the movement of the trade balance returned to levels of the nineteenth century, with £4,637,337 in exports and £5,719,045 in imports, giving a *deficit* of only £1,071,208.

If we look at trade with Britain, the balance had swung a little less in nominal values, but the market registered considerable swings. While exports totalled £5,259,667 and imports £6,709,338, in 1906 this proportion began to change when the Brazilian production jumped to £9,294,707 spent on imports while exports rose to £8,544,904, giving a negative balance of -£749,803. The following year, the jump in imports was even higher, £8,657,955 against £12,155,110, giving a negative balance of -£3,498,155.

From this moment onwards, the scenario that preceded the First World War seemed to influence the domestic economy that, in line with the need for investment, increased the amount spent on imports while export values declined to 1902 values, with a balance that was always negative for Brazil.

If we continue the trade balance analysis by looking at the United States of America, the figures are more favourable for Brazil, perhaps due to the absence of conflict in that territory and the need to import machinery and equipment. Thus, the value of Brazilian exports in 1901 stood at £17,462,650, while imports were valued at £2,659,237, generating a surplus of £14,812,413. The greatest variation in these values occurred again in 1912 when Brazil traded £29,200,594 against £9,899,036, giving a surplus of £20,311,558. From then on, until the last year of this series in 1914, trade fell with exports reaching £19,001,781 against £6,222,948 in imports, giving a surplus of only £12,873,833.

The comments made by the most successful Brazilian businessman in early 1930 about the relative importance of coffee exports in Santos in business transactions in Brazil as a whole, as of the early years in the twentieth century, appear to justify our assertions about the importance of the Port of Santos in terms of the analysis of the trade balance: 'When it comes to the importance of exportation through the port of Santos, this statement implicitly confirms the central role that coffee plays in their totals' (Ministério da Fazenda, 1934, 61).

This reality was soon revealed in the figures that the port equipment in Santos primarily assigned to the shipment of coffee. Guinle also shows us, through the dynamics of Santos, that the agricultural production of coffee had accompanied the building of port facilities, thereby surpassing the growth in all other products exported in the area. This is clearly seen in the following:

To get a complete idea of the value of coffee, in the exports performed in the port of Santos, during the last century, that is, from 1900 to 1926, we should say that in the past 26 years, 241,239,906 sacks of coffee worth 17,328,140 *contos de réis*, corresponding, in international currency, to £724,806,000 were exported through Santos. When these values are compared with the total export figures for Santos, we see that in the same period, they amounted to 18.482.560 *contos de réis*, or £50,073,000, so less than the value of coffee exported in just any one of the recent years. (Ministério da Fazenda, 1934, 59)

6   Conclusion

Throughout this chapter, we have sought to describe the importance of coffee exports for the emergence and development of the Port of Santos as a Brazilian capitalist port complex from the late nineteenth century until the beginning of the First World War, when international businesses were heavily damaged. To this end, we have used several, mainly statistical, sources that fully validate this assertion.

As the main product of Brazilian exportation, coffee, even when produced under the old production techniques, expanded to more productive regions in the interior of southeastern Brazil, especially in the vast plateau of São Paulo, where fortunes were made based on this product that gave rise to the creation of many urban centres associated with human settlement of the interior. And major investment was committed to railways and new production processes, all of which gave rise to a brutal demand for port equipment consistent with the country's new economic dynamics.

It is in this context that we understand the emergence of concessions for the building of the Port of Santos and the emergence of Companhia Docas de Santos S/A. In fact, our analysis of Brazilian exports of general products and coffee, between 1880 and 1914, allows us to conclude that Santos was characterised by the loading of coffee onto ships. Thus, taking coffee as the main product of the national economy, we understand the important role the Port of Santos in the construction of a political and economic system that sustained the newly created Republic as the basis for the subsequent urban and industrial transformations that the country would experience, especially industrialisation and the urban expansion of São Paulo.

Notes

1. In 1882, the Trade Association of Santos estimated that, of the value of a coffee plantation, 20 per cent could correspond to the value of the land (Martins, 1981, 25).
2. This popular expression contained the idea that the monoculture of coffee suited Brazil, and was therefore criticised by Dr Nicolau Moreira of SAIN, O *Auxiliador da Indústria Nacional* (1884), 27–31.
3. The setbacks and changes occurring in the political life of the Empire were reflected in the financial system, making it complex and difficult to analyse. For a better understanding of the issue, see Stein, 1961; Levy, 1988; Fragoso, 1990, 1992; Machado, 1993; Almeida, 1994; Caldeira, 1995.
4. *O Auxiliador da Indústria Nacional* (1891), 93.

5. The number of slaves in the province of Espírito Santo was not included in the statistics presented by Sen. Godoy in 1875 for *O Auxiliador da Indústria Nacional* (1882), 163.
6. *O Auxiliador da Indústria Nacional* (1886), 231.
7. In 1816, the governor of Bahia authorised the Earl of Arcos to open a canal in the tributary between Itapajipe and Jequitaia. See Honorato, 1996, 83.
8. There is insufficient space in this chapter to offer an in-depth description of the problems in the Brazilian port in the previous period. In this regard, see Honorato, 1996.
9. Decree No. 9979 of 7/12,1888. Collection of Laws and Decrees of the Empire.
10. The contract between the Imperial Government and José Pinto de Oliveira and Other to Implement Works of Improvement in the Port of Santos, São Paulo.ACDS/A. The document is reproduced in Ministry of Transportation and Public Works. Federal Inspectorate of Ports, Rivers and Canals (1926) – *Collection of Laws, Decrees, Other Officials and Informal Acts relating to the Port of Santos* (RJ: Pap. Americana).
11. Decree No. 10277 of 07/30, 1880. Collection of Laws and Decrees of the Empire.
12. Decree No. 966 of 11/7, 1890 Provisional Government.
13. Decree No. 966 of 11/7, 1890 Provisional Government.
14. This is expressed in the Brazilian currency of 1895. The currency of Brazil was the *real* (*réis* in plural), which lasted from the Portuguese colonial period until 1942, but the standard was the *mil-réis* = 1000 *réis*, while a *conto* was worth 1,000,000 *réis*. In 1895, 1 mil-réis was equal to 0.24 American dollars. The value expressed is 14,627 *contos*, 194 *réis* and 777 *mil-réis*. That means 14,627,707 *mil-réis* or 3,510,649 dollars.
15. Decree No. 942 of 7/15,1892.
16. Decree No. 9979 of 7/12,1888. Article VII.
17. About the construction of geographical space, see Moreira, 1985.
18. The contract between the Imperial Government and José Pinto de Oliveira and Other to Implement Works of Improvement in the Port of Santos, São Paulo.ACDS/A.
19. Decree No. 74 of 3/21, 1891 Provisional Government.
20. Act No. 33 of 01/29, 1892. Ministry of Transportation and Public Works. Federal Inspectorate of Ports, Rivers and Canals (1926) – *Collection of Laws, Decrees, Other Officials and Informal Acts relating to the Port of Santos* (RJ, Pap. Americana), 44.
21. Decree No. 943 of 05/7, 1892 and Term of Renewal of 07/20, 1892.
22. Decree No. 9979 of 7/12, 1888.
23. Decree No. 74 of 3/21, 1891 Provisional Government.
24. Decree No. 1069 of 10/5, 1892.
25. Act No. 426 of 10/19, 1894; Decree No. 6587 of 07/18,1907.
26. Act No. 109 of 04/15, 1899.
27. Cia. Docas de Santos – Memorial Presented to the Ministry of Industry, Transportation and Public Works on 06/11, 1909. ACDS/A.
28. This is a derogatory identification created by the opposition press for Santos Dock Co., due to its expansion into the various activities related to the port.
29. Act No. 342 of 08/28, 1894; Ministry of Transportation and Public Works. Federal Inspectorate of Ports, Rivers and Canals (1926) – *Collection of Laws,*

Decrees, Other Officials and Informal Acts relating to the Port of Santos (Rio de Janeiro: Pap. Americana), 73.

30. Cia. Docas de Santos (1911) *Report of the Board of the Year* (Rio de Janeiro: Jornal do Comércio), 24.
31. Act No. 426 of 10/19, 1894. Ministry of Transportation and Public Works. Federal Inspectorate of Ports, Rivers and Canals (1926) – *Collection of Laws, Decrees, Other Officials and Informal Acts relating to the Port of Santos* (Rio de Janeiro: Pap. Americana), 75.
32. Decree No. 4088 of 07/22, 1901.
33. Decree No. 4235 of 11/11, 1901.
34. Decree No. 6139 of 09/11, 1906.
35. Federal Law No. 429 of 12/10, 1896 – Federal Budget Act – Brazil: Laws and Decrees.
36. Decree No. 3807 of 10/15, 1900.
37. Decree No. 6080 of 07/3, 1906.
38. On the introduction of machinery to improve coffee in Brazil, see Ribeiro, 1995, 282.
39. Statistics based on the information supplied by Ortigão, n.d., 90.

Bibliography

Almeida, G. R. (1994) 'Hoje é dia de branco. O trabalho livre na província fluminense: Valença e Cantagalo, 1870–1888', masters dissertation. Niterói ICHF/UFF.
Caldeira, J. (1995) *Mauá – empresário do Império* (São Paulo: Cia. da Letras).
Camargo, R., and A. Q. Telles Jr (1953) *O café no Brasil. Sua aclimação e* industrial-ização, 2 vols (Rio de Janeiro: Serviço de Informação Agrícola/MA).
Cano, W. (1984) 'Padrões diferenciados das principais regiões cafeeiras', *Anais do XII Encontro Nacional de Economia*, 1, 461–80.
Centro da Memoria da Eletricidade (1988) *Panorama do Setor de Energia Elétrica no Brasil* (Rio de Janeiro: Memoria da Eletricidade).
Centro da Memoria da Eletricidade (1993) *A Cerj e a História da Energia Elétrica no Rio de Janeiro* (Rio de Janeiro: Memoria da Eletricidade).
Costa, I. D. N. , V. A. Hernandes and J. L. Lima (eds) (1990) *Estatísticas básicas da agricultura paulista (1839–1988)* (São Paulo: FEA-USP).
Fontana, C. F. et al. (2009) 'Technological Model for Application of Mobile Technology in the Process of Highway Transportation of Imported Sulfur', *Proceedings of the 13th WSAES international conference on Systems*, 441–8.
Fragoso, J. L. (1990) 'O império escravista e a república dos plantadores', in M. Y. Linhares (ed.), *História Geral do Brasil* (Rio de Janeiro: Campus).
Fragoso, J. L. (1992) *Homens de grossa aventura* (Rio de Janeiro: Arquivo Nacional).
Gitahy, M. L. C. (1992) *Ventos do Mar* (Santos: UNESP/PMS).
Hardma, F. F. (1988) *Trem fantasma. A modernidade na selva* (São Paulo: Cia. das Letras).
Honorato, C. (1995) *A montagem do complexo portuário capitalista em Santos* (Montevideo: Primeras Jornadas de Historia Econômica).
Honorato, C. (1996) *O Polvo e o Porto: A Cia. Docas de Santos e a Montagem do Complexo Portuário Capitalista de Santos* (Santos: Hucitec/PMS).

Honorato, C. et al. (2012) 'A formação do complexo portuário capitalista no Brasil', in *The Sixth International Congress of Maritime History* (Gante), 2–6 July.

Kemp, T. (1987) *A Revolução Industrial na Europa no século XIX* (Lisboa: Edições 70).

Levy, M. B. (1988) 'A indústria do Rio de Janeiro através de suas sociedades anônimas', doctoral thesis. Rio de Janeiro, FEA/UFRJ.

Lobo, H. (1936) *Docas de Santos, Suas Origens, Lutas e Realizações* (Rio de Janeiro: Jornal do Commercio).

Machado, H. F. (1993) *Escravos, senhores e café* (Niterói: Cromos).

Martins, A. L. (1990) *Império do café. A grande lavoura no Brasil 1850 a 1890*, 4th edn (São Paulo: Atual).

Martins, J. S. (1981) *O cativeiro da terra*, 2nd edn (São Paulo: LECH).

Ministério da Fazenda, Brasil. Departamento Nacional do Café (1934) *Relatório de 1934* (Rio de Janeiro).

Monbeig, P. (1984) *Pioneiros e fazendeiros de São Paulo* (São Paulo:Hucitec).

Moreira, R. (1985) *O Movimento Operário e a Questão Cidade-Campo no Brasil: Estudo sobre Sociedade e Espaço* (Petropólis: Vozes).

Ortigão, Ramalho (n.d.) 'A influência do café na economia e nas finanças nacionais', in M. W. Reis (ed.), *O Café no Rio de Janeiro. Textos selecionados de história fluminense* (Niterói: ICHF-UFF).

Ribeiro, F. (2011) 'A Política Econômica e o Convênio de Taubaté na Economia Cafeeira (1889–1906)', *Pesquisa & Debate*, 22(1), 75–93.

Ribeiro, L. C. (1995) 'Ofício criador: invento e patente de máquina de beneficiar café no Brasil (1878–1910)', masters dissertation. São Paulo: FFLCH/USP.

Sobrinho, C. S. (1953) *Santos Noutros Tempos* (São Paulo: Prefeitura Municipal de Santos).

Stein, S. J. (1961) *Grandeza e decadência do café no vale do Paraíba* (São Paulo: Brasiliense).

Index

Printed and bound by CPI Group (UK) Ltd, Croydon, CR0 4YY